I0876412

V&R unipress

Sara Taglialatela

Ars memoriae and *scriptura interna*

A metaphorological account on the *De umbris idearum*

With 8 figures

V&R unipress

MIX
Papier aus verantwortungsvollen Quellen
FSC www.fsc.org FSC® C083411

Bibliographic information published by the Deutsche Nationalbibliothek
The Deutsche Nationalbibliothek lists this publication in the Deutsche Nationalbibliografie; detailed bibliographic data are available online: https://dnb.de.

Printed and bound by CPI books GmbH, Birkstraße 10, 25917 Leck, Germany
Printed in the EU.

Vandenhoeck & Ruprecht Verlage | www.vandenhoeck-ruprecht-verlage.com

ISBN 978-3-8471-1396-6

To Lia and Antonio

Prelude
Descent into Hell

Deep is the well of the past. Should we not call it bottomless?

Indeed we should, if – in fact, perhaps only if – the past subjected to our remarks and inquiries is solely that of humanity, of this enigmatic life-form that comprises our own naturally lusty and preternaturally wretched existence and whose mystery is quite understandably the alpha and omega of all our remarks and inquiries, lending urgency and fire to all our speech, insistence to all our questions. And yet what happens is: the deeper we delve and the farther we press and grope into the underworld of the past, the more totally unfathomable become those first foundations of humankind, of its history and civilization, for again and again they retreat farther into the bottomless depths, no matter to what extravagant lengths we may unreel our temporal plumb line. The salient words here are "again" and "farther," because what is inscrutable has a way of teasing our zeal for placing it under scrutiny; it offers us only illusory stations and goals, behind which, once we reach them, we discover new stretches of the past opening up – much like a stroller at the shore whose wanderings find no end, because behind each backdrop of loamy dunes that he strives to reach lie new expanses to lure him onward to another cape.

Thus some origins are of a conditional sort, making both in practice and in fact the primal beginning of the particular tradition kept by a given community, people, or family of faith, but in such a way that memory, even when advised that the well's deeps can in no way be considered earnestly plumbed, may find national reassurance in some primal event and come to historical and personal rest there.

For example, …

– Thomas Mann, *The Stories of Jacob*

Contents

Preface 13

List of figures 15

Notes on the text 17

Introduction 19

Chapter 1: Mnemonics and theories of the memory 31
1. Definition of the field of research (1): Mnemonics and memory theories 31
2. Definition of the field of research (2): Selection of the sources for the history of mnemonics 32
2.1 Latin sources for mnemonics 34
2.1.1 *Rhetorica ad Herennium* 36
2.1.2 Cicero, *De oratore* 42
2.1.3 Quintilian, *Institutio oratoria* 44
2.2 Greek philosophical sources for mnemonics: Aristotle's doctrine of the soul 48
2.3 Mediaeval sources for mnemonics (1): Albertus Magnus and Thomas Aquinas 50
2.4 Mediaeval sources for mnemonics (2): Augustine and Ramon Llull 53
3. Definition of the field of research (3): Mnemonics in the sixteenth century 55

Chapter 2: Studying Giordano Bruno's *ars memoriae* from a metaphorological perspective 57
1. Definition of the research objective (1): Giordano Bruno's *ars memoriae* 57

2. Definition of the research object (2): Analysis of three methodological approaches 60
2.1 Paolo Rossi: "Landing on the continent of memory" 61
2.2 Frances A. Yates: Mnemonics and the Hermetic tradition 64
2.3 Mary Carruthers: Creative thinking in mediaeval memory systems 65
3. Definition of the research objective (3): The metaphor of inner writing in Giordano Bruno's *ars memoriae* 66

Chapter 3: Hans Blumenberg as an interpreter of the Modern Age: A critique of the historical category of secularization 69
1. The twofold centrality of *Die Legitimität der Neuzeit* 69
2. Critique of the historical-interpretative category of secularization (*Säkularisierung*) 72
2.1 The legitimization of a historical period 73
2.2 Against the underlying theologism of the secularization category (1): On the use of the secularization concept 74
2.3 Against the underlying theologism of the secularization category (2): A functionalistic vision of the concepts or of the good use of analogies 77
3. The formation of the Modern Age 79
3.1 The thesis: The Modern Age as a second overcoming of Gnosis . 80
3.2 The 'epochal threshold' (*Epochenschwelle*) 82
3.3 The origin of evil in the world 83
3.4 'Self-assertion' (*Selbstbehauptung*) and the first of the two key comparative analyses 87

Chapter 4: From metaphorology as an auxiliary discipline of the history of philosophy to metaphorology as a discipline of attention 91
1. Metaphorology as an auxiliary discipline of the history of philosophy 91
1.1 Metaphor, concept, and history 92
1.2 The Kantian origins of the problem of the absolute metaphor . . 93
1.3 Absolute metaphors have history (beyond the Kantian historical apriorism) 95
2. Historical reconstruction of philosophical theories of the metaphor, with reference to Hans Blumenberg's metaphor theory 99
2.1 Aristotle: Definition of the research space 99
2.2 A history of the reception of *Poetics* and *Rhetoric* 101
2.3 The twentieth century: "The age of metaphoromania" 103

2.4 Hans Blumenberg and the revival of the Aristotelian discussion framework 106
3. Metaphorology as a discipline of attention 107
3.1 Stimulus-reaction or stimulus-dilation 107
3.2 The rise of philosophy from 'pensiveness' (*Nachdenklichkeit*) . . 108
3.3 A phenomenological-anthropological reply to Kant 110

Chapter 5: On Blumenberg's interpretation of Giordano Bruno 113
1. Giordano Bruno, philosopher of Copernicanism 113
1.1 The second of two comparative model analyses: Nicholas of Cusa and Giordano Bruno 115
2. The metaphor of the world as a book 117
2.1 Ernst R. Curtius, Erich Rothacker, Hans Blumenberg: Three approaches to the study of the metaphor of the book . . . 117
2.2 The absolute metaphor of the world as a book: A metaphor for the experimentability of everything 120
3. A critique of Blumenberg's interpretation of Bruno 122
4. Metaphors for memory and mnemonics 125
4.1 Metaphors for natural memory 126
4.2 Metaphors for artificial memory 127
5. The metaphor of inner writing as an absolute metaphor 131

Chapter 6: "Ad internam scripturam, et non vulgares per memoriam operationes explicates" 135
1. Giordano Bruno's *ars memoriae* (1): Consistency, novelty, and excess as regards the tradition of the mnemonic arts 136
2. Giordano Bruno's *ars memoriae* (2): Consistency and novelty as regards the tradition of the mnemonic arts 138
2.1 The *subiecta* 138
2.2 The *adiecta* or *formae* 143
2.3 The *organum* 145
2.4 A technique of inner writing for images: The metaphor of inner writing as a leading paradigm of conceptual formulation 147
3. Giordano Bruno's *ars memoriae* (3): An excess in the wake of the tradition of the mnemonic arts 150
3.1 Criticism of *ars memoriae* 151
3.2 A unique *ars:* Metaphor of the shadow and metaphor of inner writing 152

Concluding remarks 157

Bibliography 161

Figures 175

Preface

In the following pages I present to the reader my PhD dissertation in history of philosophy, which was defended in 2018 in Berlin at the end of a joint-doctoral program between the Freie Universität Berlin and the Scuola Normale Superiore, Pisa.

After the defence I planned to revise the text thoroughly, giving more space to one of the theses of the dissertation i. e. that in his first mnemonic works Giordano Bruno had already elaborated those notions of language, nature, and creativity that he later presented in a more philosophical context in the Italian works. This plan would have resulted in writing a completely new text and I decided to postpone it, because I did not want to lose the methodological perspective of my dissertation.

When I started working on Giordano Bruno from a metaphorological perspective Renaissance philosophy was a new research field for me, having been educated in theoretical philosophy and having focused during my first PhD studies in Venice both on the contemporary debate on metaphors and the twentieth-century interpretations of Modernity. After my first PhD, a professor in Berlin challenged me by asking to conduct a research project on Giordano Bruno's mnemonics using Blumenberg's metaphorological perspective and what the reader holds in their hands now is the result of that intellectual challenge that led me to approach Renaissance philosophy.

Relinquishing this work I would like to aknowledge those who guided me through my philosophical studies: Franco Tonon, my first teacher at the Liceo Ginnasio Marco Foscarini in Venice, my professors at the Department of Philosophy and Theories of Sciences at the Ca' Foscari University in Venice, among them Prof. Mario Ruggenini and Prof. Luigi Perissinotto, Prof. Anne Eusterschulte (Freie Universität Berlin), and Prof. Michele Ciliberto (Scuola Normale Superiore, Pisa, and Istituto Nazionale per gli Studi sul Rinascimento, Florence).

The English version of the dissertation, that was partially composed in Italian, has been improved under the supervision of Katherine Bird, whom I would like to thank not only for her help but also for her patience in allowing me to explore another language and learning how to work philosophically in this language.

All mistakes, inaccuracies, misunderstandings that the reader may find in the text are mine and will be an opportunity for me to keep working on these topics.

Sara Taglialatela
University of Copenhagen, Faculty of Theology, Section of Church History
January 2022

List of figures

Figure 1. Johannes Romberch, *Congestorium artificiose memorie*, 1520. Head with areas annotated. Credit: Wellcome Collection, London.

Figure 2. Cosma Rosselli, *Thesaurus artificiosae memoriae*, 1579. Diagram of the faculties of the soul arranged in cells within the brain. Credit: Wellcome Collection, London.

Figure 3. Johannes Romberch, *Congestorium artificiose memorie*, 1520. Illustration of the rule for choosing the *loci*, according to which the proportions of the human body should be respected to ensure that the mnemonic *locus* is suitable for its use. Credit: The Royal Danish Library, Copenhagen.

Figure 4. Johannes Romberch, *Congestorium artificiose memorie*, 1520. The shops in a city as a set of *loci* for the creation of an artificial memory system. Credit: The Royal Danish Library, Copenhagen.

Figure 5. Cosma Rosselli, *Thesaurus artificiosae memoriae*, 1579. Hell as a set of *loci* for the creation of an artificial memory system. Credit: Wellcome Collection, London.

Figure 6. Cosma Rosselli, *Thesaurus artificiosae memoriae*, 1579. Paradise as a set of *loci* for the creation of an artificial memory system. Credit: Wellcome Collection, London.

Figure 7. Johannes Romberch, *Congestorium artificiose memorie*, 1520. Visual alphabet: an example of images that may be used to count or assign an order to both the *loci* and *imagines*. Credit: Wellcome Collection, London.

Figure 8. Johannes Romberch, *Congestorium artificiose memorie*, 1520. Visual alphabet: V, X, Y. Credit: Wellcome Collection, London.

Notes on the text

In the book I have used the following standard abbreviations:

	Rhetorica ad Herrennium	*Rhet. Her.*
Aristotle	*De anima*	*De an.*
	De insomniis	*Insomn.*
	De memoria et reminiscentia	*Mem.*
	Topica	*Top.*
Augustine	*Confessiones*	*Conf.*
Cicero	*De inventio*	*Inv. rhet.*
	De oratore	*De or.*
Plato	*Phaedo*	*Phd.*
	Phaedrus	*Phdr.*
	Philebus	*Phlb.*
Quintilian	*Institutio oratoria*	*Inst.*

Unless otherwise stated in notes, all translations are mine.

Introduction

1. I pick up my tablet and read a book.

It is an exciting experience, but at the same time bewildering. The page I am reading is not a defined space that determines the rules of composition and unambiguously establishes the aspect of the text as does the page of a paper book. Indeed, the program I use to read the book makes it possible to modify the aspect of the page whenever and however I like. For instance, I can change the font size, or the orientation of the tablet, or do these two things together, or else change the aspect of each page according to what happens while I am reading: the brightness of the light may alter, I may have left my reading glasses in the other room and I do not feel like getting up to look for them, or even my own personal taste dictates the type of spacing between the lines and number of characters per line.

Initially, it is rather fun experimenting with the different alternatives the program has to offer, but eventually I realize that I am lost. I find it quite difficult to recall the page where I read something because the electronic page has no fixed layout compared to the printed or handwritten page. Indeed, the digital page is fluid, without a paper page's spatial or geometric physical reference, so that it is difficult to build a mind map of the text as I would with a hard copy version.

I strive to pin down a part of the text to help my memory: I mentally go through the text, but it no longer belongs to one page or another. I find my memory going backwards, as it does in the *Prelude* of Thomas Mann's *Joseph and his Brothers.*[1] All in vain. My memory does not find a firm point where to rest and from where to start to remember. Indeed, it almost seems as if such a point no longer exists, or rather that its recall no longer observes our usual reading habits, based on the connection between memory, time, and space. Indeed, what we remember is an ordered sequence that is frequently recalled, a sequence arranged in an imagined space, and therefore there is a connection between time and space

1 Thomas Mann, *Joseph and His Brothers*, transl. John E. Woods (New York: Everyman's Library, 2005), 3.

– if it is true that the first element that enables us to perceive the passage of time is the ordered arrangement of phenomena in a sequence.

2. In *De oratore*[2] Cicero narrates that Simonides of Ceos, a famous Greek poet, had composed a poem in honour of a nobleman of Thessaly, Scopas, who had invited him to a banquet. The poem also included a long ode to Castor and Pollux, which irritated the nobleman as the poem was supposed to be composed solely in his honour. As a result, Scopas told Simonides that he would only pay half of the agreed fee, and the other half could be paid by the Dioscuri. The response of the twin deities was immediate and saved Simonides' life. As soon as Scopas had uttered these words, Simonides was summoned outside the palace as he was told two young men were waiting for him. He went outside, but no one was there. Suddenly, the roof of the palace fell in and crushed all the banqueters, including Scopas. The corpses were unrecognizable and so it was impossible to give them a decent burial. However, thanks to Simonides and his ability to recall exactly where each person had been sitting before the collapse of the roof, the relations could identify each corpse for separate burial.

Cicero concludes this story noting that, according to the tradition, after some reflection on what had occurred the poet realized that orderly arrangement was the key to accurate recall, and thus the discovery of mnemonic principles is attributed to Simonides. In Cicero's time mnemonics (*ars memoriae*) was one of the rhetoric techniques and it was adopted by orators to strengthen memory recall and memorize long speeches. The technique itself consisted of a few rules, quite simple and intuitive. The teachers of rhetoric taught that to memorize something the first thing to do was to associate an image to each item to be memorized and then place the image in a specific imaginary location, making sure that the arrangement of the locations reflected the sequence of items in the speech. The repetition of this orderly scheme would ensure recollection.

At the end of the section on the origin of mnemonics, Cicero reminds us that together with this account tradition has also passed down an analogy to facilitate understanding of the rules for the *ars memoriae*. Allocating an image to each item and placing it in order within a mental location is rather similar to writing. In fact, assigning a word to each item and then arranging these words in a specific order to describe reality or to communicate an idea resembles the mnemonic process taught to the pupils of rhetoric. The analogy between memory and writing clearly exploits the analogy between images, written words, and letters.

2 Cicero, *De or.*, II, lxxxv, 350–lxxxviii, 360, in Cicero, *On the Orator: Books 1–2*, trans. E. W. Sutton and H. Rackham (Cambridge, MA: Harvard University Press, 1942), 462–473.

3. The experience of reading a tablet highlights how the analogy between memory and writing is neither naïve nor without a certain impact on understanding the phenomenon of memory, even if only intuitively. While reading an e-book I think about the fact that when my experience of reading and writing changes, so does the way of recalling information and how I understand the concept of order. My disorientation stems from the fact that the digital text has no fixed location already given to the reader, since the minimum unit of meaning, that is the page, is missing, unlike for a hardcopy text. Indeed, the page of a printed or handwritten text defines the first level of order on which the words are set. This minimum unit of meaning is also the unit of reference for memory: the page is the space where memory arranges in a specific order what it needs to recall the text on that page.

There may be some ways to tackle the difficulty in reading a digital text. For instance, I could define the criteria to set the format of the pages beforehand to resemble a printed paper text and hence facilitate recall. However, even in this case the two types of experience would still be different to a great extent, because there would be no way to form a common memory of a text, unless the configuration criteria of the page format were shared between readers before starting to read, as well as any later modifications made during reading.

Apart from the difference in the two ways of reading and the measures taken to facilitate more familiar reading practices, reading an e-book prompts me to consider a type of memory that does not adapt to – does not move in – a pre-established order.

4. I suggested a way to tackle disorientation by defining pre-established criteria for setting the format of the digital page and sharing these parameters between readers, both before and during reading. However, there may be more than one way to tackle the problem of disorientation since we know from the neurosciences that the use of new technologies leads to new cognitive processes.

By this I am not implying that the evolution of writing techniques is something negative, nor do I specifically wish to address the issue of the impact of new technologies on humans in this study, even if this is an underlying problem. What I do wish to focus on instead is the recurrence and mutual implication of certain historical phenomena that seem to be connected. I refer to the fact that the history of writing techniques seems to be linked to the history of philosophical and scientific memory theories and to mnemonics, through the conceptual processing of our writing and reading experience.

This conceptual connection between the writing and reading experience, mnemonics, and memory theories is evident if we analyse the leading paradigm in the conceptual formulation of the two fields of research on memory. The paradigm that guides the methodological considerations of mnemonics and the philosophical considerations of the theories of memory is the paradigm of "inner writing": this is the hermeneutic hypothesis that I will formulate in this book, and my research objective, the analysis of Giordano Bruno's first mnemonic work, *De umbris idearum*,[3] aims to discuss this hermeneutic hypothesis.

The importance of this hypothesis emerges if one reflects upon further potential research not only in Bruno's studies but also in the new phenomenological research field called "philosophy of memory."[4] Once the hermeneutic hypothesis has been discussed and confirmed, from the perspective of the philosophy of memory one could try to argue that, despite the differences inherent in the history of memory theories, the paradigm has been able to preserve its general underlying criteria because the evolution of writing techniques has never modified the relationship with writing and the space in which it is written, i. e. the spatial notion of order. Should this thesis also be confirmed, one could further hypothesize that the experience of reading and writing with a tablet could decrease the validity of the paradigm or could force one to reconsider the concept of spatial order. In fact, the experience of writing and reading on a tablet eliminates the absoluteness of the space given to the writing. I shall return briefly to this hypothesis, which is not discussed in the present book, in the conclusion when I comment on the results that have been achieved and formulate a further discussion of the connections between the history of writing, the history of memory theories, and the history of mnemonics. But for now, let us focus on Bruno's studies.

5. The invention of writing implied almost immediately the awareness of the interaction between writing and memory. This interaction has often been highlighted by philosophers, though at times with little enthusiasm.

It is well known how much the impact of the use of writing on memory troubled Plato. His *Phaedrus* is an excellent example on this theme, although we should highlight some aspects that could be neglected, because it is there that the text may be apprehended as the expression of a literary style and not of philosophical argument. Let us take as an example the initial scenes.[5] Socrates admonishes the young Phaedrus, who, after a day spent indoors attending a rhetorical lecture, needs to stretch his legs, and brings a book to keep exercising

3 Giordano Bruno, *De umbris idearum*, in *Opere mnemotecniche: Tomo I*, eds. Marco Matteoli, Rita Sturlese, and Nicoletta Tirinnanzi (Milan: Adelphi, 2004).

4 *The Routledge Handbook of Philosophy of Memory*, eds. Sven Bernecker and Kourken Michaelian (London and New York: Taylor and Francis, 2017); *New Directions in the Philosophy of Memory*, eds. Kourken Michaelian, Dorothea Debus, and Denis Perrin (London and New York: Taylor and Francis, 2018).

5 Plato, *Phdr.*, 227a–228e, in Plato, *Phaedrus*, ed. and transl. C. J. Rowe (Oxford: Aris and Phillips, 2013), 20–25.

the declamation of speeches. Socrates berates Phaedrus because the young man carries the book with him, being afraid of not being able to remember everything.

This is a dramatic rendering of Plato's critique of writing. Phaedrus is impatient. He needs to stretch his legs after a day spent indoors listening to the same identical speech being read without any variation. Phaedrus' impatience is the dramatic representation of the soul's exasperation as it is forced into an artificial *ordo* and prevented from tracing alone the dialectic connection of reality in which the *ordo* of truth is expressed, being the ideal image of the cosmos (*kosmos*), the 'world-order' or 'universe'.[6] The main point of Plato's critique lies in the fact that writing constrains the soul, whose primary faculty is memory, to move in a defined space and let the soul believe that this is recollection. According to Plato, instead, writing and the kind of memory that derives from it limits the soul when it needs to be set free to move to take part in the ascension to the world of Ideas, which is the aim of true recollection.[7]

Therefore, the scene described by Plato is so violent, almost catastrophic: Phaedrus is not satisfied with just leaving the house where he has spent all day listening to and repeating one speech. The young man is restless, and needs to walk far, going outside of the city walls that to Plato means political and cultural order. Hence, Plato must have been deeply suspicious of the perils of writing as a substitute for oral memory, able to subvert and steer the soul away from order, not only gnoseological but also political and civil order, represented by the city and its walls.[8]

While Plato considered the order and permanency that writing imposed on thought to be harmful for the soul and damaging for memory recall, thus denying access to true knowledge, this was not so for Aristotle and Greek and Latin rhetoricians. Being able to guarantee a specific order in the composition and declamation of speeches not only through writing, but also through the defi-

6 On Plato's critique to writing as a visual representation of reality, see: Marie-Pierre Noël, "Plato, Alcidamas, and Isocrates on Logography," in *New Chapters in the History of Rhetoric*, ed. Laurent Pernot (Leiden: Brill, 2009), 91–107.

7 See also: Plato, *Phlb.*, 34b–c; *Meno*, 98a; *Phd.*, 73b ff.

8 On the importance of the dialogue's setting, see: G. R. F. Ferrari, *Listening to the Cicadas: A Study of Plato's* Phaedrus (Cambridge: Cambridge University Press, 1990), 1–36. On the theme of space in Ancient Greek narrative, see: *Space in Ancient Greek Literature: Studies in Ancient Greek Narrative*, ed. Irene J.F. de Jong (Leiden/Boston: Brill, 2012), chapter 22 of the volume is dedicated to Plato: K.A. Morgan, "Plato," 415–437. On the association between wandering and the wanderer as a man of learning, see: Silvia Montiglio, *Wandering in Ancient Greek Culture* (Chicago: University of Chicago Press, 2005). On the symbolic meaning of Athens' walls in Ancient Greek literature, see: Carol Dougherty, "Ships, Walls, Men: Classical Athens and the Poetics of Infrastructure," in *Space, Place, and Landscape in Ancient Greek Literature and Culture*, eds. Kate Gilhuly and Nancy Worman (Cambridge: Cambridge University Press, 2014), 130–170.

nition of a series of argumentative schemas that could be used in various contexts meant providing an aid to memory recall.[9]

Apart from the two philosophers' notions of the souls and from the history of their reception, a further interesting aspect from the point of view of the history of ideas emerges here: how the concept of the soul and the function of memory in both systems of thought is developed also in reflecting on the writing experience, and the attitude the two philosophers had towards it. Whereas Plato was convinced that the soul would be deeply affected by the act of writing, Aristotle, who belonged to a generation that had already assimilated the invention of writing as a tool for communication, believed it would have no effect at all on the soul.

6. In the following pages I would like to bring attention to this connection between memory theories, mnemonics, and the reading-writing experience. Above all, I am interested in exploring from a philosophical and historical point of view this long-lasting connection between phenomena throughout the history of thought and in submitting a hermeneutic hypothesis, that the analogy between writing and memory led the conceptual development of philosophical memory theories and of mnemonics, contributing to the definition of the notion of spatial order.

It could be argued that other analogies were used in the past to explain the function of memory – such as the seal-in-wax metaphor, or the ark metaphor, and the stomach metaphor, to name some of the most common – which is true, but also these analogies stem from the writing and reading experience and refer to its semantics as we will see. Hence, the analogy with writing was the most prolific in terms of the development of the theories and their conceptuality.

One of the specific aspects of this question is that from a historical point of view no undisputed priority has ever been established regarding memory theories and mnemonic techniques. Indeed, during the gradual process of understanding memory the two lines of research prevailed alternately; writing provided

9 This kind of aid must have been quite important in a culture that had very few technical tools to record data and in a limited manner. On the connections between the emerging of new technical tools, the ways we store data, and their impact on the knowledge production in the Modern Age and in the digital age, see for instance: Paolo Rossi, *Il passato, la memoria, l'oblio: Sei saggi di storia delle idee* (Bologna: Il Mulino, 2001); Anna M. Blair, *Too much to know: Managing Scholarly Information before the Modern Age* (New Haven and London: Yale University Press, 2010); Lorraine Daston, "The Sciences of the Archive," *Osiris* 27, 1 (2012), 156–187; *Science in the Archives: Pasts Presents Futures*, ed. Lorraine Daston (Chicago: University of Chicago Press, 2015); Luciano Floridi, *Information: A Very Short Introduction* (Oxford: Oxford University Press, 2010); Luciano Floridi, *The Ethics of Information* (Oxford: Oxford University Press, 2013); Luciano Floridi, *The Philosophy of Information* (Oxford: Oxford University Press, 2013); Luciano Floridi, *The Fourth Revolution. How the Infosphere Is Reshaping Human Reality* (Oxford: Oxford University Press, 2016).

the leading paradigm for their conceptual development; and the reflections on the evolution of writing techniques, modifying the leading paradigm, gradually made the conceptual shifts in memory theories and mnemonics comprehensible in another way.

7. The Renaissance and Giordano Bruno's *ars memoriae* provide a wealth of material concerning the relationship between these themes. Since the cutting-edge studies on the history of mnemonics by Frances A. Yates and Paolo Rossi,[10] Giordano Bruno is usually cited as the mnemonist who combined the various souls of the art of memory in the sixteenth century. That is to say, prior to its decline in a period in which the dissemination of print made the function of mnemonics redundant and before its partial incorporation into late seventeenth- and eighteenth-century studies on the *ars combinatoria* and language.

What I aim to explain is that Bruno's importance in the history of mnemonics and in an understanding of the development of philosophical memory theories also lies elsewhere. Firstly, Bruno strongly expresses in an innovative manner his awareness of the link between technical and conceptual evolution of the *ars memoriae*, between mnemonics as such and memory theories, and his awareness of their conceptual dependence to the evolution of writing techniques. Furthermore, it is precisely beginning with his reflections on the *ars memoriae* that Bruno develops a philosophy in which human creativity plays a central role in rearranging previous gnoseological, physical, and ethical orders and thereby laying the basis for modern ones. Thus, from this point of view it is the *ars memoriae* itself which Bruno forces into a philosophical theory of the soul seeking an ontological basis for mnemonics, which plays a role in the shift from the rearrangement of medieval philosophical conceptuality to the composition of a modern one.[11]

Thus, paraphrasing Thomas Mann, I have decided to find rest in this beginning and to establish Bruno's *De umbris idearum*, his first work on mnemonics, as my research objective in this book, with its underlying philosophical problems

10 Paolo Rossi, *Clavis universalis: Arti della memoria e logica combinatoria da Lullo a Leibniz* (Milan: Ricciardi, 1960); Frances A. Yates, *The Art of Memory* (London: Routledge and Kegan Paul, 1966).

11 Here I am implying the centrality of Bruno's thought in the transition from the Middle Ages to the Modern Age. In the following pages I shall not address the question of the legitimacy of this interpretation, because it oversteps the bounds of the present research. For this interpretation of Bruno's philosophy, see for instance: Ernst Cassirer, *Das Erkenntnisproblem in der Philosophie und Wissenschaft der neuren Zeit. Erster Band*, in Ernst Cassirer, *Gesammelte Werke. Hamburger Ausgabe. Band 2.* (Hamburg: Meiner, 1999), 225–261; Ernst Cassirer, *Individuum und Kosmos in der Philosophie der Renaissance* (Leipzig: G.B. Teubner, 1927); Hans Blumenberg, *Die Legitimität der Neuzeit*, 2nd revised edition (Frankfurt am Main: Suhrkamp, 1988).

mentioned earlier, namely: the impact of the writing experience on the understanding of the relationship between man and reality and the concept of spatial and temporal order in understanding the notion of memory.

8. Giordano Bruno's works on mnemonics have always been open to debate for scholars who either consider them as merely an expression of Bruno's interest in aspects of contemporary culture such as magical practices, Cabalistic and Hermetic interpretations, and mnemonics itself, which would bear little weight on the history of thought,[12] or else they attempt to adopt a holistic approach to Bruno's works.[13]

This makes the history of the interpretations of Bruno's mnemonics also highly relevant to understanding how the historical reception of mnemonics was affected by the conception of rationality that inspired the historiography on which this research was based. In fact, as long as the historiographic research model was dictated by the Enlightenment, so that all previous history moved towards modern rationality, mnemonics, magical practices and Cabalistic interpretation could only be viewed as mistakes to be corrected on the path towards the mature expression of modern rationality. Thus, according to this historiographic perspective, Giordano Bruno's works on the art of memory were considered expressions of a modern but immature spirit inclined to "dreams of reason", in a period moving towards eighteenth-century modern rationality that would triumph over imperfect historical manifestations.[14]

Not until the middle of the twentieth century would it be conceivable to interpret Bruno's works on the art of memory through perspectives that were outside the Enlightenment tradition. This new scholarship sought to restore those aspects of the Renaissance that had been adjusted to suit eighteenth-century interpretation in the light of the philosophy of modern history that was well entrenched in the Enlightenment tradition, but that had disappeared in the last century, amended from its interpretation in the perspective of the modern philosophies of history which were born during the Enlightenment, but that had disappeared in the last century.

Those who sought a more holistic and scholarly approach to Bruno's works on mnemonics by considering them within the culture of his time were Paolo Rossi

12 Felice Tocco, *Le opere latine di Giordano Bruno esposte e confrontate con le italiane* (Florence: Le Monnier, 1889).

13 Rossi, *Clavis universalis*, Yates, *The Art of Memory*, and more recently, Marco Matteoli, *Nel tempio di Mnemosine: L'arte della memoria di Giordano Bruno* (Pisa: Edizioni della Normale, 2019).

14 For a preliminary reconstruction of this debate, see: Michele Ciliberto, *Il Rinascimento: Storia di un dibattito* (Florence: La Nuova Italia, 1975).

and Frances A. Yates. Paolo Rossi[15] highlighted Bruno's continuation of the legacy left by Ramon Llull and the search for a *clavis universalis*, a universal science that would enable one to acquire complete knowledge of the universe and make it easily accessible to everyone. Conversely, Frances A. Yates[16] set Renaissance mnemonics and Bruno's *ars memoriae* within the history of the Renaissance Hermetic tradition. In this way, the English historian set the works on mnemonics in a context that was crucial to gaining a better understanding of the Renaissance, but at the same time rendered it more difficult to understand the texts, interpreting them as initiatory. This was completely in contrast to what Paolo Rossi sought to achieve, by proposing a semiotic reading of Bruno's mnemonics, as well as by seeking to position the history of mnemonics within the history of the development of the modern scientific method.

Although these two scholarly contributions are still essential for an understanding of the role of Bruno's works on mnemonics in relation to the history of this tradition and sixteenth-century thought, they leave open the question regarding the relationship between Bruno's works on memory and his philosophical works while still concentrating on the relationship between Bruno's *ars memoriae* and the culture of his day.

In conclusion, this book aims to make two contributions: first, to establish a hermeneutic paradigm for the history of philosophical and scientific memory theories that identifies the metaphor of inner writing as the leading metaphor for understanding memory; second, by applying the hermeneutic paradigm to Giordano Bruno's first mnemonic work, I aim to open up the path to an interpretation that enables us to understand the role of Bruno's mnemonic works within Bruno's works as a whole and more specifically in the development of his philosophy.

9. To establish this new hermeneutic paradigm, I will elaborate Hans Blumenberg's interpretation of Giordano Bruno, since it is Blumenberg who stresses Bruno's attempt to reconsider the concept of order. Following a critical analysis of this interpretation, I shall propose a metaphorological analysis of the *De umbris idearum* that will be the basis for a future examination of the use of the metaphor of inner writing in Bruno's philosophy.

Therefore, two parallel lines of argument will be developed in this book: one methodological and the other concerning textual analysis. The former will seek to identify the most effective hermeneutic paradigm to later study the role of Bruno's mnemonic works in relation to the development of his philosophical

15 Rossi, *Clavis universalis.*

16 Yates, *The Art of Memory*, and *Giordano Bruno and the Hermetic tradition* (Chicago: University of Chicago Press, 1964).

works. In the textual analysis, I shall discuss the hypothesis that the metaphor of inner writing is the leading paradigm in the conceptual formulation of mnemonics and that this paradigm enables us to place and understand Bruno's *ars memoriae* within his philosophical works because it highlights the importance of the concepts of order, nature, language, and creativity, which will be at the core of his philosophy.

The two lines of argument are developed over six chapters.

The first chapter defines the field of research beginning with a discussion of the distinction between theories of memory and mnemonics. Then I go on to provide examples of the rules and principles of mnemonics, and subsequently demonstrate that these elements, partly technical and partly of philosophical origin, remained the same throughout the mnemonic tradition, while their function changed in relation to the knowledge system and to the philosophical memory theories.

The second chapter is a transitional one. Through the analysis of three methodological approaches in studies of mnemonics, I re-define the research objective as the inner writing metaphor in Bruno's *De umbris idearum*. This redefinition is then substantiated in the next two chapters, where I present Blumenberg's *Die Legitimität der Neuzeit*,[17] focusing on the interpretation of historical transitions as re-modelling of conceptual order, and Blumenberg's *Paradigmen zu einer Metaphorologie*,[18] Blumenberg's first work on metaphorology, in which he argues that the reshaping of conceptual order (hence of historical epochs) occurs through the substitution or metamorphosis of leading metaphors by conceptual formulations.

Chapter five begins with an examination of Blumenberg's *Die Lesbarkeit der Welt*,[19] in which he analyses the absolute metaphor of the world as a book as a metaphor for the testability of reality. I argue that the metaphor of the world as a book, which also implies the notion of order, may be further explored and placed in the more general context of the metaphor of writing. Here I distance myself from Blumberg's interpretation of Bruno as the philosopher of Copernicanism and establish the scope and methods of my metaphorological research. Not only focusing on how Bruno uses the inner writing metaphor in his mnemonic works to be an aid to better understanding the mnemonic tradition, but we will also better grasp Bruno's philosophy itself, reinstating Bruno's independent thinking.

17 Hans Blumenberg, *Die Legitimität der Neuzeit* (Frankfurt am Main: Suhrkamp, 1966; 2nd edition revised, Frankfurt am Main: Suhrkamp, 1988).

18 Hans Blumenberg, "Paradigmen zu einer Metaphorologie", *Archiv für Begriffsgeschichte* 6, (1960): 7–142.

19 Hans Blumenberg *Die Lesbarkeit der Welt* (Frankfurt am Main: Suhrkamp, 1981; 2nd edition revised, Frankfurt am Main: Suhrkamp, 1983).

Chapter six completes the metaphorological account on Giordano Bruno's first mnemonic work, *De umbris idearum*. The textual analysis of the *De umbris idearum* will serve to reveal how the metaphor of inner writing is an aid to understanding three traits of Bruno's *ars memoriae*, namely its *consistency*, *continuity*, and *excess* in the mnemonic tradition. Referring to *excess*, I will conclude showing how Bruno's *ars memoriae* preludes to the central notions of his philosophy.

Chapter 1: Mnemonics and theories of the memory

(...) this circumstance suggested to him the discovery of the truth that the best aid to clearness of memory consists in orderly arrangement. He inferred that persons desiring to train this faculty must select localities and form mental images of the facts they wish to remember and store those images in the localities, with the result that the arrangement of the localities will preserve the order of the facts, and the images of the facts will designate the facts themselves, and we shall employ the localities and images respectively as a wax writing tablet and the letters written on it.

– Cicero, *De or.*, II, lxxxvi, 353–354

1. Definition of the field of research (1): Mnemonics and memory theories

The history of mnemonics as an artificial aid to memory, which was widespread prior to the advent of the printing press, began in Greek Antiquity and continued until the seventeenth century. As this is a long, complex, multifaceted history involving long-lasting rules and features, which interacted with several other disciplines and raised issues of a theoretical nature, it would be best to start by distinguishing between mnemonics and memory theories.

Since Antiquity philosophers have sought to define and explain the various functions of the soul, namely the different ways that the soul interacts with reality. The function that enables the soul to retain in some form what has been experienced once and enables it to be available for other functions later and without the physical stimulus that originally produced that which has been retained is called *memory.*

Memory theories were the philosophical interpretations that investigated the role and functioning of memory within a theory of the soul. In other words, they were theories that examined the function of memory within a theory of knowledge which also investigated the other functions of the soul. This theory of knowledge had to be capable of summarizing the various functions of the soul in order to apprehend how we relate to the world and are able to operate in it. On the other hand, mnemonics gathered a series of precepts that originated in ancient Greece within the rhetorical tradition to improve natural memory, by using a series of images that were placed in a certain order and sequence in mental locations, whether real or imaginary ones.

Thus, what distinguishes memory theories from mnemonics is the relationship they have with the theory of knowledge and the theory of the soul. Memory theories are part of the theory of knowledge and contribute to the comprehension of how the soul works, while mnemonics is a technique that does not challenge the principles and doctrine of an implicit memory and soul theory but allow us an occasional glimpse of them during their treatises.

2. Definition of the field of research (2): Selection of the sources for the history of mnemonics

If we consider the history of the *ars memoriae* from the point of view of the role it played in Western systems of knowledge prior to the advent of the printing press, then it could be argued that the model of historical development proposed by Frances A. Yates is still convincing and could be summarized in three moments.[20] Mnemonics, originating in ancient Greece, was further developed in Roman times for rhetorical purposes (rhetorical use of memory). It was then thoroughly reformed in the Middle Ages through the application of Aristotle's memory theories (ethical use of artificial memory). While the late Renaissance was a period of great advances in mnemonic theories and prolific output of works on the subject, at the same time this period also saw the gradual decline of its popularity due to the ever-increasing use of printed books which made this artificial support to natural memory largely obsolete (*ars memoriae* and universal knowledge).

20 Frances A. Yates, *The Art of Memory* (London: Routledge and Kegan Paul, 1966; London: Pimlico, 2000). Citations refer to the Pimlico edition. Although Frances A. Yates' interpretation of the *ars memoriae* was the subject of considerable debate, some of the points that the British historian proposed, apart from the widespread Hermeticism in which Yates places Renaissance and Bruno's mnemonics, are still didactically valid as an introduction to the study of the history of mnemonics in relation to the philosophical theories of memory. It is therefore only from this perspective that I am referring here to the course of the history of mnemonics, as outlined in the work first published in 1966. On the critiques to Frances A. Yates' interpretations, see for instance: Francesca Dell'Omodarme, "Frances A. Yates interprete di Giordano Bruno: appunti per una ricerca," *Rinascimento* 41, (2001): 353–374; Guido Giglioni, "Who is afraid of Frances Yates? 'Giordano Bruno and the Hermetic tradition' (1964) fifty years later," *Bruniana and Campanelliana* 20, no. 2 (2014): 421–432.

However, if we consider mnemonics not in reference to the role it played in Western systems of thought, but within a broader cultural context, we can only agree with Paolo Rossi who speaks of a persistence of the presence of mnemonic systems up to the present day in the form of "intellectual fossils".[21] Indeed, it is still quite common to see posters on the walls of our cities advertising courses to improve our memory, or else to read more or less scientific articles that recommend the best lifestyle or diet to enhance or boost powers of recall and maintain them over time. Those who have studied the history of mnemonics easily recognize rhetorical precepts of ancient Greek origin, observations made over the centuries and even some rules that came from other disciplines, such as medicine, intended to improve one's memory. They are termed "fossils" because their cultural function no longer reflects their original one in the centuries predating the printing press, nor do they have much in common with their function in the seventeenth century, a period that marks the beginning of the decline of mnemonics as a distinct discipline. In fact, the final applications of mnemonics may be traced to studies that would ultimately lead to Leibniz' *ars combinatoria*, to classification systems and the introduction of encyclopaedias during the Enlightenment, and to eighteenth- and nineteenth-century language studies.

The precise boundaries of the history of mnemonics are unimportant here. What is important is that throughout the history of the *ars memoriae* its definition remained the same, as did its core precepts, as illustrated by the following summary of key sources for mnemonic wsystems and how they evolved up to the sixteenth century.

The sources under examination have been chosen because they are representative for each period and for the reception of mnemonics in different epochs. The selection was made using the following criteria: sources that defined the discipline, its rules, and problems associated with the discipline (Latin rhetorical sources); memory theories that may not be counted as mnemonic systems but contributed to reshaping some aspects of the classical conception of memory, above all in the Middle Ages and during the Renaissance (Aristotle's memory theory); medieval sources that combined mnemonic traditions with Aristotelian philosophical theories (Albertus Magnus and Thomas Aquinas) and those that sought to define the criteria of a universal science accessible to everyone (Augustine and Ramon Llull).

21 Paolo Rossi, *Clavis universalis: Arti della memoria e logica combinatoria da Lullo a Leibniz* (3rd ed. Bologna: Il Mulino, 2000). Translated by Stephen Clucas as *Logic and the Art of Memory: The Quest for a Universal Language* (Chicago: Chicago University Press, 2000), xxi. Citations refer to the translation of Stephen Clucas. About the "intellectual fossils" also in relation to the meaning and the study of the history of ideas, see: Paolo Rossi, *Il passato, la memoria, l'oblio: Sei saggi di storia delle idee* (Bologna: Il Mulino, 2001), 59–62.

The limited number of texts dealt with here do not reflect the wealth and variety of texts produced throughout the history of the art of memory. However, the choice of texts is research-oriented, namely the aim is: to explain the nature of mnemonics and how it is different from philosophical memory theories; to explain the rules and principles of memory techniques; to illustrate how the core of mnemonics, which consists of technical elements (mnemonic rules) and elements of philosophical origin (mnemonic principles) remained unchanged, even if the function of mnemonics changed in relation to knowledge systems and to philosophical memory theories that mnemonists followed.

2.1 Latin sources for mnemonics

In Antiquity, memory was one of the five canons of rhetoric,[22] apart from being considered part of the soul and therefore of philosophical interest. Not only was mnemonics related to treatises on rhetoric, but it was also actually at the heart of them, being a set of rules through which the orator could improve their memorization of various, long and complex speeches that would then be declaimed from memory.

The classical sources for the mnemonic arts are of Latin origin, in textbooks dealing with rhetoric: the anonymous text *Rhetorica ad Herennium*,[23] *De oratore*[24] by Cicero, and Quintilian's *Institutio oratoria*.[25] As regards Greek sources

22 The five canons of rhetoric were: *inventio*, *dispositio*, *elocutio*, *memoria*, and *pronuntiatio*. Cicero defined them thus: "Therefore the material of the art of rhetoric seems to me to be that which we said Aristotle approved. The parts of it, as most authorities have stated, are Invention, Arrangement, Expression, Memory, Delivery. Invention is the discovery of valid or seemingly valid arguments to render one's cause plausible. Arrangement is the distribution of arguments thus discovered in the proper order. Expression is the fitting of the proper language to the invented matter. Memory is the firm mental grasp of matter and words. Delivery is the control of voice and body in a manner suitable to the dignity of the subject matter and the style," "Quare materia quidem nobis rhetoricae videtur artis ea quam Aristoteli visam esse diximus; partes autem eae quas plerique dixerunt, inventio, dispositio, elocutio, memoria, pronuntiatio. Inventio est excogitatio rerum verarum aut veri similium quae causam probabilem reddant; dispositio est rerum inventarum in ordinem distributio; elocutio est idoneorum verborum ad inventionem accomodatio; memoria est firma animi rerum ac verborum perceptio; pronuntiatio est ex rerum et verborum dignitate vocis et corporis moderatio," Cicero, *Inv. rhet.*, I, vii, 9, in Cicero, *On Invention. The Best Kind of Orator. Topics*, trans. H.M. Hubbel (Cambridge, MA: Harvard University Press, 1949), 18–21.

23 [Cicero], *Rhetorica ad Herennium*, trans. Harry Caplan (Cambridge, MA: Harvard University Press, 1954).

24 Cicero, *On the Orator: Books 1–2*, trans. E. W. Sutton and H. Rackham (Cambridge, MA: Harvard University Press, 1942).

25 Quintilian, *The Orator's Education, Volume V: Books 11–12*, ed. and trans. Donald A. Russell (Cambridge, MA: Harvard University Press, 2001).

for mnemonic texts, none have survived to this day, even if Latin sources refer to an important authoritative Greek mnemonic tradition which the Latin textbooks on rhetoric were in fact based on.[26]

The *precepts* of classical mnemonic systems as dealt with in the three Latin textbooks on rhetoric were the following: 1. To impress on the mind a series of places (*loci*) that were either real or imaginary; 2. to associate each object (*res*) or word (*verbum*) of the speech to be memorized with an image (*imago*); 3. to arrange the images in the places according to the order or sequence (*ordo*) in which the objects or words were placed in the speech to be memorized; 4. to exercise the memory by mentally revisiting the places to become accustomed to seeing the images located therein.

In addition to these precepts, there were five *general principles* on which the precepts were based. These principles, which reflect ancient Greek philosophical conceptions, were the underlying prerequisites for all extant treatises on mnemonics. Although the authors refer to the principles, they never discuss them, assuming that the reader would be already familiar with them.

The first principle concerns the distinction between natural memory (*memoria naturalis*) and artificial memory (*memoria artificiosa*). *Memoria naturalis* is the natural faculty of the soul to retain past sensations as images and recall them even when the physical sensation that produced them is no longer present. *Memoria artificiosa* is the product of the application of mnemonic precepts, namely the memory system created with the use of mnemonic *loci* and *imagines*. The simplest artificial memory system that can be constructed is the one that helps us remember a list of things. For example, if I want to remember in the following order: horse, dog, eagle, shoe, book, cork, first I choose a place where I can put the images of these objects. To simplify memorizing, I can imagine a room with six recesses, each of which is large enough to contain the image of the object so that it is clearly visible inside the recess. Then I place each object in a recess, in the same order that I wish to recall the images. Revisiting the room and following the same itinerary from the first to the last recess ensures that I will memorize the list I wish to recall.

The second principle stresses the importance of order (*ordo*) itself, both during the creation of the artificial memory (creation of the system of images composed of *loci* and *imagines* and fixing them firmly in the mind), as well as during the phase of recall of the objects (namely, when I revisit the mnemonic *loci* to retrieve the *imagines* of the objects there). Indeed, order is the principle that ensures the success of the technique: memory is required to retain and reproduce

---

26 See, for example: *Rhet Her.*, III, xxiii, 38, in [Cicero], *Rhetorica ad Herennium*, 220–223; Cicero, *De or.*, II, lxxxviii, 360, in Cicerone, *On the Orator*, 470–471; Quintilian, *Inst.*, XI, ii, 22–26, in Quintilian, *The Orator's Education*, 68–71.

an existing order in reality, and this is possible by virtue of the fact that the soul is able to order information on experience.

The third and fourth principles are linked together. One asserts the primacy of the sense of sight over the other senses, and the other consequently focuses on the central importance of wonder during the learning process as well as during memorization. These three principles clearly express the origins of mnemotechnics within the philosophical system in Antiquity. Sight was considered superior to the other senses since the cosmos (*kosmos*) was apprehended through conceptual forms, such as ideas, but also through sensory forms, such as the images that came from sense experience.

Finally, the fifth principle, which is also linked to the previous two, recalls the central role of analogy in the creation of the artificial memory system. Here analogy should be interpreted broadly to mean imitation of nature and it is applied to the choice of mnemonic images as well as the general conception of the relationship between souls and nature. Since the artificial memory system is a support for natural memory, the choice of images is based on their similarity to the objects or words that need to be remembered. However, this is possible by virtue of the fact that the mnemonic rules to create *memoria artificiosa* are based on the principles that determine the functioning of *memoria naturalis* and imitate them through analogy.

2.1.1 *Rhetorica ad Herennium*

As the *Rhetorica ad Herennium* is the most detailed and complete treatise on mnemonic techniques, as well as being the most influential in the history of the *ars memoriae*, I shall discuss this text more thoroughly to illustrate the precepts of mnemonic systems and show how the authors of texts on mnemonics used its principles.

The *Rhetorica ad Herennium* is an anonymous text, probably written between AD 86 and AD 82, for a long time attributed to Cicero.[27] It is a manual on rhetoric

27 In the Middle Ages it was still attributed to Cicero and, in fact, this text was referred to as *rhetorica nova* or *secunda* to distinguish it from Cicero, *De inventione*, which was known as *rhetorica vetus* o *rhetorica prima.* In 1491, however, the Venetian humanist Raphael Regius demonstrated that this attribution was incorrect and proposed another two possible authors, including Cornificio: Raphael Regius, *Utrum ars rhetorica ad H. Ciceroni falso iscribatur*, in *Duecenta problemata in totidem institutionis oratoriae Quintiliani depravationes*, Venezia, 1491. This information can be found in Rossi, *Logic and the Art of Memory*, chap. 1, note 18, 246. According to Frances A. Yates, *Rhetorica ad Herennium* is the text responsible for passing mnemonics not only down to the Middle Ages, but also to the Renaissance: Yates, *The Art of Memory*, 21. For an introduction to the history of the reception of *Rhetorica ad Herennium* in the Middle Ages and the early Renaissance, see: Virginia Cox and John O.

and the part devoted to memory (*Rhet. Her.*, III, xvi–xxiv)[28] is divided into two sections: one addresses general questions concerning the distinction between natural and artificial memory (*Rhet. Her.*, III, xvi) and the other goes into the details of the precepts of mnemonics, discussing difficulties linked to the study of mnemonics, and provides some advice on how to make it more effective in the context of rhetorical practice (*Rhet. Her.*, III, xvii–xxiv).

The section on memory begins with the question of whether a natural memory and an artificial memory exist, as each mnemonic treatise claims. The author declares that, although this is not the place to deal with the problem (which he clearly regards as a philosophical and not rhetorical one)[29] he agrees with this distinction, taking it as the starting point for his interpretation. He then goes on to present the definition of natural memory and artificial memory according to rhetorical tradition and states that natural memory is innate in the soul, like thought, whereas artificial memory is obtained through the practice of specific techniques (*ars*).[30]

Whilst accepting as a fact the existence of the two types of memory, the author of *Rhetorica ad Herennium* also explains the relationship between them and posits that natural memory is pre-eminent over artificial memory. This is because although it is true that technique and constant training may result in artificial memory competing with natural memory, it is also true that without a well-established natural memory, technique and training would be of little help.

When the author addresses the rules for *ars memoriae*, he introduces the elements that artificial memory is built on, namely the mental places (*loci*) and images (*imagines*) that are defined as follows:

> By backgrounds I mean such scenes as are naturally or artificially set off on a small scale, complete and conspicuous, so that we can grasp and embrace them easily by the natural memory – for example, a house, an intercolumnar space, a recess, an arch, or the like. An image is, as it were, a figure, mark, or portrait of the object we wish to remember; for example, if we wish to recall a horse, a lion, or an eagle, we must place its image in a definite back-ground.[31]

Ward, eds., *The Rhetoric of Cicero in its Medieval and Early Renaissance Commentary Tradition* (Leiden: Brill, 2006).

28 *Rhet. Her.*, III, xvi, 28–xxiv, 40, in [Cicero], *Rhetorica ad Herennium*, 204–225.

29 It is a problem concerning the theories of memory and not mnemonics, according to the categories introduced here, pp. 31–32.

30 *Rhet. Her.*, III, xvi, 28, in [Cicero], *Rhetorica ad Herennium*, 206–207.

31 "Locos appellamus eos qui breviter, perfecte, insignite aut natura aut manu sunt absoluti, ut eos facile naturali memoria conprehendere et amplecti queamus; ut aedes, intercolumnium, angulum, fornicem, et alia quae his similia sunt. Imagines sunt formae quaedam et notae et simulacra eius rei quam meminisse volumus; quod genus equi, leonis, aquilae memoriam si volemus habere, imagines eorum locis certis conlocare oportebit," *Rhet. Her.*, III, xvi, 29, in [Cicero], *Rhetorica ad Herennium*, 208–209.

The effectiveness of the technique to improve natural memory is completely reliant on the choice of mnemonic places and images and therefore specific rules need to be followed, which are based on the natural characteristics of thought and memory.

For the choice of places (*Rhet. Her.*, III, xvii–xix), the text recommends that there should be several, and arranged in a sequence because it is easier to recall something which is placed in a certain order: they should be consistent in the memory system to avoid confusion by juxtaposing places that are too different. The places should also be quiet and devoid of any crowds of people that could disturb memory, and they should be well-defined, in order not to confuse the mind. The size of the place should be such that the object itself is in sharp relief, and the lighting adequate. Finally, the space between the places should not exceed thirty feet so that moving from one place to another is swift and the flow of images uninterrupted. Moreover, the *loci* may be real or fictitious, although if a fictitious place is used it is advisable to have a strong imagination to avoid problems mentioned above.

As regards the rules for choosing images (*Rhet. Her.*, III, xx), the author explains that as the images should resemble the things to memorize, they should be based on the principle of likeness (*similitudo*).[32] There are two types of likeness, reflecting the two kinds of things to be remembered: likeness of things (*rerum similitudines*) and likeness of words (*verborum similitudines*),[33] where the things (*res*) are both objects and physical reality corresponding to the material world, and the subject matter of the speech, and words (*verba*) are the individual words in the speech. The choice of a specific image that will best resemble the word or thing to be remembered is left to the nature of the soul. For example, it is well known that what is unusual or bizarre attracts our attention much more than a normal, everyday occurrence, and hence is also recalled much more easily. Consequently, it is preferable to choose unusual or striking mnemonic images to accommodate the soul and boost the natural memory faculty.

Hence, *memoria artificiosa* should *imitate nature.* This underlying premise of mnemonic precepts should be kept in mind when reading mnemonic treatises. Not only does it follow that mental images and places should imitate nature, but also that general criteria concerning the nature of thought and its function that are like the ones for natural memory should be used to define the rules for the

32 *Rhet. Her.*, 212–213, in [Cicero], *Rhetorica ad Herennium*, III, xx, 33.

33 "Likenesses of matter are formed when we enlist images that present a general view of the matter with which we are dealing; likenesses of words are established when the record of each single noun or appellative is kept by an image," "Rerum similitudines exprimuntur cum summatim ipsorum negotiorum imagines conparamus; verborum similitudines constituuntur cum unius cuiusque nominis et vocabuli memoria imagine notator," *Rhet. Her.*, III, xx, 33, in [Cicero], *Rhetorica ad Herennium*, 214–215.

composition of artificial memory. As we have seen, while the choice of mental places should meet the criteria of order and uniformity, the choice of images focuses on what is unusual or repugnant, anything that can draw our attention and provoke an emotional reaction.[34]

The importance of analogy, but also the problems that arise from its use when creating a system of artificial memory, emerges in the distinction between *rerum similitudines* and *verborum similitudines*, in other words in the distinction that in the medieval and Renaissance tradition would become a distinction between *memoria rerum* and *memoria verborum*. This was one of the most discussed and criticized problems in mnemotechnics, but it was also the one that was focused on to a greater extent and enabled the discipline to develop. Hence, let us examine the examples given by the author of *Rhetorica ad Herennium* for the choice of *agentes*.

There is no specific problem in choosing images for the *memoria rerum*. The term *res* refers to the subject and themes of the speech, to the "things of the speech" and, as author provides an example of a law suit, the things are concrete and the situations may easily be represented by images. In this hypothetical law suit we are supposed to defend a client accused of poisoning a man to in order to gain an inheritance and there are many witnesses and accomplices in this crime:

> We are forming a memory system about the whole case and we shall wish to put in our first memory *locus* an image to remind us of the accusation against our client. This is the image: "We shall imagine the man in question is lying ill in bed, if we know him personally. If we do not know him, we shall yet take some one to be our invalid, but not a man of the lowest class, so that he may come to mind at once. And we shall place the defendant at the bedside, holding in his right hand a cup, in his left, tablets, and on the fourth finger, a ram's testicles. In this way we can have in memory the man who was poisoned, the witnesses, and the inheritance [*Rhet. Her.*, III, xx, 33]." The cup would remind of the poisoning, the tablets of the will or the inheritance, and the testicles of the ram through verbal similarity with testes – of the witnesses. The sick man is to be like the man himself, or like someone else whom we know (though not one of the anonymous lower classes). In the following *loci* we would put other counts in the charge, or the details of the rest of the case, and if we have properly imprinted the places and images we shall easily be able to remember any point that we wish to recall.[35]

As Frances A. Yates illustrates so well in this passage, there is no difficulty in creating a memory system for *memoria rerum* and its efficacy is evident. Indeed, even without deliberately creating a memory system according to mnemonic rules, we naturally turn to analogies that we place in a certain order when we wish to memorize a series of events or a particular situation. *Memoria rerum* just

34 See fig. 8.
35 Yates, *The Art of Memory*, 27.

exploits the natural features of memory and makes it a conscious process that uses codified rules to recall and improve the natural memory faculty.

This point is worth stressing as it shows how in the mnemonic systems in Antiquity a highly specific performance was required of artificial memory, but at the same time it could be minimal in the sense that effective functioning of memorizing was ensured through technically consolidating the rules of natural memory. This request for minimal participation by artificial memory should come as no surprise, but rather could be helpful in gaining an in-depth understanding of the relations between natural and artificial memory, and more generally the relation between *ars* and nature. We have already seen that artificial memory cannot substitute natural memory, but rather serves to make it more efficient. The tool to make it more efficient is the *ars* that should make use of and enhance the natural features of the memory faculty. Unable to substitute or modify nature, the *ars* has an analogical relationship with it and serves to enhance nature through the perfection of its own characteristics.

The choice of images becomes more problematic when one turns to the practice of *memoria verborum*, namely when a mnemonic system is created to remember all the words in a speech. Indeed, *memoria verborum* means memorizing a far greater number of images compared to *memoria rerum*, as the relation between words and images should be one to one. Furthermore, one should be able to find phonetic or linguistic associations that enable us to recollect the words, as Frances A. Yates explains so well when commenting on the example provided in *Rhetorica ad Herennium* (*Rhet. Her.*, III, xxi, 34):

> We are setting out to memorise this line of verse: "Iam domum itionem reges Atridae parant (And now their homecoming the kings, the sons of Atreus are making ready)." (…) It is to be memorised through two very extraordinary images.
>
> One is 'Domitius raising his hands to heaven while he is lashed by the Marcii Reges'. The translator and editor of the text in the Loeb Edition (H. Caplan) explains in a note that 'Rex was the name of one of the most distinguished families of the Marcian *gens*; the Dominitian, of plebeian origin, was likewise a celebrated *gens*'. The image may reflect some street scene in which Domitius of the plebeian gens (perhaps bloodstained to make him more memorable) is being beaten up by some members of the distinguished Rex family. It was perhaps a scene which the author himself had witnessed. Or perhaps it was a scene in some play. It was a striking scene in every sense of the word and therefore suitable as a mnemonic image. It was put on a place for remembering this line. The vivid image immediately brought to mind 'Domitius-Reges' and this reminded by *sound resemblance of 'domum itionem reges'*. It thus exhibits the principles of a 'memory for words' image which brings to mind the words which the memory is seeking through their sound resemblance to the notion suggested by the image. (…)
>
> The other image for memorising the rest of the line is 'Aesopus and Cimber being dressed for the roles of Agamennon and Menelaus in *Iphigenaia*'. Aesopus was a well-known tragic actor, a friend of Cicero; Cimber, evidently also an actor, is only men-

> tioned in this text. (…) In the image these actors are being dressed to play the parts of the sons of Atreus (Agamennon and Menelaus). It is an exciting off-stage glimpse of two famous actors being made up (to smear an image with red paint makes it memorable according to the rules) and dressed for their parts. Such a scene has all the elements of a good mnemonic image; we therefore use it to remember *'Atridae parant'*, the sons of Atreus are making ready. This image immediately gave the word *'Atridae'* (though not by sound resemblance) and also suggested 'making ready' for the home-coming through the actors making ready for the stage.[36]

Although this is an extremely good example because the author of *Rhetorica ad Herennium* has no trouble finding phonetic analogies or references to episodes in the cultural life of his time that attract his attention and help the soul to recall, it is immediately evident that finding such analogies is not always simple. Indeed, a much greater effort would have to be made than that made by natural memory if one were to memorize the verse without creating a system of artificial memory.

In fact, the main criticism of the use of mnemonics concentrates on the difficulties linked to the *memoria verborum*, as we shall now see with both Cicero and Quintilian. The most common criticism of the mnemonic system concerns the efficacy of a technique that requires a great effort to memorize a speech with a certain number of words, in which not only do the speakers have to memorize a number of images that exceeds the number of words, but they also have to establish analogies that may be difficult to memorize because they have no relation to reality.

The section on the *ars memoriae* in *Rhetorica ad Herennium* ends with some practical recommendations regarding the study of the techniques that have just been explained, perhaps as an indirect answer to this critique. Specifically, the first piece of advice is that pupils should be allowed to choose *their* personal places and create *their own* images. The author of *Rhetorica ad Herennium* criticizes the teaching that was typical of the Greek authors of textbooks on rhetoric that usually provided long lists of pre-codified images that were ready for use. This pedagogical approach was considered wrong because it failed to consider the kind of attention and memory kept alive by those things and associations that strike us most. Providing a ready-made list of mnemonic places and images forces the pupil to make an immense effort to memorize a speech, defeating the original purpose, especially if the image were not able to attract the pupil's attention and the faculty of natural memory. Finally, the last exhortation is to practise mnemonic exercises daily, whether the person has a strong natural memory or is an expert at artificial memory, because only by revisiting inner places and the images placed within every day can the orator ensure that he has mastered the speech he will declaim by heart. Daily exercise is also essential for

36 Yates, *The Art of Memory*, 29–30.

the *memoria verborum*, because less evident analogies are made more obvious through habit and in some way the pupil will become accustomed to recognizing and "seeing" them immediately.

2.1.2 Cicero, *De oratore*

Written in 55 BC, Cicero's *De oratore* is the result of his mature conception of rhetoric as a discipline that is founded not only on the rules of the school, but also on a broader cultural education of the rhetorician that includes philosophy and history. The work is in the form of a Platonic philosophical dialogue, and not only does it discuss the precepts of rhetoric, but above all it refers to the general principles on which the precepts are founded.

This model may also be found in treatises on memory, so that among the Latin sources Cicero's work is the one that insists most on the general and philosophical principles that we mentioned earlier, namely: the distinction between natural and artificial memory, the concept of order, the function of wonder in learning, analogy as imitation of nature, and the predominance of sight. However, even Cicero, like the anonymous author of *Rhetorica ad Herennium*, does not focus on the principles of mnemonic techniques, but limits himself to emphasizing that it is thanks to these that the mnemonic rules are an effective aid for the rhetorician. Considering the importance of Cicero in spreading Greek philosophy in Rome, his choice is a good example of the distinction made between memory theory and *ars memoriae*.

Cicero begins the section on memory[37] by explaining why it is effective and valuable for the orator, going on to say that even if nature is the main source for memory, it is evident that it may be consolidated and improved through exercise. For those who believe that the *ars memoriae* is not a help to natural memory because it burdens the natural faculty, Cicero argues that although mnemonic techniques are no substitute for the natural faculty, they are certainly able to strengthen it if it is weak.[38]

37 Cicero, *De or.*, II, lxxxv, 350–lxxxviii, 360, in Cicero, *On the Orator*, 462–473.

38 Cicero deals with this criticism in reference to the opportunity to speak of *ars* referring to mnemonics, and not of the natural characteristics of the faculty of memory: "And consequently for my own part I confess that the chief source of this endowment, as of all the things I have spoken of before, is nature; but the efficacy of the whole of this science, or perhaps I should say pseudoscience, of rhetoric, is not that it wholly originates and engenders something no part of which is already present in our minds, but that it fosters and strengthens things that have already sprung to birth within us," "Quare confiteor equidem huius boni naturam esse principem, sicut earum rerum de quibus ante locutus sum omnium: sed haec ars tota dicendi, sive artis imago quaedam et similitudo est, habet hanc vim, non ut totum aliquid cuius in ingeniis nostris pars nulla sit pariat et procreet, verum ut ea quae sunt orta

Thus, like the author of *Rhetorica ad Herennium,* Cicero also makes the distinction between memory as a natural faculty and artificial memory as the result of the application of the *ars*, which he believes are at the basis of the mnemonic arts. However, unlike the author of *Rhetorica ad Herennium*, what Cicero seeks to do is to establish the efficacy of the *ars* and by referring to the key principles of the mnemonic arts that concern the nature of the soul and knowledge. The two fundamental principles he cites are the principle of order, by virtue of which artificial memory creates a copy of the real order, and the principle of the primacy of the sense of sight, founded on the theory of perception which states that sensory experience is stored in the soul in the form of images.

The two principles are then brought together and illustrated by the story that attributes the invention of mnemonics to Simonides of Ceo,[39] who developed a system founded on order as an essential aid to recollection[40] since it was based on the sense of sight that was the most perceptive of the senses. This also explains why the choice of places is important to store the images. Indeed, according to the theory of perception Cicero refers to, images conveyed by our senses are stored in our mind and since images are bodies and bodies are recognizable if positioned within a place, it is thus suitable to use a system of mental places in which mental images are placed.[41]

As regards mnemotechnic rules, Cicero cites in more or less detail the precepts as they are found in the *Rhetorica ad Herennium* and so we need not examine them here. However, what he says concerning the *memoria verborum* and *memoria rerum* is interesting:

> But a memory for words, which for us is less essential, is given distinctness by a greater variety of images; for there are many words which serve as joints connecting the limbs of the sentence, and these cannot be formed by any use of simile – of these we have model images for constant employment; but a memory for things is the special property of the orator – this we can imprint on our minds by a skillful arrangement of the several masks that represent them, so that we may grasp ideas by means of images and their order by means of localities.[42]

---

iam in nobis et procreata educet atque confirmet," Cicero, *De or.*, II, lxxxviii, 356, in Cicero, *On the Orator*, 468–469.

39 See here, Introduction, p. 20.

40 Cicero, *De or.*, II, lxxxvi, 353–354, in Cicero, *On the Orator*, 466–467.

41 Cicero, *De or.*, II, lxxxvii, 358, in Cicero, *On the Orator*, 468–469.

42 "Sed verborum memoria, quae minus est nobis necessaria, maiore imaginum varietate distinguitur; multa enim sunt verba quae quasi articuli connectunt membra orationis quae formari similitudine nulla possunt; eorum fingendae nobis sunt imagines quibus semper utamur; rerum memoria propria est oratoris; eam singulis personis bene positis notare possumus ut sententias imaginibus, ordinem locis comprehendamus," Cicero, *De or.*, II, lxxxviii, 359, in Cicero, *On the Orator*, 470–471.

The memory of things is the part that is characteristic of the orator's speech, and the precepts of mnemonic techniques are perfect for this. Indeed, the orator is asked to create and declaim speeches that have as their subject tangible cases from daily life, so there is no problem in finding images in the sensory world. On the other hand, recalling words is the hardest part in mnemonics, since there are words that may be impossible to represent as analogies with things. Cicero is not referring to abstract words here, but to parts of the speech such as conjunctions. In this case, Cicero recommends using a certain number of fixed images that are repeated identically in each new memory system.[43]

Here Cicero perceives one of the limits of artificial memory closely connected to sight as a privileged sense, and to the fact that the possibility of spatial memory is based on sight. The problem is that not every word may have a natural image associated with it, as there are words that do not refer directly to things in the real world. Thus, to represent these words that have no reference in nature, one needs to make use of stock images that have the same meaning in the various systems of artificial memory that the mnemonist creates.

The solution suggested by Cicero is effective and makes sense, but from the philosophical point of view raises a problem that would weaken the reliability of mnemotechnics as an *ars* able to imitate nature and ensure order in the mental images that correspond to the order of perceived reality. In other words, Cicero provides no answer to the question of how the connection between words and what they stand for is made, nor to the question of the correspondence of natural order to that of mental images. We shall see that it is above all the latter question that would arise later in the Renaissance and would be one of the problems of mnemonic systems that Giordano Bruno would try to find a solution to.

2.1.3 Quintilian, *Institutio oratoria*

Quintilian's key work, the *Institutio oratoria* (probably written between AD 93 and AD 96 when it was published), sets out the rhetorician's educational programme of cultural and moral reform. His section on *ars memoriae* is one of the classical sources that expresses the most doubts and criticisms on the educational efficacy of mnemonic systems. This aspect in itself is highly important as a source and is worth exploring in order to highlight the critical points in the *ars memoriae*, that is to say those points that would be developed later in order to improve the technique.

43 On the birth of stenography, which Plutarch attributes to Cicero, see: Yates, *The Art of Memory*, chap. 1, note 16, 375.

The chapter on the *ars memoriae*[44] can be divided into three sections: memory as a natural faculty (*Inst.*, XI, ii, 1–10); critique of the *ars memoriae* (*Inst.* XI, II, 11–26); several suggestions and recommendations on memorizing the text that fall outside the traditional mnemotechnical precepts (*Inst.*, XI, ii, 27–51).

Book XI of the *Institutio oratoria* opens with a eulogy to memory, considered by most people a gift of nature, but for an orator this needs to be trained through specific exercises. Quintilian then discusses the kind of exercises that are most suitable. As a rhetorician interested in the various aspects of education he is rather sceptical about the use of mnemonic devices, specifically as regards the efficacy of superimposing artificial memory on natural memory, and so is more inclined to train and strengthen natural memory directly. Nevertheless, as we shall see, Quintilian still outlines memory techniques and urges the student of rhetoric to acquaint themselves with these devices and use them, if only according to each student's needs.

According to Quintilian, memory is the essential element in the learning process and in knowledge, as it enables us to combine the individual masters' teachings to their pupils and because it allows us to have a collection of examples, laws, everyday phrases at hand as well as all those elements that a good orator needs when producing a speech. However, memory is not considered a passive faculty, as – together with thought (*cogitatio*) – it is involved in the composition (*inventio*) and style (*elocutio*) of the subjects of a speech.[45] Memory is an extraordinary faculty, since on the one hand it acts independently because we cannot always decide what to remember (we often remember events better that occurred in the more distant past than more recent ones). Indeed, sometimes it is the memory itself that emerges unbidden. However, on the other hand our experience shows that memory and reason interact providing mutual aid and this may be proof that there must be a feature of memory that is unnatural, which depends on an *ars* that can enhance this cooperation.

Quintilian is firm in his belief that suggestions and recommendations may be made to strengthen natural memory, and deep concentration and a sharp eye, as well as regular training, may help memorization, as the story of Simonides suggests. Apart from the reliability of the attribution to Simonides of this invention,[46] it appears that this event inspired the supposition that memory may be

---

44 Quintilian, *Inst.*, XI, ii, 1–51, in Quintilian, *The Orator's Education*, 58–85.

45 Quintilian links this active aspect of memory to Plato's criticism in *Phaedrus*, 275 A, perhaps Plato meant that once we have entrusted what we want to say to pen and paper, we are no longer involved personally: Quintilian, *Inst.*, XI, ii, 9–10, in Quintilian, *The Orator's Education*, 62–63.

46 Quintilian starts the second section of book XI by telling the story of Simonides, the inventor of the *ars memoriae*, as handed down from Cicero; he also adds a philological comment and concludes that he believes the story to be a myth as Simonides never mentions it and he would

improved if places are used to remember things. Unlike Cicero, who justified this through the principle of the primacy of the sense of sight, Quintilian refers to common experience to justify the use of *loci* and observes that everyone is familiar with this, as it is common for us to visit a place after a long time and still remember people and things, as well as what was said in this location. Thus, the technique of *ars memoriae* derives from this common experience.[47]

Quintilian believes that this technique is extremely useful for remembering long lists of words, similar to when we have to memorize a long list of objects.[48] However, when one has to remember a speech, the technique becomes useless and may even compromise natural memory, above all because ideas do not have

surely have spoken about it if such an extraordinary event had taken place: Quintilian, *Inst.*, XI, ii, 11–16, in Quintilian, *The Orator's Education*, 62–67.

47 Quintilian is the only author who describes in detail how rhetoric students were taught the *ars* and therefore his testimony is of such importance: "Students learn Sites (*loca*) which are extensive as possible and are marked by a variety of objects, perhaps a large house divided into many separate areas. They carefully fix in their mind everything there which is notable, so that their thoughts can run over all the parts of it without any hesitation or delay. The first task is to make sure that it all comes to mind without any hold-up, because a memory which is to help another memory has to be something more than secure. The next stage is to mark what they have written or are mentally preparing with some sign which will jog their memory. This may be based on the subject as a whole (on navigation or warfare, for example) or on a word, because even people who lose the thread of what they are saying can have their memory put back on track by the cue of a single word. Let us suppose a symbol of navigation, such an anchor, or of warfare, such as a weapon. Then this is how they arrange it. They place first the idea, as it were, in the vestibule, the second, let us say, in the atrium, and then they go round the open areas, assigning ideas systematically not only to bedrooms and bays, but to statues and the like. This done, when they have to revive the memory, they begin to go over these Sites from the beginning, calling in whatever they deposited with each of them, as the images remind them. Thus, however many things have to be remembered, they become a single item, held together as it were by a sort of outer shell, so that speakers do not make mistakes (?) by trying to connect what follows with what goes before by the sole effort of learning by heart," "Loca discunt quam maxime spatiosa, multa varietate signata, domum forte magnam et in multos diductam recessus. In ea quidquid notabile est animo diligenter adfigunt, ut sine cunctatione ac mora partis eius omnis cogitatio possit percurrere. Et primus hic labor est, non haerere in occursu: plus enim quam firma debet esse memoria quae aliam memoriam adiuvet. Tum quae scripserunt vel cogitatione complectuntur aliquo signo quo moneantur notant, quod esse vel ex re tota potest, ut de navigatione, militia, vel ex verbo aliquo; nam etiam excidentes unius admonitione verbi in memoriam reponuntur. Sit autem signum navigationis ut ancora, militiae ut aliquid ex armis. Haec ita digerunt: primum sensum vestibulo quasi adsignant, secundum (puta) atrio, tum impluvia circumeunt, nec cubiculis modo aut exhedris, sed statuis etiam similibusque per ordinem committunt. Hoc facto, cum est repetenda memoria, incipiunt ab initio loca haec recensere, et quod cuique crediderunt reposcunt, ut eorum imagine admonentur. Ita, quamlibet multa sint quorum meminisse oporteat, fiunt singula †necaeta quodam coria onerant† coniungentes prioribus consequentia solo ediscendi labore," Quintilian, *Inst.*, XI, ii, 18–20, in Quintilian, *The Orator's Education*, 66–69.

48 See fig. 8.

the same images as things and this means creating another symbol for each idea.[49] With this comment Quintilian has no intention of initiating a philosophical reflection on the relation between the content of thought and what it refers to in the real world, but rather as a rhetorician and teacher defining the best educational tools to teach rhetoric, he is interested only in highlighting a problem which consists in the huge number of images to remember. This problem on its own would suffice to prove the inefficacy of artificial memory, but Quintilian is also rather dubious about the possibility to even memorize the structure of a discourse effectively using the system of *loci*, as also in this case he is convinced that natural memory is overburdened with too many elements to memorize. Interestingly, Quintilian does not challenge the possibility of constructing an artificial memory system based on mnemonic rules, but rather he is only interested in assessing and discussing the real efficacy of the *ars*. Whether two types of memory exist – one natural and one artificial – holds no interest for him and indeed, he seems inclined to accept the real possibility of creating an artificial memory. He considers the difficulties with mnemonic devices only from the point of view of practicality and when considering Cicero's problem of tying images to parts of the speech such as conjunctions, deems it to be easily solved. As suggested by Cicero, one only has to establish a series of symbols for these parts that do not have any correspondence to sensory reality.

The book ends with further suggestions and recommendations on how to memorize texts (*Inst.*, XI, ii, 27–51) that are based on the exercise of natural memory and not on a complex construction of a system of artificial memory. For example, Quintilian suggests working on the composition of the speech and on its structure to facilitate memorizing it. If the speech is well structured and composed in independent sections that correspond to a single, well-defined subject for each section, it will be easier to train natural memory to remember the speech, because it is easier to remember thematic chunks rather than the whole text.

According to Quintilian, this expedient, in addition to composing well-structured speeches and repeating parts of the speech daily, is enough to ensure that the orator memorizes his speech or subject matter without recourse to the creation of an artificial memory system.

49 Quintilian, *Inst.*, XI, ii, 24, in Quintilian, *The Orator's Education*, 70–71.

2.2 Greek philosophical sources for mnemonics: Aristotle's doctrine of the soul

Aristotle's works make several references to the art of memory as practised in ancient Greece. The four passages where he discusses the creation of rules for an artificial memory system are the following:[50] *De anima*, III, iii, 427b, 20–21; *De insomniis*, 458b, 18–24; *De memoria et reminiscentia*, 452a, 12–16; *Topica*, VIII, xiv, 163b, 17–34.

In the first two passages Aristotle cites as an example of mental images the advice given by mnemonists when creating an artificial memory system:

> (...) for it is possible to call up mental pictures, as those do who employ images in arranging their ideas under a mnemonic system (...)[51]

Aristotle goes on to say that these images are like the ones to be found in imagination as the product of sensory experience, but are also similar to the images conjured up in dreams:

> And so in sleep we sometimes have other thoughts besides the mental pictures. This will become obvious to anyone if he concentrates and tries to remember his dream immediately upon rising. Indeed some men have seen such dreams, *e.g.*, those who think that they are arranging suggested subjects according to some principle of memorizing; for they often find themselves envisaging some other imaginary concept, apart from the dream, into position.[52]

Aristotle stresses that the pictures in the imagination or in dreams, just like the mental images produced by mnemonists, do not require the presence of the object at the time of perception but enable the soul to perform mental acts on them.

However, in the other two passages in which Aristotle cites mnemonic practice, he discusses the importance of orderly arrangement both during recollection and during the construction of the arguments in a speech:

> This is why acts of recollection are achieved soonest and most successfully when they start from the beginning of a series; for just as the objects are related to each other in an order of succession, so are the impulses. Those subjects which possess an orderly arrangement, like mathematical problems, are the easiest to recollect; ill-arranged subjects are recovered with difficulty. It is in this that the difference between recollecting and learning afresh lies, that in the former one will be able in some way to move on by his own effort to the term next after the starting-point. When he cannot do this himself, but only through another agency, he no longer remembers.

50 Richard Sorabji, *Aristotle on Memory* (Chicago: University of Chicago Press, 2004), 22.

51 Aristotle, *De an.*, III, iii, 427 b, 20–21, in Aristotle, *On the Soul. Parva Naturalia. On Breath*, trans. W. S. Hett (Cambridge, MA: Harvard University Press, 1957), 156–157.

52 Aristotle, *Insomn.*, I, 458b, 18–24, in Aristotle, *On the soul*, 350–351.

> It often happens that one cannot recollect at the moment, but can do so by searching, and finds what he wants. This occurs by his initiating many impulses, until at last he initiates one such that it will lead to the object of his search. For remembering consists in the potential existence in the mind of the effective stimulus; and this, as has been said, in such a way that the subject is stimulated from himself, and from the stimuli which he contains within him. But one must secure a starting-point. This is why some people seem, in recollecting, to proceed from *loci*. The reason for this is that they pass rapidly from one step to the next; for instance from milk to white, from white to air, from air to damp; from which one remembers autumn, if this is the season that he is trying to recall.[53]

The ability of the soul to recollect past experience is not the result of a single, mental act, but rather of a combination of mental acts to identify and select what is to be recalled. The emphasis on process rather than the single, distinct act when describing the faculty of recollection suggests that the Aristotelian doctrine of the soul is more interested in the temporal rather than the spatial aspect of memory:

> You ought thoroughly to learn arguments dealing with questions of frequent occurrence and especially primary propositions; for answerers often become discouraged in dealing with these. Moreover, you should have a good supply of definitions and have those familiar and primary ideas ready to hand; for it is by means of these that reasonings are carried on. You should also try and grasp the categories into which the other arguments most often fall. For just as in geometry it is useful to have a ready knowledge of the multiplication table up to ten times helps much to the recognition of the other numbers which are the result of multiplication, so too in arguments it is important to be prompt about first principles and to know your premisses by heart. For just as to a trained memory the mere reference to the places in which they occur causes the things themselves to be remembered, so the above rules will make a man a better reasoner, because he sees the premisses defined and numbered. A premiss of general application should be committed to memory rather than an argument, since it is pretty difficult to have a first principle or hypothesis ready to hand.[54]

Likewise, when we wish to build an argument, it is better to do so by applying the general rule to each part so that its legitimacy is confirmed. Indeed, we recall the general rules more easily than specific cases. However, if we insert a specific case within its rule, as if the rule were a mnemonic *locus*, it will be easier to recall the case drawn from the general.

Apart from being a witness to the circulation and importance of mnemonic devices in the ancient Greek world, Aristotle should also be considered among the most important philosophical sources for the history of the mnemonic arts, specifically for medieval history as we shall see later. Indeed, medieval mne-

53 Aristotle, *Mem.*, II, 452a, 2–16, in Aristotle, *On the soul*, 302–305.

54 Aristotle, *Top.*, VIII. xiv, 163b, 17–34, in Aristotle, *Posterior Analitics. Topica*, trans. Hugh Tredennick and E. S. Forster, (Cambridge, MA: Harvard University Press, 1960), 734–737.

monists regularly cite Aristotle's two treatises on psychology, the *De anima* and its appendix, the *De memoria et reminiscentia.*

Aristotle's *De anima* is a treatise on the faculties of the soul and it is also where he expounds his theory of knowledge. According to Aristotle, all knowledge is drawn from the five senses and their impressions on the mind. The imaginative faculty works on the perceptions brought through the senses and these are turned into images. The images are thus the material for the intellectual faculty, which always thinks in mental pictures.

Based on this theory of perception, Aristotle explains in the *De memoria et reminiscentia* that memory (*mneme*) belongs to the same part of the soul that imagination belongs to. Hence, memory is also a collection of mental images stemming from sense impressions, but as such is not a unique feature of humans, as animals also have a memory. The distinctive aspect of human memory is that thought can work on it and retrieve a previous sensation or a piece of knowledge (*anamnesis*) through a decision-making act based on association by likeness and on the principle of order. Thus, the special nature of the mental pictures that define the specific memory of humans, the *anamnesi*, is that they have a temporal element in that they draw on the perception of past things.[55]

2.3 Mediaeval sources for mnemonics (1): Albertus Magnus and Thomas Aquinas

The history of the reception of Aristotle's doctrine of the soul and memory is bound up with the history of the mnemonic arts in the Middle Ages, which results in a shift in the function of artificial memory within the system of medieval knowledge. The *ars memoriae* is no longer considered part of the tradition of rhetoric, but now part of ethics and thus also becomes a tool for preaching in the most important religious orders.[56]

This shift in the function of artificial memory derives from mistaken attribution in the reception of the *Rhetorica ad Herennium*, and from the interpretation of mnemonic principles as described in Aristotle's works on the soul. In

55 A profound distinction between mnemonics and memory theories emerges here. By virtue of this principle, in that mnemonics underline the spatial aspect of artificial memory to a greater extent they can be defined as "spatial memory", while the philosophical theories of memory, starting with Aristotle, place more emphasis on the temporal aspect of the memory function, that is, of the *memoria naturalis.* For more about the distinction between "spatial memory" and "temporal memory", see: Mary Carruthers, *The Craft of Thought: Meditation, Rhetoric, and the Making of Images, 400–1200* (Cambridge: Cambridge University Press, 2003), 12–13.

56 For more on the role of the *ars memoriae* in the *ars predicandi*, see: Rossi, *Logic and the Art of Memory*, 11–15, Lina Bolzoni, *La rete delle immagini: Predicazione in volgare dalle origini a Bernardino da Siena* (Turin: Einaudi, 2002).

the Middle Ages it was believed that the *Rhetorica ad Herennium*, also known as the *rhetorica secunda*, was the continuation of Cicero's *De inventione*, thus also known as *rhetorica prima*. This false attribution of the *Rhetorica ad Herennium* to Cicero led scholars to read the two works on rhetoric together, as if one completed the other. Indeed, Cicero's first work on rhetoric, the *De inventione*, is an unfinished work which focuses on ethics and virtue. According to this interpretation Cicero wrote the *rhetorica secunda* as a sequel to the *rhetorica prima*, here providing rules for a technique whereby ethical themes discussed in the first work could be recalled. The *Rhetorica ad Herennium* and its treatment of memory was thus a closer examination of memory in reference to the system of virtue and ethics discussed in the *De inventione*.

It is at this point in the history of the mnemonic arts and of memory theories that they first find points of contact: the mnemonic arts are now explicitly associated with philosophical treatises on memory, and specifically with Aristotle's conception of the soul. In Aristotle's philosophy, which was the maximum authority in the Middle Ages, we find doctrines that could be traced back to the principles of the mnemonic arts and could be used to establish its precepts philosophically. Scholars referred to four Aristotelian doctrines. The first was the idea of a double memory, which coincided with the distinction between natural and artificial memory (where the first was called *mneme* and the artificial memory was known as *anamnesis*). The second is the doctrine of images (*phantasma*) in which the image is a kind of weakened sense as it is immaterial and is stored as memory which can recall past sensory perception. This doctrine implies that there is a close link between sensation, imagination, and memory. The third doctrine deals with the fact that recollection (*anamnesis*) is facilitated by order and uniformity. Finally, the fourth doctrine deals with images again and the fact that they are associated with ideas according to relations of similarity, dissimilarity, and contiguity.

Albertus Magnus is responsible for merging mnemonic techniques and Aristotelian theory of the soul through the false attribution of the *Rhetorica ad Herennium* to Cicero, and Thomas Aquinas consolidated this: both make explicit references to the *Rhetorica ad Herennium* and Aristotle's *De memoria et reminiscentia* in their treatises. The two treatises are based on what Cicero affirms in the *De inventione* when he states that memory is part of prudence[57] and since it

57 Cicero, *Inv. rhet.*, II, 53, 160, in Cicero, *On Invention. The Best Kind of Orator. Topics*, trans. H.M. Hubbel (Cambridge, MA: Harvard University Press, 1949), 326–327: "Wisdom is the knowledge of what is good, what is bad and what is neither good nor bad. Its parts are memory, intelligence, and foresight. Memory is the faculty by which the mind recalls what has happened. Intelligence is the faculty by which it ascertains what is. Foresight is the faculty by which it is seen that something is going to occur before it occurs," "Prudentia est rerum bonarum et malarum neutrarumque scientia. Partes eius: memoria, intellegentia, provi-

was believed that art and virtue added perfection to nature, the precepts for the mnemonic arts assumed fundamental importance in the discussion on memory as part of rhetoric.

In the *De Bono*, IV, qu. 2, art. 1 and art. 2[58] Albertus Magnus begins with Cicero's definition of prudence and addresses all the precepts in the *Rhetorica ad Herennium*. His attempt to combine Aristotle with pseudo-Cicero is evident in his definition of prudence:

> Let us say that memory is a part of prudence, in as much as it is part of the essence of reminiscence. In fact, as prudence chooses what facilitates and not what hinders its action, one must proceed following a specific principle and through the possible one arrives at a possible action; and therefore, since it proceeds from things from the past, it uses memory, as it is part of reminiscence.[59]

It is also evident in the section on the principle of order or arrangement:

> (1) One must say that recalling past things occurs in two ways, that is, owing to a potentia, and this revocation is only in intensity and imperfect, because it does not have instructions for how it is to proceed. Then there is revocation on the strength of an instruction, with which, if one wants, one remembers the past. And this remembering can be a cognitive instruction, and then it is theoretical, and it can be a moral instruction, and then it is practical, and is a virtue that concerns prudence.[60]

Similarly, Thomas Aquinas in *Summa theologiae*, II, ii, qu. 49, art. 1[61] sets out four rules for artificial memory drawn from the *rhetorica secunda* and provides comments that are also inspired by Aristotle. The first rule deals with the creation of images, which should be extraordinary so as to be easily recalled, and which should have corporeal similitudes, since human cognition is more suitable for

---

dentia. Memoria est per quam animus repetit illa quae fuerunt; intellegentia, per quam ea perspicit quae sunt; providentia, per quam futurum aliquid videtur ante quam factum est."

58 Albertus Magnus, *De bono, Tr. IV: De prudentiae*, in Albertus Magnus, *Opera omnia. Tomus 28: De bono*, ed. Heinrich Kühle et al. (Monasterii Westfalorum in aedibus Aschendorff, 1951), 245–252.

59 "Dicimus, quod memoria est pars prudentiae, secundum quod memoria cadit in rationem reminiscentiae. Cum enim prudentia eligat ea quibus adiuvatur, ab his a quibus impeditur in opere, oportet ipsam procedere inquirendo et sic necesse est eam progredi a principio determinato et per media probabilia devenire in propositum operabile; et ideo cum proceditur ex praeteritis, utitur memoria, secundum quod est pars reminiscentiae," Albertus Magnus, *De bono*, IV, qu. 2, art. 1, 470, in Albertus Magnus, *Opera omnia*, 245a.

60 "(1) Dicendum ergo, quod repetere ea quae fuerunt, dupliciter contigit, scilicet ex potentia, et haec repetitio est in potentia tantum et imperfecta, eo quod non habeat habitum, unde procedere debet. Et est repetitio ex habitu, qua repetitur praeteritum, quando vult repetens. Et haec potest esse in habitu cognitivo, et tunc est theoretica et potest esse in habitu morali, et tunc est practica et est virtus pertinens ad prudentiam," Albertus Magnus, *De bono*, IV qu. 2, art. 1, 470, in Albertus Magnus, *Opera omnia*, 245b–246a.

61 Thomas Aquinas, *Summa theologiae. Volume 36: Prudence (2a2æ. 47–56)*, ed. Thomas Gilby (Cambridge: Blackfriars, 1974), 61–64.

what may be sensed (and the reason why memory may be found in the sensitive part of the soul). The second rule states the principle of order: to move easily from one memory to another the things we wish to remember should be arranged in an orderly manner since what we wish to recall is inspired by its location. The third rule asserts that an effort should be made to practice mnemonics regularly, and the fourth rule insists on frequent revisiting of what we wish to recall, so that the habit of repetition becomes second nature to memory.

2.4 Mediaeval sources for mnemonics (2): Augustine and Ramon Llull

There is another medieval philosophical line of research that has certain points of contact with the *ars memoriae* and is worth discussing in order to understand the various strands of scholarly studies that later made up Renaissance mnemonic systems. This line of research arose out of Augustine's works and in particular his section on memory that the rhetorician and philosopher discusses in *Confessions*, X, 8 (12).[62]

Augustine bases his idea of memory on the mnemonic model, as is evident in the following passage:

> So I shall transcend even my natural life force, and climb in stages to him who made me. I come to the fields and the grand palaces of my memory, where there are treasure stores of countless impressions brought there from every imaginable kind of thing that my senses perceived. Stowed away there is everything we reflect upon either by accentuating or depreciating it or in any way whatever modifying the actual things which our sense apprehended; and anything else that has been preserved and deposited and that forgetfulness has not yet consumed and buried. When I am there, I call for whatever I want to be produced: some things are immediately forthcoming; others take longer to look for, and are, as it were, unearthed from more inaccessible places; and yet others cascade out in a rush, and while one particular item is searched and hunted for, they thrust themselves forward en masse as if saying "Can we be the ones?" With the hand of my heart I drive them away from the forefront of my recollection, until what I am after emerges from obscurity and comes out of hiding into plain sight. Other things are produced in the correct order as required, easily and without any fuss; and the earlier things make way for those that come later, and by making way they return into storage, ready to come forth again whenever I want them. This is exactly what happens when I recite something from memory.[63]

62 Augustine, *Confessions, Volume II: Books 9–13*, ed. and trans. Carolyn J.-B. Hammond, (Cambridge, MA: Harvard University Press, 2016), 86–89.

63 "Transibo ergo et istam naturae meae, gradibus ascendens ad eum qui fecit me, et venio in campos et lata praetoria memoriae, ubi sunt thesauri innumerabilium imaginum de cuiuscemodi rebus sensis invectarum. ibi reconditum est quidquid etiam cogitamus, vel augendo vel minuendo vel utcumque variando ea quae sensus attigerit, et si quid aliud commendatum

This passage is extraordinary because it provides a rare description of what a mnemonist's experience must have been when applying the *ars*.[64] What is striking is the fact that Augustine speaks of his memory system as if it were a real place and he was drawing a map of it. This helps us understand that the mnemonic experience required a high level of concentration, like that used in meditation or prayer.[65] Thus, it is hardly surprising that the practice of artificial memory led Augustine not only to reflect on memory as a faculty of the soul, but that it also led him to find God through this extraordinary faculty.

Augustine seeks God through memory, one of the central themes in Book X of the *Confessions* and makes distinctions between different types of memory. For example, if we name a stone or animal, we may find a picture of that reality in memory, even if the objects are not present at the moment of recollection. However, the question becomes more complex when we name abstract words

et repositum est quod nondum absorbuit et sepelivit oblivio, ibi quando sum, posco ut proferatur quidquid volo, et quaedam statim prodeunt, quaedam requiruntur diutius et tamquam de abstrusioribus quibusdam receptaculis eruuntur, quaedam catervatim se proruunt et, dum aliud petitur et quaeritur, prosiliunt in medium quasi dicentia, 'ne forte nos sumus?' et abigo ea manu cordis a facie recordationis meae, donec enubiletur quod volo atque in conspectum prodeat ex abditis. alia faciliter atque imperturbata serie sicut poscuntur suggeruntur, et cedunt praecedentia consequentibus et cedendo conduntur, iterum cum voluero processura. quod totum fit cum aliquid narro memoriter," Augustine, *Conf.*, X, 8 (12), in Augustine, *Confessions, Volume II: Books 9–13*, 86–89.

64 There are descriptions of how Thomas Aquinas, another great mnemonist, worked, as we have already seen, but there are no direct testimonies. Mary Carruthers cites this extract from a biography of Thomas Aquinas, written shortly after his death by Bernard Gui: "Of the subtlety and brilliance of his intellect and the soundness of his judgment, sufficient proof is his vast literary output, his many original discoveries, his deep understanding of the Scriptures. His memory was extremely rich and retentive: whatever he had once read and grasped he never forgot; it was as if knowledge were ever increasing in his soul as page is added to page in the writing of a book. Consider, for example, that admirable compilation of Patristic texts on the four Gospels which he made for Pope Urban [the *Catena* aurea or "golden Chain"] and which, for the most part, he seems to have put together from texts that he had read and committed to memory from time to time while staying in various religious houses. Still stronger is the testimony of Reginald his *socius* and of his pupils and of those who wrote to his dictation, who all declare that he used to dictate in his cell to three secretaries, and even occasionally to four, on different subjects at the same time … No one could dictate simultaneously so much various material without a special grace. Nor did he seem to be searching for things as yet unknown to him; he seemed simply to let his memory pout out its treasures (…)," in Mary Carruthers, *The Book of Memory* (Cambridge: Cambridge University Press, 2008), 3.

65 As Mary Carruthers often underlines, implicitly criticizing Frances A. Yates. Yates did not believe that the obscurity of mnemonics is to be attributed to abandoned practices and, therefore, to the faculty of the memory and the mind that changed as the result of a different use being made of them. For more about this type of meditative experience associated with the *ars memoriae*, see also "A Little Book About Constructing Noah's Arch", in Mary Carruthers, Jon Ziolkowski, eds., *The Medieval Craft of Memory: An Anthology of Texts and Pictures* (Philadelphia, University of Pennsylvania Press, 2002), 41–70.

such as beauty, health or even memory itself, which are not related to sensory memories and thus have no image. Thus, he concludes that our minds may store images for material objects, but there are no images for general concepts, which are the result of the processing of the images for material objects. Exploring memory in this way Augustine perceives God, who is neither an image nor may be found in a specific part of his memory:

> Where do you abide in my memory, Lord, where in that place do you abide? What kind of resting place have you fashioned for yourself? What kind of sanctuary have you built for yourself?[66]

He finds God in memory by uncovering the truth of God.

An important medieval scholar who not only drew from Augustine's works, but took Augustine's conception of memory as the place where God could be experienced to the extreme, was Ramon Llull. Inspired by his religious mission to convert the infidels and establish unity in faith, Llull sought a universal language that could combine all knowledge. Llull's *ars memoriae* aimed to create a model to understand reality and in which one could know God through the quality of things that were also divine attributes, or as he called them "dignities" (*dignitates Dei*). Starting from the fundamental attributes of God, which as such are real, we can attain a logical and ontological definition of the simple, principal elements of reality, which are also the principles of art. Llull drew on Augustine's symbolic conception of the sensory world and transformed it into a symbolism that was expressed by a finite number of letters and symbols beginning with the divine dignities.

3. Definition of the field of research (3): Mnemonics in the sixteenth century

In the fourteenth century the Dominican reflections on this theme had been made popular through the spread of mnemonic techniques as a tool for the *ars predicandi*, and a distinction emerged between the Ciceronian-rhetoric and Dominican-Aristotelian traditions. In the fifteenth century, interest in this topic gradually declined and scholars dealing with the *ars memoriae* were there to elucidate the *ars*, explaining already codified rules in a simpler manner that would be useful for learning and use.

66 "Sed ubi manes in memoria mea, domine, ubi illic manes? quale cubile fabricasti tibi? quale sanctuarium aedificasti tibi?", Augustine, *Conf.*, X, 25 (36), in Augustine, *Confessions, Volume II: Books 9–13*, 130–131.

This tendency continued into the sixteenth century, when Llull's *ars combinatoria* was coupled with the mnemonic arts, now interpreted as the *clavis universalis*, a discipline that collected all knowledge into one single doctrine. It is in this context that Giordano Bruno's studies on the mnemonic arts are situated, that is as a discipline that enables us to gather knowledge into one, single doctrine.

To sum up what we have seen so far: 1. to identify the research field where the role of Bruno's mnemonic works will be examined in relation to his other works it is necessary to first understand the relation between mnemonics and philosophical treatises on memory; 2. the distinction between the two fields was clear and constantly revisited up to the Middle Ages, when through an error of attribution of the *Rhetorica ad Herennium*, mnemonics shifted from a rhetoric context, which had already lost its primacy in the medieval system of knowledge, to an ethical and philosophical context; 3. this shift was assimilated in the *ars predicandi* and it would be above all the Dominican and Franciscan orders that would practice mnemonics and thus transmit it to Renaissance scholarship; 4. mnemonics in the sixteenth century was ready to weave the different strands of this tradition, seeking to provide a universal key to understanding and communicating knowledge.

Chapter 2: Studying Giordano Bruno's *ars memoriae* from a metaphorological perspective

> "Rational arguments" [...] are of the greatest importance, I have always regarded them as a very important and relevant part of history, but certainly not the only one that deserves to be studied or in function of which everything else should be used. I have always had a strong preference for the world that is often ambiguous and evasive with its ideas, metaphors, ways of perceiving and interpreting the world, choices, and "preference" (or to use the expressions that went on to become more fashionable), the paradigms, theme, images of science, research traditions, tacit or unexpressed knowledge, and styles of thought. All things that act with strength even if very often how they act is not immediately clear, even on the most respectable "theories" and on the choice amongst the countless possible argumentations philosophers and scientists resort to, to support them, to propagandise them.
>
> – Paolo Rossi, *Il passato, la memoria, l'oblio*

1. Definition of the research objective (1): Giordano Bruno's *ars memoriae*

If we look at the trajectory Frances A. Yates chose to depict in the history of mnemonic tradition, Giordano Bruno's mnemonic works are to be found in the last stage, taking a foreground role as they represent the most thorough synthesis and reworking of the diverse theoretical proposals of that period on the *memoria verborum.*

The first work by Bruno that we have is one on mnemonics[67] and Bruno's publishing commitment in this field continues over the years, until his return to

67 The *De umbris idearum* was printed in Paris in 1582. According to what Bruno reports in later works, he had already written and published several works before he published the *De umbris. L'arca di Noè* (1574), was probably presented to Pope Pius V, and the *De' segni dei tempi* (1575), was published during his first stay in Venice: see the dedicatory epistle of *La cabala del cavallo pegaseo*, in Giordano Bruno, *Dialoghi filosofici italiani*, ed. Michele Ciliberto, 5th ed. (Milan: Mondadori, 2005), 679, and *La cena de le Ceneri*, in Giordano Bruno, *Dialoghi filosofici italiani*, 153. In the *De umbris idearum* Bruno frequently refers to another text he

Italy and the commencement of his trial.[68] Giordano Bruno not only dedicates a considerable amount of his writings to mnemonic works, but he also repeatedly demonstrates his interest in and commitment to the development of this discipline. Considering that mnemonic techniques were important for the development of preaching in the Dominican and Franciscan orders, it is likely that they appealed to the young Bruno in Naples and may have even persuaded him to join the Dominican order:

---

wrote on mnemonics, the *Clavis magna*, citing it as the main text for the presentation of his *ars memoriae*. Not one copy of this work has survived. In his early works Bruno uses the expression *clavis magna*, not necessarily in reference to a text, but to his mnemotechnics. Nicoletta Tirinnanzi, who analysed in detail the occurrences of the expression in the *De umbris idearum* and in the *Cantus Circaeus*, hypothesized that the text of *Clavis magna* was never actually published as a book and that it only circulated amongst Bruno's students in the form of a manuscript and lesson handbook, before being subsumed into different sections of his later mnemonic works such as *Explicatio triginta sigillorum*, *Sigillus sigillorum*, and *De imaginum compositione:* Nicoletta Tirinnanzi, introduction to *Opere mnemotecniche: Tomo I*, by Giordano Bruno, eds. Marco Matteoli, Rita Sturlese, and Nicoletta Tirinnanzi (Milan: Adelphi, 2004), xiv–xix.

68 The mnemonic works include: *De umbris idearum* (Paris, 1582), *Cantus Circaeus* (Paris, 1582), *Ars reminiscendi* (London, 1583), *Explicatio triginta sigillorum* (London, 1583), *Sigillus sigillorum* (London, 1583), and *De imaginum compositione* (Frankfurt, 1591). However, references to mnemonics and, more generally, to the topic of memory are also to be found in the philosophical dialogues. See for instance, *La cena de le Ceneri*, "Proemiale epistola", in Giordano Bruno, *Dialoghi filosofici italiani*, 10: "Che vuol dire cena de le ceneri? fu vi posto forse questo pasto innante? potrassi forse dir qua *cinerem tamquam panem manducabam?* Non; ma è un convito, fatto dopo il tramontar del sole, nel primo giorno de la quarantana, detto da nostri preti *dies cinerum*, e talvolta 'giorno del *memento*'," "What does a supper of ashes mean? Was a plate of ashes put before you? Could you perhaps say here: 'I have eaten ashes like bread'? No, it is a banquet held after sunset on the first day of Lent, which is called by our priests the day of ashes, and sometimes the day of remembrance," in Giordano Bruno, *The Ash Wednesday Supper*, trans., annotated and with an introduction by Hilary Gatty, 9 (Toronto, ON: University of Toronto Press, 2018). See also, *La cena de le Ceneri*, "Dialogo primo", in Giordano Bruno, *Dialoghi filosofici italiani*, 23: "E tu, Mnemosine mia, ascosa sotto trenta sigilli, e rinchiusa nel tetro carcere dell'ombre de le idee, intonami un poco ne l'orecchio," "And you, Mnemosyne my, hidden beneath thirty seals and immured within the dark prison of the shadows of ideas, whisper to me in my ear," in Giordano Bruno, *The Ash Wednesday Supper*, 27. In the second quotation the reference to the mnemonic works is clear (the expression 'shadow of ideas', as we will see in the textual analysis, refers to the *De umbris*, and the seals under which memory is hidden is a reference to another mnemonic work, namely the *Explicatio triginta sigillorum*); but of even greater interest for the hermeneutic hypothesis we are discussing is the fact that in the *La cena* Bruno places the dialogue on Copernicus and the "paradoxes of the new philosophy" under the auspice of Mnemosyne. Bruno clarifies immediately that he does not see with the eyes of Copernicus or Ptolemy, but with his own and that, even if the observations of the two illustrious astronomers are beyond discussion and constitute material for reflection for his own philosophy as well, the results achieved by Bruno's philosophy are the fruit of diverse reasoning. It seems evident here that in presenting his philosophy Bruno was elaborating ideas already developed in his mnemonic works.

(…) he took his vows as priest when he heard them disputing in Saint Dominic in Naples, and thus said that those were worldly gods (…)[69]

Moreover, the art of memory was linked to several episodes in the life of Bruno. His first stay in Paris was facilitated by his fame as a master of *ars memoriae*, as he claimed in the "Secondo costituto" of his trial,[70] not to mention his fatal return to Venice prior to being delivered to the Inquisition, his long trial and death at the stake, all episodes linked in one way or another to his interest in mnemonics.[71]

69 "(…) e si fece frate con occasione che sentì disputare a San Domenico in Napoli, e così disse che quelli erano dii della terra," deposition by Francesco Graziano, in Luigi Firpo, *Il processo di Giordano Bruno* (Rome: Salerno Editrice, 1993), 251.

70 "(…) acquistai nome tale che il re Henrico terzo mi fece chiamare un giorno, ricercandomi se la memoria che havevo et che professava era naturale o pur per arte magica; al qual diedi sodisfattione; et con quell oche li dissi et feci provare a lui medesmo, conobbe che non era per arte magica ma per scientia. Et doppo questo feci stamper un libro de memoria sotto il titolo *De umbris idearum*, il quale dedicai a Sua Maestà; et con questa occasione mi fece lettor straordinario et provisionato; et seguitai in quella città a legger, come ho detto, forsi cinqu'anni (…)," in Luigi Firpo, *Il processo di Giordano Bruno* (Rome: Salerno Editrice, 1993), 161–162, "(…) such renown did I acquire that King Henry III summoned me one day, wanting to know whether the memory I had and what I professed was natural or magical art; my reply gave him satisfaction; and with what I told him and made him also experience, he admitted it was not magical arts, but science. And after this I had a book on memory published with the title *De umbris idearum*, which I dedicated to His Majesty; and on this occasion I was made extraordinary, waged lecturer; and I went on to read in that city, as I have already said, perhaps five years (…)". See also the testimony of Johan von Nostiz, a pupil of Bruno's, in Giovanni Aquilecchia, *Schede bruniane (1950–1991)* (Rome: Vecchiarelli, 1993), 283–285. For an analysis of Bruno's experience in Paris, see: Saverio Ricci, *Giordano Bruno nell'Europa del Cinquecento* (Rome: Salerno Editrice, 2000), 142–177.

71 See the deposition of the bookseller Giovan Battista Ciotti: "Questo Iordani è venuto in questa città, per quell oche so io, perché un giorno il signor Zuane Mocenigo, gentilhomo venetiano, comprando un libro dato fuori dal detto Iordano, intitolato *De minimo, magno et mensura*, me domandò se io conoscevo costui et se sapevo dove egli era all'hora. Io gli dissi di sì, et che io l'havevo visto in Francforte, et che credevo che fosse tuttavia lì. Et il detto signor Mocenigo soggionse: 'Io vorrei ch'egli venisse a Venetia per insegnarmi li secreti della memoria et li altri che egli professa, come si vede in questo suo libro': et io a questo risposi: 'Crederò che, se sarà ricercato, venirà.' Et così doppo alcuni giorni esso signor Mocenigo mi portò una littera direttiva al detto Iordano, con farmi instantia, che io gli la mandasse, come feci, dicendomi che gli scriveva per veder se voleva ven[i]r a Venetia. Et doppo comparve egli qui, saranno circa sette mesi o otto," in Luigi Firpo, *Il processo di Giordano Bruno* (Rome: Salerno Editrice), 149–150, "This Iordani came to this city as far as I know, because one day Signor Zuane Mocenigo, a Venetian nobleman, purchasing a book published by the aforesaid Iordano, called *De minimo, magno et mensura*, asked me if I knew him and if I knew where he was now. I said yes, and that I had seen him in Frankfurt, and that I believed he was still there. And the aforesaid Signor Mocenigo said: 'I would like him to come to Venice to teach me the secrets of memory and the other ones he professes, such as the ones in this book;' and I replied: 'I believe that if he is asked after, he will come.' Thus, a few days later Signor Mocenigo brought me a letter for the aforesaid Iordan, asking me to send it to him immediately, which I did, telling me that he had written to ask if he wanted to come to Venice. And afterwards he showed up here, seven or eight months later."

Thus, what is Giordano Bruno's relationship with the tradition of the *ars memoriae* and how does he refer to it? As was the case in theology and philosophy, Bruno had no intention of doing away with the traditions that had fed into his own studies. However, he knew his *ars memoriae* – but also his philosophical and theological positions – went beyond tradition. In other words, whilst not renouncing the classical and Renaissance mnemonic precepts, he transformed their philosophical premises and meaning, while at the same time seeking to express the system in a more complete form. To explain the precepts of mnemonic systems and make the system more effective, thus in line with mnemonic literature in the sixteenth century, Bruno reorganized the gnoseology that underlay the *ars memoriae* and made some important alterations to the *memoria verborum*, which in Germany would later develop into combinatory calculus. Hence, Bruno's memory systems go beyond the traditional definition of the *ars memoriae* as a technical system to improve natural memory, and move towards the field of gnoseology, merging with what had hitherto been studied in memory theories, namely how humans and the world relate together.

This thus brings me to the articulation of the research topic I intend to develop: if the *ars memoriae* is the context in which the relations between humans and the world are formulated, we should investigate the nature of the relation between the *ars memoriae* and Giordano Bruno's philosophy, as well as whether the *ars memoriae* could be defined as the philosophical place where Bruno sets out his gnoseological framework for his philosophy, as it is here that he redefines the concept of order, which he will seek to change compared to traditional concepts in three fundamental areas: theology (nature), gnoseology (language), ethics (*praxis* or creativity, using a non-Brunian term).

2. Definition of the research object (2): Analysis of three methodological approaches

The history of the tradition of mnemonics in the Renaissance is a relatively new field of study. It developed in the second half of the twentieth century alongside new studies and disciplines in Renaissance studies that challenged the primacy of the Age of the Enlightenment as the final rational goal towards which all previous centuries strove and cast aside the model of philosophy of history based on the idea of rationality.[72]

72 Michele Ciliberto, "Fortune e (sfortune) di un maestro 'onnisciente' e 'quasi divino'," introduction in Giordano Bruno, *Opere Lulliane*, eds. Marco Matteoli, Rita Sturlese, and Nicoletta Tirinnanzi (Milan: Adelphi 2012), xi–xli.

The history of the interpretations of Renaissance mnemonics depends to a great extent on the interpretation of rationality in the Modern Age. We have already highlighted the fact that the history of mnemonics is linked to the understanding of the system of knowledge, and this applies not only to when the systems were developed, but also subsequently when the systems were studied and placed in a historical context. Since the history of the interpretation of Bruno's mnemonics is an excellent example of what has been discussed, I shall now provide an overview of it.

Between the late nineteenth and early twentieth centuries Bruno scholars, albeit with different motivations, were still unanimous in considering Bruno's works on mnemonics as inferior to his philosophical works, as they expressed an aspect of Renaissance culture that questioned the role of this period as the cradle of the origin of the enlightened rationality that was regarded as the mature, complete result of Renaissance criticism of the centuries of the Dark Ages of reason. Thus, from the 1940s onwards, Bruno scholars began to be influenced by the change in direction of studies on the Renaissance that took place in the early decades of the twentieth century. They started to abandon the conception of Renaissance that was hinged mainly on the relationship with Enlightenment (Konrad Burdach) and had begun to place Hermeticism and magic at the centre of research, thus revealing the subject of the practical, reformative dimension of Renaissance culture (Paul Oskar Kristeller and Eugenio Garin). A decade on, Garin's pupils worked on the final rehabilitation of magic, Hermeticism, and Llullism in the Renaissance, bringing forth new essential themes for the development of Renaissance philosophical traditions, such as that of Giordano Bruno: the relationship between logic and rhetoric, the incidence of magical and astrological questions, the meaning and function of the art of memory, and the attempt to find a universal language to investigate the world.

It was in this fertile intellectual climate that Paolo Rossi and Frances A. Yates developed their works, which today are still the key reference works for those who wish to study the *ars memoriae* in the Renaissance and Bruno's mnemonics.

2.1 Paolo Rossi: "Landing on the continent of memory"

The cultural atmosphere that surrounded the studies on the *ars memoriae* in the twentieth century is described succinctly, but very effectively, by Paolo Rossi in the introduction to *Il passato, la memoria e l'oblio*, which is significantly entitled 'promemoria' (*memorandum*).[73] At the end of the 1950s there were very few

73 Paolo Rossi, "Promemoria", in *Il passato, la memoria, l'oblio: Sei saggi di storia delle idee* (Bologna: Il Mulino, 2001), 7–11.

scholars working on these topics. Historical-philosophical research concentrated on two main currents: on the one hand, the perspective of idealistic philosophy, which regarded topics such as mnemonics as being not truly philosophical and, on the other, the perspectives of neo-Enlightenment directed towards a scientific philosophy that regarded mnemonics as an expression of vague, imprecise ideas that were of little interest and difficult to juxtapose with the extremely pure, scientific nature of philosophy, which was believed to be superior to history.

It was through his mentor, Eugenio Garin, that Paolo Rossi ventured into two unexplored territories: the Llullian tradition and mnemonics, and the magical-hermetic tradition. The "landing on the continent of memory"[74] took place in 1957, when Paolo Rossi published his celebrated work on Francis Bacon.[75] Seeking to determine Bacon's standpoint on the prolific literary Renaissance output of treatises on *ars memoriae*, Rossi decided to organize the wide range of works that were produced on this topic in the fifteenth and sixteenth centuries.[76]

Paolo Rossi organizes this vast collection of mnemonic manuals from just before the decline of the ancient discipline into three topics. The first topic deals with an encyclopaedia of knowledge; the second addresses artificial memory as the basis for the creation of a perfect science; and the third topic deals with the art of memory as a tool to organize the subjects of a speech. The first topic, represented by Ludovico Dolce, is traced back to Llullism; the second, represented by Jean Bellot, Giordano Bruno, and Cornelius Agrippa, is closely linked to the first, although the authors here do not refer solely to Llull; the third topic, finally, finds its roots in Peter Ramus and his idea to use the art of memory as a tool to introduce order in knowledge and speech.[77]

The attempt to thematically organize the treatises produced on the *ars memoriae* that define the history of mnemonics from Antiquity to the Renaissance was also the approach adopted by Rossi when he embarked on new studies on the art of memory and wrote the *Clavis universalis.*[78]

---

74 Rossi, *Il passato, la memoria, l'oblio*, 2.

75 Paolo Rossi, *Francesco Bacone: Dalla magia alla scienza* (Turin: Einaudi, 1974).

76 Paolo Rossi, "La mnemotecnica e la 'ministratio ad memoriam': luoghi retorici e luoghi naturali," in Rossi, *Francesco Bacone*, 329–337.

77 Peter Ramus identifies the *ars memoriae* with the doctrine of discourse. For more about the influence of Llull and Ramus in the Renaissance, see: Cesare Vasoli, *La dialettica e la retorica dell'Umanesimo: "Invenzione" e "Metodo" nella cultura del XV e XVI secolo* (Milan: Feltrinelli, 1968).

78 Rossi, *Clavis universalis: Arti della memoria e logica combinatoria da Lullo a Leibniz* (Milan: Ricciardi, 1960; 3rd ed., Bologna: Il Mulino, 2000). Translated by Stephen Clucas as *Logic and the Art of Memory: The Quest for a Universal Language* (Chicago: Chicago University Press, 2000). Citations refer to the translation of Stephen Clucas. This was a new series of studies, although there were several monographs on the history of mnemonics in specific periods and also entries in encyclopedias, such as: Johann Christoph Aretin, *Systematische Anleitung zur Theorie und Praxis der Mnemonik: nebst den Grundlinien zur Geschichte u. Kritik dieser*

The title of this 1960 work reflected Rossi's approach to Renaissance memory techniques:

> The term *clavis universalis* was used in the sixteenth and seventeenth centuries to designate a method or general science which would enable man to see beyond the veil of phenomenal appearances, or the 'shadow of ideas', and grasp the ideal and essential structure of reality. Deciphering the alphabet of the world; reading the signs imprinted by the divine mind in the book of nature; discovering the correspondence between the original forms of the universe and the structure of human thought; constructing a perfect language capable of eliminating all equivocations and putting us in direct contact with things and essences rather than signs; the construction of total encyclopaedias and ordered classifications which would be the true 'mirrors' of cosmic harmony – these were the objectives of the numerous defenders, apologists and expositors of Llullism and artificial memory between the fourteenth and seventeenth centuries. They formulated systematic rules for improving the memory, compiled grandiose encyclopaedias and complicated "theatres of the world", sought to reduce the complexities of human thought to a primordial 'alphabet' of simple notions, and harboured pansophic aspirations and hopes for a universal reformation and pacification of human-kind.[79]

The *clavis universalis* is the key to the universal knowledge that was at the speculative centre of Ramon Llull's undertaking to find the matrix of all languages and thought. Hence, Paolo Rossi landed on the continent of memory and sought to map it out by following the development of classical rhetorical sources and their medieval links to Aristotelianism. Although he criticized and openly challenged the aprioristic historical approach, which tended to exclude all those phenomena that would "taint" the legacy of Classical Greek rationality from the history of logic, Paolo Rossi's mapping tended towards seventeenth-century treatises on method and he sought to show how even historical phenomena like mnemonics could be considered part of the history of modern rationality.[80] Thus, this was Rossi's perspective from which he viewed this almost unexplored territory.

Paolo Rossi's exploration is not only a detailed survey of the protean nature of the history of Renaissance mnemonics, defining the countless themes linked to it. One of the more significant themes is images and imagery. The Italian scholar frequently draws our attention to the fact that Renaissance culture was the fruit of an age of images, and little would be understood of memory techniques in the Renaissance if texts were separated from pictures.

Wissenschaft: mit 3 Kupfertaf (Sulzbach, 1810); Edward Pick, *Memory and its Doctors* (London: Thurber, 1888); Ludwig Volkmann, "Ars memorativa", *Jahrbuch des Kunsthistorischen Sammlungen in Wien* 3, n.s., (1929): 111–200; Helga Hajdu, *Das Mnemotechnische Schrifttum des Mittelalters* (Vienna: F. Leo and Comp., 1936).

79 Rossi, *Logic and the Art of Memory*, xv.

80 Rossi, *Il passato, la memoria, l'oblio*, 59–62.

2.2 Frances A. Yates: Mnemonics and the Hermetic tradition

Frances A. Yates came across Giordano Bruno while she was writing the biography of another Italian in Elizabethan London, John Florio, and she dedicated a whole chapter in her first book to the relationship between the two and their mutual influence.[81]

Based on the works by Italian scholars, Gentile and Spampanato, Yates interpreted Bruno's philosophy as the attempt to include modern scientific discoveries, especially those by Copernicus in the field of astronomy, in a much broader theoretical discourse, which was antagonistic to the theological and scholastic authorities in Elizabethan England.[82] From this point of view the work that best represents Bruno's relation to Copernicanism is the *La cena de le Ceneri*, to which Yates dedicates several pages of commentary.

In the years following the biography of Florio, Yates embarked on a project to translate the *La cena de le Ceneri* into English and to write a preface on how Bruno had assimilated and philosophically explained Copernicus' innovative astronomical theory.[83] While she was working on the project, she began to realize that the *La cena de le Ceneri* could be read on a level that was not based on Copernicanism. The more Yates worked on the project and studied Bruno's thought in more detail, the more this idea became plausible. However, she was unable to define the terms of this reading, and the nature of this different level of interpretation.

Help in defining the new perspective came in the form of a series of studies that had been published between the mid-1940s and mid-1960s. During those two decades numerous scholars of the Renaissance drew attention to the importance of the Hermetic tradition to understand the characters of the age between the late Middle Ages and the Modern Age. These were studies by such pioneers as P. O. Kristeller and Eugenio Garin on the Hermetic tradition in Renaissance thought.[84] This is how the initial project to translate the *La cena de le Ceneri* turned into the project to seek traces of the Hermetic tradition in Bruno's philosophy and works.

81 Frances A. Yates, "Florio and Bruno", chap. 5, in Frances A. Yates, *John Florio. The Life of an Italian in Shakespeare's England* (London: Cambridge University Press, 1934), 87–123.

82 "It has been said that Bruno's work forms 'the greatest philosophical thought-structure executed by the Renaissance'. His was an early attempt to build a philosophy to include the discoveries of modern science, represented in his day by the work of Copernicus. (…) By a leap of the imagination he extended the Copernican theory far beyond the limit laid down by its author (…)," Yates, *John Florio*, 91.

83 Yates, "Preface," in *Giordano Bruno and the Hermetic Tradition*, ix–xii.

84 Eugenio Garin, *Medioevo e Rinascimento* (Bari: Laterza, 1954), and *La cultura filosofica del Rinascimento: Ricerche e documenti*, 2nd ed. (Firenze: Sansoni, 1979), but also the works by many of Garin's pupils who studied different aspects of the research field identified by the philosopher and historian, also including Rossi, *Logic and the Art of Memory*.

The works that Yates deemed to yield more evidence on links to Hermeticism were the works on magic, which she immediately realized were to be read together with the works on mnemonics. In this way her research extended to include that of the history of mnemonics,[85] which became famous for having defined a new line of research, as well as providing a Hermetic key to interpreting Renaissance *ars memoriae.*

This interpretation has been strongly criticized and nowadays has been partly dismissed.[86] The main criticism concerns the fact that Yates tends to use Hermeticism to explain the understanding of historical phenomena that are complex and obscure owing to their historical distance from us, but for which there are explanations that lie outside Hermeticism.

As it addresses the problem of the interpretation of mnemonic tradition as a cultural one that intersects with the history of different disciplines and has consequences for contemporary cultural history, Yates' approach is still valid. Moreover, the chronology suggested by Yates is an interpretative framework which can still be used to set out a historical reconstruction of mnemonics. It is true to say that her interpretation of Bruno and other Renaissance authors is strongly influenced by the Hermetic tradition, but here, too, there are some possible points that could be useful. Indeed, the historian proposed a research hypothesis that up to that time had not been applied to Bruno, and she did this just to see what results would emerge, without claiming to have produced the final interpretation.

2.3 Mary Carruthers: Creative thinking in mediaeval memory systems

Owing to the importance of the linkages between the *ars memoriae* and the *ars predicandi* in the mediaeval monastic orders, and to the fact that it was in this area that Bruno studied and encountered the mnemonic tradition, the works by Mary Carruthers on mnemonics and mediaeval rhetoric are also invaluable to the study of Bruno's mnemonics. Although the American scholar explored the *ars memoriae* in the Middle Ages but not in the Renaissance, and so a brief overview of her studies will suffice, I consider her methodological approach and the two conclusions that she reached fundamental for my research.

Her first conclusion is the explanation that treatises on memory in the Middle Ages attributed the function of memory to the creativity of the soul and thought,

85 Frances A. Yates, *The Art of Memory* (London: Routledge and Kegan Paul 1966; London: Pimlico, 2000).

86 See, for example: Francesca Dell'Omodarme, "Frances A. Yates interprete di Giordano Bruno: appunti per una ricerca," *Rinascimento* 41, (2001): 353–74.

and not to imagination, which would become the norm in the Modern Age. Thus, since the Middle Ages memory has expressed a productive feature of thought and the American historian reached this conclusion through a detailed analysis of the metaphor of the world as a book, which we shall see is closely linked to the metaphor of inner writing.

The second conclusion that is important for my research is that she demonstrated that the art of memory was a practice that could lead to results that would be difficult to imagine in our times, precisely because it was a practice, exercise, and training of the faculty of thought. This training eventually declined due to the introduction of new techniques to store information and knowledge.

3. Definition of the research objective (3): The metaphor of inner writing in Giordano Bruno's *ars memoriae*

From a methodological perspective, it seems necessary to devise a new interpretative theoretical model of mnemonics which could be used as a general interpretative model of the relationship between mnemonics and memory theories. Looking at this more closely, one is forced to consider the relationship between the concepts, their formation, and their history.

This requirement works on two levels: the first level is historical (how to show the way in which Bruno stepped away from the mnemonic tradition while still making use of the same concepts and precepts); the second level is historiographical (how to address the problem of rationality and history following the decline of the philosophy of history).

In Hans Blumenberg's metaphorology projects (*Metaphorologie*) one can find a method of inquiry that could help grasp the problems at hand. In fact, Blumenberg interprets metaphorology as an auxiliary discipline to the history of philosophy that can draw out specific moments in which conceptual systems come into conflict, the order of knowledge is rearranged, and the function of the concepts themselves are redefined.

I therefore suggest reading both the mnemonic and philosophical works of Giordano Bruno from a metaphorological perspective and reformulating the questions I began with from this angle, i. e. the conviction that the *ars memoriae* is where Bruno questions and rethinks the concept of order, which is the central idea of his philosophical reflections. In fact, even if Bruno can be criticized for not having reached univocal descriptions of the subjects he is dealing with, one must still acknowledge that he is always striving to force a previous order: the cosmological order, the metaphysical order, the ethical order, and the theological order. Bruno's intention is not to overturn or destroy, but is clearly to reformulate notions and problems, since he believes they are unsuited to explaining reality.

From a metaphorological perspective, my problem is thus reformulated as follows: if Bruno's philosophy depends on the reworking of the philosophical concept of order, starting with different points of view, such as the gnoseological, the physical and the ethical, and if the *ars memoriae* is where Bruno begins his redefinition of the concept of order, which absolute metaphor guided this conceptual reformulation? I thus reach the following hypotheses, which I shall present in the following chapters:

1. The most productive interpretative model to study the relationship between *ars memoriae* and Bruno's philosophy can be formulated by starting with Hans Blumenberg's interpretation of Giordano Bruno in *Die Legitimität der Neuzeit*[87] and in *Die Lesbarkeit der Welt*;[88] the conclusions do, however, need to be revisited as they were hampered by the model of modern rationality based on the Enlightenment, which not only Blumenberg wants to criticize but that, as we have seen, has so far conditioned and restricted the understanding of mnemonics.
2. If one adopts the analysis of the metaphors that guided the formation of the theories as the research methodology, in the field of mnemonics and memory theories one comes across several analogies whose development has a long history, for example, the metaphor of the seal and inner writing, the ark and the stomach. However, by analysing their use, it emerges that the most performative is the metaphor of inner writing; furthermore, there is a part of the semantic field of writing that is tangent to that of the ark and the stomach, considered as containers, as places for filing.
3. From a gnoseological point of view, Bruno's *ars memoriae* is related to his philosophy and is interwoven with another absolute metaphor that is fundamental in the understanding of Giordano Bruno's thought: the metaphor of shadow.

Thus, through an interpretation of the metaphor of inner writing I intend to show how Bruno developed a philosophy that locates the new principle of order that guides knowledge as well as the relation between humans and the world in memory. I shall seek to demonstrate how Bruno's central conception of philosophy, represented in the themes of nature, language, and *praxis*, originates in his *ars memoriae*. I would like to point out here that I have no intention of

87 Hans Blumenberg, *Die Legitimität der Neuzeit*, 2nd rev. ed. (Frankfurt am Main: Suhrkamp, 1988).

88 Hans Blumenberg, *Die Lesbarkeit der Welt*, 2nd rev. ed. (Frankfurt am Main: Suhrkamp, 1983).

reducing Bruno's philosophy to his *ars memoriae*. I only intend to draw attention to an important connection and ascertain whether as a result we may acquire new understandings of Giordano Bruno's thought.

Chapter 3: Hans Blumenberg as an interpreter of the Modern Age: A critique of the historical category of secularization

1. The twofold centrality of *Die Legitimität der Neuzeit*

Blumenberg worked on *Die Legitimität der Neuzeit* for almost twenty years, making it both the achievement of his early works, which stand out in their direct comparison with Martin Heidegger[89] and Edmund Husserl,[90] and the starting point for his subsequent research. The thematic ties interwoven with the other works and the fact that it took Blumenberg from 1966 to 1988 to write the work as

For the themes dealt with in this chapter I not only took into consideration Hans Blumenberg, *Die Legitimität der Neuzeit*, 2nd rev. ed. (Frankfurt am Main: Suhrkamp, 1988), but also: Hans Blumenberg, "Kosmos und System. Aus der Genesis der Koperikanischen Welt," *Studium Generale* 10, (1957): 61–80; Hans Blumenberg, "Kritik und Rezeption antiker Philosophie in der Patristik. Strukturanalysen zur einer Morphologie der Tradition," *Studium Generale* 12, no. 8 (1959): 485–497; Hans Blumenberg, "Augustinus Anteil an der Geschichte des Begriffs der theoretischen Neugierde," *Revue des Études Augustiniennes* 7, (1961): 35–70; Hans Blumenberg, "Weltbilder und Weltmodelle," *Nachrichten der Gießener Hochschulgesellschaft* 30, (1961): 67–75; Hans Blumenberg, "Ordnungsschwund und Selbstbehauptung. Über Weltverstehen und Weltverhalten im Werden der technischen Epoche," in *Das Problem der Ordnung*, eds. Helmut Kuhn and Franz Wiedmann (Meisenheim am Glan: A. Hain, 1962), 37–57; Hans Blumenberg, "Curiositas und Veritas. Zur Ideengeschichte von Augustin, Confessiones X 35," in *Studia Patristica VI, Texte und Untersuchungen zur altchristlichen Literatur*, ed. F.L. Cross (Berlin: Akademie, 1962), 294–302; Hans Blumenberg, "'Säkularisation'. Kritik einer Kategorie historischer Illegitimität," in *Die Philosophie und die Frage nach dem Fortschritt*, eds. Helmut Kuhn and Franz Wiedmann (Munich: Pustes, 1964), 240–265; Hans Blumenberg, "Neugierde und Wissenstrieb. Supplemento zu 'Curiositas'," *Archiv für Begriffsgeschichte* 14, (1970): 7–40; Hans Blumenberg, "Selbsterhaltung und Beharrung. Zur Konstitution der neuzeitlichen Rationalität," in *Abhandlungen der Geistes- und Sozialwissenschaftlichen Klasse*, Jahrgang 1969, no. 11 (Mainz: Akademie der Wissenschaften und der Literatur, 1970), 333–383; Hans Blumenberg, "Neoplatonismen und Pseudoplatonismen in der Kosmologie und Mechanik der frühen Neuzeit," in *Le Néoplatonisme*, eds. M.P.M. Schuhl and M.P. Hadot (Paris: Éditions du CNRS, 1971), 447–471.

89 Hans Blumenberg, *Beiträge zum Problem der Ursprünglichkeit der mittelalterlich-scholastischen Ontologie*, eds. Benjamin Dahlke and Matthias Laarmann (Frankfurt am Main: Suhrkamp, 2020).

90 Hans Blumenberg, "Die ontologische Distanz. Eine Untersuchung über die Krisis der Phänomenologie Husserls" (Habilitationsschrift, Universität Kiel, 1950).

we know it today, explain the centrality of this work in his philosophical oeuvre. In fact, if one excludes *Paradigmen zu einer Metaphorologie*[91] (1960), *Matthäuspassion*[92] (1988), and *Höhlenausgänge*[93] (1989), all Blumenberg's great works were written in this twenty-year period, and if they are read bearing *Die Legitimität* in mind, it appears evident that the origin of their themes and problems lies in that work.

Considering Blumenberg's work before 1966, *Die Legitimität der Neuzeit* is a continuation of both his doctoral dissertation and the work he submitted to be awarded the *venia legendi:* While the former was dedicated to a reconstruction of Scholasticism and the latter was a reinterpretation of Husserl's phenomenology, the starting point for both was a harsh criticism of Heidegger, of his conception of historicity and the direction he gave to phenomenology. In the 1970s Blumenberg returned to the concept of theoretical curiosity (*theoretische Neugierde*), which had been a key theme in *Die Legitimität* since it could immediately be related to the historical category of self-assertion (*Selbstbehauptung*) on which Blumenberg predicated the rational authenticity of Modernity.[94] In the same period he continued his reflections on the narrative nature of history and signification through the study of the relationship between myth and conceptuality;[95] finally, with the analysis of the metaphor of shipwreck as the metaphor of existence,[96] he also brought to the fore the anthropological theme that had been the background in *Die Legitimität.* In the 1980s Blumenberg dealt once more the theme of history, which he now understands as the theme of the narrative relationship between man and the world, and when related to theory, it is interpreted as a form of sclerosis of the narrations with which man, the animal who is the least suited to surviving because nature did not assign him a habitat (*Umwelt*), gives himself a world (*Welt*).[97] This theme then leads to both the analysis of the metaphor of the world as a book[98] and his research on the problem of historical time,[99] enriched and made more complex by a much more mature comparison with Husserl's

91 Hans Blumenberg, "Paradigmen zu einer Metaphorologie," *Archiv für Begriffsgeschichte* 6, (1960): 7–142. Translated by Robert Savage as *Paradigms for a Metaphorology* (Ithaca, NY: Cornell University Press, 2010). Subsequent citations refer to the translation of Robert Savage.

92 Hans Blumenberg, *Matthäuspassion* (Frankfurt am Main: Suhrkamp, 1988).

93 Hans Blumenberg, *Höhlenausgänge* (Frankfurt am Main: Suhrkamp, 1989).

94 Hans Blumenberg, "Der Sturz des Protophilosophen. Zur Komik der reinen Theorie," in *Das Komische. Poetik und Hermeneutik: Band 7.*, eds. Wolfgang Preisendanz and Rainer Warning (Munich: Wilhelm Fink, 1976), 11–64.

95 Hans Blumenberg, *Arbeit am Mythos* (Frankfurt am Main: Suhrkamp, 1979).

96 Hans Blumenberg, *Schiffbruch mit Zuschauer: Paradigma einer Daseinsmetapher* (Frankfurt am Main: Suhrkamp, 1979).

97 Hans Blumenberg, *Wirklichkeiten in denen wir leben* (Stuttgart: Reclam, 1981).

98 Hans Blumenberg, *Die Lesbarkeit der Welt* (Frankfurt am Main: Suhrkamp, 1981; 2nd rev. ed., Frankfurt am Main: Suhrkamp, 1983).

99 Hans Blumenberg, *Lebenszeit und Weltzeit* (Frankfurt am Main: Suhrkamp, 1986).

phenomenology. Finally, almost as if wanting to close the circle of the line of thought that had been started with a comparison with Heidegger and Husserl, Blumenberg returned to a comparison regarding the meaning of theory[100] and the relationship between theory and lifeworld (*Lebenswelt*).

If one broadens the perspective and looks more closely at the context in which *Die Legitimität* was born, developed and discussed, one can see that it plays a key role in contemporary philosophy; this is because by openly contrasting an interpretative tradition that adopts secularization as a privileged, exclusive historical category for the understanding of the Modern Age, it marked the start of the so-called debate on secularization.[101]

The centrality of this debate in the post-World War II German philosophical context can also be seen in the fact that *Die Legitimität* is a stratified work. The edition that is usually referred to, the second, is the fruit of numerous, continuous revisions of the first, all of which were aimed at clarifying the text and explaining its argumentative structure, rather than modifying or going into it in more detail.[102] As far as the themes and subjects are concerned, the work was

100 Hans Blumenberg, *Das Lachen der Thrakerin: Eine Urgeschichte der Theorie* (Frankfurt am Main: Suhrkamp, 1987), Hans Blumenberg, *Die Sorge geht über den Fluß* (Frankfurt am Main: Suhrkamp, 1987).

101 The literature on secularization as a historiographic subject is vast. Here I shall mention only one work, because it offers a historical reconstruction of the debate from Hegel to Blumenberg and is thus more relevant here: Jean-Claude Monod, *La querelle de la sécularisation de Hegel à Blumenberg* (Paris: Vrin, 2002).

102 Blumenberg knew his philosophical writing style hindered the comprehension and diffusion of his works. Testimony to this awareness is the extensive documentation contained in his *Nachlaß*, for example, in his personal correspondence with some translators, see: "Briefwechsel Rigotti-Blumenberg (1983)," in *Nachlaß Blumenberg*, Deutsches Literaturarchiv, Marbach am Neckar. Irrespective of this awareness, the subject of Blumenberg's philosophical style is not irrelevant when interpreting his works; on the contrary, many other important matters are affected. Scholars agree in their description of Blumenberg's philosophical style as one in which it is difficult to trace fundamental themes and theses. Therefore, it is difficult to assign Blumenberg to a specific philosophical school. Furthermore, although his skilful ability to control language has been recognized, for which he was also awarded two prizes for the literary value of his scientific prose, the main characteristic of his philosophical writings is the attempt to hide the philosophical reasonings. It was Jürgen Habermas who, when discussing Blumenberg's philosophical style and, more generally, the question of the relationship between philosophical writing and literature, showed that Blumenberg's works are based on a critical approach that is characteristic of philosophy. For Habermas in fact, the approach, the perspective of the viewpoint rather than Blumenberg's style dictates the difference between philosophy and literature: Jürgen Habermas, "Philosophy and Science as Literature?" in Jürgen Habermas, *Postmetaphysical Thinking: Philosophical Essays*, transl. William Mark Hohengarten (Cambridge, MA: MIT Press, 1992), 205–228. For more about these problems see, for example: Robert Buch and Daniel Weidner, eds., *Blumenberg lessen: Ein Glossar* (Frankfurt am Main: Suhrkamp, 2014), 11–25; Franz J. Wetz, *Hans Blumenberg zur Einführung* (Hamburg: Junius, 1993), 7–11; Franz J. Wetz and Hermann Timm, eds., *Die Kunst des Überlebens: Nachdenken über Hans*

therefore already complete in 1966, the year in which the first edition was published, and the need to revise it came from the countless objections and stimuli it had aroused in German philosophical circles,[103] following Blumenberg's first presentation[104] of his thesis at the Seventh German Philosophy Congress.

2. Critique of the historical-interpretative category of secularization (*Säkularisierung*)

At the Seventh German Philosophy Congress, which was held in 1962 in Münster, many of the most important German philosophers, including Karl Löwith, Hans Georg Gadamer and Theodor W. Adorno, were invited to reflect upon how historical progress should be understood. The unprecedented and systematic violence of the Second World War had cast doubt on and led to accusations against the way the philosophies of history born in the Enlightenment had developed the concept of historical progress. Therefore, the questions that sparked the debate dealt with the meaning of the Modern Age, its ties with the theological-Christian tradition in the Middle Ages, and the degree of originality with which the Modern Age had presented itself on the scene of history. Therefore, the key words in the ensuing debate were "civilization," "secularization," "revolution," and "dialectics."

Blumenberg (Frankfurt am Main: Suhrkamp, 1999), 8. As regards the interpreters' difficulties, I believe that certain facts have either been repeatedly ignored, or not considered with sufficient honesty. As to the issue of assigning Blumenberg to a philosophical current – leaving aside the questionability of such attempts (as if merely belonging to a philosophical school could make it easier to understand a philosopher), one must remember that Blumenberg studied with phenomenologists such as Ludwig Landgrebe and more than once Blumenberg stated that his research was to be ascribed to phenomenology. It was no coincidence, as I shall show later in this chapter, that the philosophical terminology he works with most frequently and repeatedly is all phenomenological in nature: 'world,' 'lifeworld,' 'horizon,' to name but a few.

103 For example, the reviews by Karl Löwith and Hans Georg Gadamer: Hans Georg Gadamer, Review of *Die Legitmität der Neuzeit*, by Hans Blumenberg, *Philosophische Rundschau* 15, (1968): 201–209; Karl Löwith, Review of *Die Legitmität der Neuzeit*, by Hans Blumenberg, *Philosophische Rundschau* 15, (1968): 196–201.

104 Hans Blumenberg, "'Säkularisation'. Kritik einer Kategorie historischer Illegitimität," in *Die Philosophie und die Frage nach dem Fortschritt*, eds. Helmut Kuhn and Franz Wiedmann (Munich: Pustes, 1964), 240–265.

2.1 The legitimization of a historical period

In his presentation Blumenberg dealt with the topic of progress and the Modern Age, discussing the problem of the 'legitimacy of the Modern Age.' Whilst on the one hand, the issue of legitimacy is one that is common to all the problems of historical legitimacy, on the other, it is the main characteristic trait of the Modern Age because for the very first time the subjects of a historical period are openly disputing and breaking with tradition, questioning the historical continuum. According to Blumenberg, the problem of the legitimacy of the Modern Age can be interpreted from two different perspectives: the Modern Age is either the result of a historical period, the Middle Ages, which was theologically conditioned and in whose shadow the new period is asserting itself authoritatively by turning against it with disputes; or, it is the metamorphosis of the theological substance of the Middle Ages, in other words, a simple derivative of the latter, which can only be understood through the category of secularization. The first thesis can legitimize human self-assertion (*humane Selbstbehauptung*), that is, can explain the distinctive trait of the Modern Age in its full legitimacy; the second categorizes the Modern Age as Christian heresy. Nevertheless, the first thesis, which Blumenberg intends to support, and which asserts the Modern Age's right to autonomy, has to deal with the becoming of historical reality and cannot position the Modern Age as an absolutely new beginning, disregarding the rectilinear theological cause-effect pattern – because it would lose all its meaning. For Blumenberg, the problem of the legitimacy of the Modern Age is therefore extended to the problem of how one can maintain both the justification of the autonomy of historical periods and the idea of the becoming of historical reality, that is, it directly questions the problem of a philosophy of history that is no longer based on the enlightened concept of progress.

Blumenberg expands this criticism to the category of secularization on two levels: on the one hand, he develops a metalinguistic reflection on the terminological transfer of "becoming worldly" to "secularization", where the former is the technical philosophical term derived from Hegel's philosophy[105] and the

105 The term "becoming worldly" (*Verweltlichung*) was not coined by Hegel, but the origins of the concept it refers to go back to Hegel's philosophy of history and to reflections on the role of Christianity in the formation of the modern world: G.W.F Hegel, "Glauben und Wissen oder die Reflexionsphilosophie der Subjectivität, in der Vollständigkeit ihrer Formen, als Kantische, Jakobische und Fichtesche Philosophie," in *Gesammelte Werke, Bd. 4*, eds. Hartmut Buchner and Otto Pöggeler (Hamburg: Felix Meiner Verlag, 1968), 315–324. Anticipating Weber's concept of "disenchantment" (*Entzauberung*), Hegel makes a connection between Protestantism and deconsecration (*Entheiligung*) of nature (*Natur*) in the world (*Welt*). According to Hegel, this deconsecration is not the distinctive trait of the Modern Age but rather it merely describes the relationship between Protestantism and the new conception for salvation of the world. In the later form of his philosophical system, Hegel was to

second is the technical legal term used to name the expropriation of the Church's assets, as sanctioned by the Peace of Westphalia;[106] on the other hand, he identifies the key moments in the history of thought when the object of philosophical reflection, that is, the relationship between man and the world, changes radically, thus highlighting the "metakinetics of the historical horizons of meaning and ways of seeing within which concepts undergo their modifications,"[107] in other words, the actual movement of history. Blumenberg's critical strategy concentrates on understanding how concepts are formed, that is, how meanings are chosen and how linguistic usage is determined.

2.2 Against the underlying theologism of the secularization category (1): On the use of the secularization concept

Blumenberg shows that in historical interpretations the use of the expressions "becoming worldly" and "secularization" waver between two meanings: one is descriptive while the other is explicative. The first, descriptive meaning is a quantitative observation that presupposes one already knows what preceded the becoming worldly and it establishes a correlative relationship between not becoming worldly and becoming worldly. We all understand and use the expression "becoming worldly" to indicate a lengthy process that is secularization by means of a progressive fading of religious ties, of approaches aimed at transcendent and cult behaviour. Furthermore, we are all able to understand what the expression "becoming worldly" means because we feel we are still on the horizon of the final

return to this theme, transferring it from the religious to the context of philosophy and the history of science: the characteristic of the Modern Age thus lies in the co-existence of Protestantism as a religious moment, and of the worldly moment, which is created through the twofold movement of the principles of free subjectivity becoming worldly and in the subjectivization of worldliness. This twofold movement is to be revived and made famous by Hegel's epigones. Richard Rothe is the first to identify the becoming worldly process with that of secularization: Richard Rothe, *Die Anfänge der christlichen Kirche und ihrer Verfassung: Ein geschichtlicher Versuch, Band 1* (Wittenberg: Zimmermann, 1837), 85. For the history of the concepts of "becoming worldly (*Verweltlichung*)" and "secularization (*Säkularisierung*)", see: Anders H. Lübbe, *Säkularisierung: Geschichte eines ideenpolitischen Begriffs*. 3. Auflage mit einem neuen Nachwort (Freiburg: Alber, 2003); Walter Jaeschke, *Hegel Handbuch: Leben, Werk, Wirkung* (Stuttgart: J.B. Metzler, 2003), 416ff.; Walter Jaeschke, "Säkularisierung," in *Handbuch religionswissenschaftlicher Grundbegriffe, Band 5*, eds. Hubert Cancik, Burkhard Gladigow, and Karl-Heinz Kohl (Stuttgart: W. Kohlkammer, 1998), 9–20; Hermann Zabel, *Verweltlichung/Säkularisierung: Zur Geschichte einer Interpretationskategorie* (PhD Diss., Münster: Fakultät der Westfälischen Wilhelms-Universität, 1968).

106 J.G. von Meiern, *Acta Pacis Westphalicae publica oder Westphälische Friedens-Handlungen und Geschichte*, II.15, §14 (Hannover: 1734).

107 Blumenberg, *Paradigms*, 5.

stage of this process; in other words, we are still all able to understand such expressions as: waiting for salvation, hope in the afterlife, transcendence, divine judgement, abstinence from the world or abandoning oneself to it. If one therefore asks oneself what the expression "becoming worldly" means, the answer should be a descriptive meaning of the expression, in which "becoming worldly" is a process that leads to more profane assets than religious ones.

On the other hand, when "becoming worldly" and "secularization" are used as historical interpretative categories, their use is explanatory – or at least is meant to be. To understand the transition from the descriptive to the explicative use of the two terms, Blumenberg analyses what happens at a semantic level in the transition from the proper use of "secularization" to the analogical one, and in the transfer of this analogical meaning to the expression "becoming worldly".

In fact, by analogy the descriptive use of "becoming worldly" is derived from the technical legal use of the word "secularization", and this has two consequences. First and foremost, the analogy creates the idea of expropriation as a fundamental concept of historical comprehension.[108] Secondly, a substantialist meaning is introduced in the word "world", which can only be explained by resorting to the theological premises that are extraneous to the historical discourse. In fact, if the enunciations produced from the application of the secularization theorem are analysed, it can be observed that when speaking of "becoming worldly", phrases such as "B is secularized A" are used, determining univocal relationships between the points of departure and arrival, so that they are understood as a change of substance.[109] In this way "becoming worldly" is no

108 The analogical transfer preserves the characteristics of the expropriation experience, that is, the identifiability of the expropriated asset, the legitimacy of the original property, and the unilaterality and partiality of the expropriation (because the original property remains the legitimate one).

109 For example: modern work ethics would be the secularization of sacredness and forms of ascesis; the postulate of the political equality of all citizens would be the secularization of the equality of all men before God; the expectations of political salvation as in *The Communist Manifesto* would be the secularization of the biblical paradise and Messianism. However, Blumenberg regarded Carl Schmidt's *Political Theology* as the work in which the theorem of secularization affirmed itself for the first time and with vigour; therefore, his observations on it are of a more general nature and are, as a rule, applicable to all the declinations of the secularization theorem. According to Blumberg, Carl Schmitt opens his *Political Theology I* with the strongest secularization theorem: "All significant concepts of the modern theory of the state are secularized theological concepts", Carl Schmitt, *Political Theology: Four Chapters on the Concept of Sovereignty*, ed. and trans. George Schwab (Chicago: University of Chicago Press, 2005), 36. The exception state, for example, would have its theological correlation in the miracle and the figure of the omnipotent legislator would be derived from divine omnipotence. According to Blumenberg, Schmitt interpreted political and theological phenomena in a directly symmetrical manner, albeit only analogically. The cited examples link historically different phenomena in such a way as to present the affirmation of

longer a process of quantitative loss (such as, for example, when one says that the Peace of Westphalia went from more sacred to less sacred assets), but the sum of the qualitative, specifiable and transitive transformations of a given substance – the world – that must be postulated in the definition of what it now is. One therefore no longer dwells on the descriptive process, but on the sum of the specific changes, whose summation results in the product of secularization.

However, Blumenberg then asks: if the historical interpretative category of secularization has a descriptive and not explicative use, what truly interests the historian when he uses 'secularization' pretending it explains something that cannot be understood in another way. According to Blumenberg, secularization is not to be understood as a historical category that is able to explain the transition from the Middle Ages to the Modern Age but should be interpreted as a moment of theological self-comprehension. In other words, the secularization category is an expression of the theological attempt at self-preservation: faced with the phenomenon described by the "becoming worldly" concept, or rather the withdrawal of religious forms from the historical scene, and faced with the consequent doctrinal risk of losing the availability of the world as the eminent place of God's work, theology reduced the world to an essential body, but one of such generality that it could predicate everything. In fact, theological interest never regarded the world itself, but its position in total dependence to its own categories and as a function of its own justification and self-preservation.

However, the theological premises of the use of secularization are not theoretically available, that is, they are not at the historian's disposal and the historian must therefore reject not so much secularization in the sense of the description of a phenomenon, but the service it should provide as an argument that justifies the importance and cultural value of Christianity in the world. When the historian adopts the secularization category as a historical-interpretative one, the difficulty that emerges is that everybody believes they still understand what is meant by the expression "becoming worldly" to a certain extent, attributing it to the common use, whilst the use made of it is exclusively theological, entailing the adhesion to premises that are not available theoretically. From a historical point of view, Blumenberg concludes that the Modern Age cannot be justified with the recourse to the secularization theorem because it introduces conditions into the historical comprehension that, owing to "becoming worldly" itself, are extraneous to it.

what is subsequent because of the secularization of what is previous, one arises from the other.

2.3 Against the underlying theologism of the secularization category (2): A functionalistic vision of the concepts or of the good use of analogies

Once the dual use (descriptive and explicative) of the secularization category has been explained, and the explicative pretention of the historical category has been clarified, one can then ask whether "the possibility of a scientific use of the term 'secularization'" is possible.[110] In other words, the problem remains whether analogies can be put to good use. According to Blumenberg, what made the secularization category appear as an explanatory form for historical processes was having traced back the premise of this category to an identity in the historical process, and this identity corresponded to a presumed "firm canon of the 'great questions' that throughout history and with unchanging urgency have occupied human curiosity and motivated the pretension to world and self-interpretation".[111] Exploiting the difference that Ernst Cassirer introduced between the concept-substance (*Substanzbegriff*) and the concept-function (*Funktionsbegriff*),[112] Blumenberg thus explains what happens in the transition from one historical period to another: at a certain moment in historical becoming, the answers to the questions about the meaning and truth of the world appear to be obsolete or, simply and unexpectedly new answers appear; as a consequence, these questions require new answers, and the relationship between man and the world develops around this. Therefore, in the transition from one period to another a transfer of substances (*Substanzen*) that the concepts refer to does not take place, as those who support the interpretative secularization pattern claim, but a change of functions (*Funktionen*) of the actual concepts that make up man's experience in the world:

> Of course this identity, according to the thesis advocated here, is not one of contents but one of functions. It is in fact possible for totally heterogeneous contents to take on identical functions in specific positions in the system of man's interpretation of the world and of himself. (…)
>
> (…) What mainly occurred in the process that is interpreted as secularization, at least (so far) in all but a few recognizable and specific instances, should be described not as the *transposition* of authentically theological contents into secularized alienation from their origin but rather as the *reoccupation* of answer positions that had become vacant and whose corresponding questions could not be eliminated.[113]

---

110 Hans Blumenberg, *Die Legitimität der Neuzeit*, 2nd rev. ed. (Frankfurt am Main: Suhrkamp, 1988), translated by Robert M. Wallace as *The Legitimacy of the Modern Age* (Cambridge, MA: MIT Press, 1985), 11. Subsequent citations refer to the translation of Robert M. Wallace.

111 Blumenberg, *The Legitimacy*, 65.

112 Ernst Cassirer, *Substanzbegriff und Funktionsbegriff* (Berlin: Bruno Cassirer, 1910; Hamburg: Felix Meiner, 2000).

113 Blumenberg, *The Legitimacy*, 64–65.

By analysing the formation of concepts, Blumenberg therefore comes to an important consequence for the philosophy of history: one has to liberate oneself from the conception that there is a fixed canon of great questions that throughout history have urgently occupied the desire of man's knowledge and that would motivate the aspiration to interpreting the self and the world.[114]

To summarize, it is possible to say that criticism of the secularization category is a criticism of the use of the secularization concept. Blumenberg has no intention of proposing any kind of "linguistic prohibition."[115] Those who want to speak of "becoming worldly" or "secularization" to describe a historical process are certainly free to do so; what Blumenberg is disputing is "the claim to render intelligible by this terminology something that would otherwise not be intelligible, or would be less so."[116] Blumenberg explains that he does not wish to either be polemic or to negate the demonstrations for each individual use but rather that he would like to draw the reader's attention to a quantity of affirmations, whose established correlations are not in question, and verify the soundness of the secularization category as a historical-interpretative one. According to Blumenberg, the secularization category does not play an effective role in comprehending the Modern Age in terms of its legitimacy, or rather, in terms of its originality and rational authenticity compared to other periods; this is because it is a category that is tied to theological premises that cannot be shared by either the historian or the philosopher and which negatively condition the understanding of historical phenomena. In this sense the heaviest condition that the secularization theorem imposes on those who use it affects the conception of the world as an indeterminate substance that, throughout the period of historical

114 For example, historians should liberate themselves from the idea of progress, which in the perspective of the fixed canon of questions that develop throughout history would be interpreted as the secularization of eschatology. Blumenberg's controversial target here is Karl Löwith, *Meaning in History* (Chicago: University of Chicago Press, 1949). Blumenberg believes, however, that there is no mainstay for a transposition (*Umsetzung*) of the idea of eschatology into that of progress, and offers three explanations: a formal one, a genetic one and one that concerns the use of analogy. The formal difference lies in the fact that eschatology deals with an event that bursts into history and is transcendent and heterogeneous to it, while the idea of progress is extrapolated from a structure that is immanent to history and co-present in every present towards the future. The genetic difference is even more important than the formal one: eschatology is a reply to the question about the meaning and progress of history in its totality while the idea of progress was originally a structural formula for the theoretical process and as such comes from the aesthetic field as a protest against the constant dependency on ancient models. See: Blumenberg, *The Legitimacy*, 43–44.

115 Blumenberg, *The Legitimacy*, 5.

116 Blumenberg, *The Legitimacy*, 5. Here one can discern a reference to Gadamer who had proposed a legitimate hermeneutic function for the secularization category that is derived from the fact that there is always a dimension of hidden meaning in concepts, Hans Georg Gadamer, Review of *Die Legitmität der Neuzeit*, by Hans Blumenberg, *Philosophische Rundschau* 15, (1968): 201–209.

development has been the object of diverse attributes, while the reference itself remained unchanged. Blumenberg opposes this conceptual substantialism with an anthropological-functionalist vision of the concepts (with clear reference to Cassirer's distinction between *Substanzbegriff* and *Funktionsbegriff*), according to which the concepts are to be understood as orientation strategies in the reality imprinted by man, which is the animal most unsuitable for surviving because it is devoid of a habitat (*Umwelt*), as a reference point and thus forced to give the self a world (*Welt*) through infinite narrations.

This biological deficiency, that is, the lack of biological characteristics that would tie it to a specific environment, is remedied by man with the creation of conceptual systems that allow him to take his distance and orient himself inside the chaos and the immediacy of the lifeworld (*Lebenswelt*). However, this strategy that man uses to cope with the absolutism of reality does not occur just once. Man is forced to endlessly rethink and redefine his conceptuality because the lifeworld changes continuously, and he has to be able to respond as effectively and rapidly as possible to the new arrangement of reality, which always stimulates him in a different manner. In this anthropological-phenomenological reference framework, theories, that is, the most abstract conceptualizations, are not descriptions of reality but are narrations with which man faces absolutism, and the effort to preserve the effectiveness of their function makes it necessary to develop theories. However, this development is not without interruptions and, on the contrary, the historical process becomes clear at the moments when one theory is replaced by another. When this happens it means that voids have been created within the conceptual system that the previous theory is no longer able to fill, and they have to be reoccupied by new responses that are able to guarantee the minimum of stability necessary to live.

In conclusion, even if one questions the use of the expression secularization by comparing it with the theological usage, while the latter foresees the legitimacy of original properties, the property of an idea or of a concept does not fall under the category of legitimacy because, when the comparison is continued to the historical use, it entails no positivity for historical understanding. From a methodological perspective, it is therefore better to leave the secularization concept in the theological field, without moving it to the historical one.

3. The formation of the Modern Age

Let us now look at how the second stage of the criticism of the secularization category is structured, in other words, which categories Blumenberg uses to describe the transition from the Middle Ages to the Modern Age.

3.1 The thesis: The Modern Age as a second overcoming of Gnosis

The second part of *Die Legitimität der Neuzeit* begins with two untitled pages – almost like a prologue with a syncopated rhythm – that, introducing the thesis Blumenberg wants to support, succinctly covers the ways in which he disputes the legitimacy of the Modern Age, that is, its rational authenticity compared to other periods. According to Blumenberg, there are basically three ways: recourse to the secularization category, the accusation of 'relapse into paganism' and the accusation of 'relapse into Gnosticism.' Of these, recourse to the secularization category is certainly the most effective because without questioning the originality of the Modern Age, it defines it as a period that is clearly derived from the Middle Ages. In this manner conditioning exists between the Modern Age and the Middle Ages that, apart from the novelty the former represents, is to the detriment of its authenticity. The secularization theorem thus presents itself as a gentle refutation of the legitimacy of the Modern Age because it does not expect a past time to be restored, as in the case of the accusation of 'relapse into paganism' and, on the contrary, admits the originality of the Modern Age. The refutation does, however, concern the fact that the Modern Age has its own rational authenticity and that it might rightly lay claim to it. In fact, it is this gentle refutation, which seems to do justice to historical individuation, that Blumenberg believes is concealing the strong condition that the secularization theorem is imposing on the Modern Age, in other words, the request for recognition of conditioning, and thus a delegitimization.

This is the reason that, according to Blumenberg, despite the elements of interest in the secularization theorem, it is the 'relapse into Gnosticism' accusation that is the most effective in understanding the Modern Age because it forces one to question the event that marked the beginning of the Middle Ages and the unhealed trauma that then led to the Modern Age, in other words, the confrontation between Gnosticism and Christianity. Following in the footsteps of the Catholic theologian Adolf von Harnack,[117] who believed that Gnosticism was the stimulus for the start of the Middle Ages, understood as the Christian attempt to oppose it by resorting to its own dogmatization, Blumenberg interprets the Middle Ages as something that arose from the conflict with late-antique and early

117 Von Harnack claimed that the Hellenization of the Gospel had been a historical decision, enabling the ancient Church to preserve its identity in the difficult confrontation with Hellenistic civilization and Roman Empire: Adolf von Harnack, *Lehrbuch der Dogmengeschichte*, 3 vols. (Freiburg i. Br.: Mohr, 1886–1890), *Das Wesen des Christentums* (Leipzig: J.C. Hinrichs, 1900), *Die Mission und Ausbreitung des Christentums in den ersten drei Jahrhunderten* (Leipzig: J.C. Hinrichs, 1902), *Marcion: Das Evangelium von fremden Gott: eine Monographie zur Geschichte der Grundlegung der katholischen Kirche* (Leipzig: J.C. Hinrichs, 1921).

Christian Gnosticism. However, the medieval attempt to overcome Gnosticism failed, and it was not until the Modern Age that it was reattempted with totally different premises:

> The thesis that I intend to argue here begins by agreeing that there is a connection between the modern age and Gnosticism, but interprets it in the reverse sense: The modern age is the second overcoming of Gnosticism. A presupposition of this thesis is that the first overcoming of Gnosticism, at the beginning of the Middle Ages, was unsuccessful. A further implication is that the medieval period, as a meaningful structure spanning centuries, had its beginning in the conflict with late-antique and early-Christian Gnosticism and that the unity of its systematic intention can be understood as deriving from the task of subduing its Gnostic opponent.[118]

The reasoning to support his thesis is based on the three main themes of *Legitimacy,* which are, in the order in which they are discussed: the fundamental role of the problem of the origin of evil in the development of the history of philosophy; the self-assertion category as a privileged historical category in the understanding of the Modern Age; reflection on what is meant by historical epoch and how the transition from one period to another can be determined.

In the work, most of the treatise is devoted to the discussion of the concept of epoch and the explanation of what determines the transition from one period to another, while less space is devoted to the role of the problem of the origin of evil in the history of thought, although it does preserve its genealogical priority in the definition of the thesis. The subject of self-assertion, on the other hand, is enunciated and introduced with an explicit reference to the underlying anthropological question, and it is exemplified immediately afterwards in various forms, such as cosmogony and method; they are however, all grouped together in a single figure, that of theoretical curiosity, which makes explicit the meaning of self-assertion as an distinctive characteristic of the Modern Age.

Both the structure and the economy of the text thus show that Blumenberg's main interest lies in the definition of a hermeneutic rather than detailed, in-depth analysis of the Modern Age; indeed, if one looks closely, it is almost as if the Modern Age is absent in *Die Legitimität* and that the real protagonist is the movement of history, analysed at the precise moment of the transition from the Middle Ages to the Modern Age. For this reason, in the presentation of Blumenberg's interpretation of the Modern Age, I shall first define the hermeneutic strategy he developed, starting with the answer to the question of what a historical epoch is and what determines the transition from one epoch to another; I shall then clarify the role that the problem of evil plays in this hermeneutic

118 Blumenberg, *The Legitimacy*, 126; here Blumenberg borrows an expression from Eric Voegelin, "Philosophie der Politik in Oxford," *Philosophische Rundschau* 1, no. 1 (1953/54): 43: the Modern Age "could also rightly be called the gnostic age."

strategy, before going on to introduce the category of self-assertion as a privileged historical category for the interpretation of the Modern Age, including one of the two examples of the comparative analysis method put forward by Blumenberg. That almost brings us to Giordano Bruno's interpretation, but before doing so, I shall take a detour in the next chapter to look more closely at the subject of concept formation, followed by the question of metaphorology as an accessory discipline to the history of philosophy and as a discipline of attention.

3.2 The 'epochal threshold' (*Epochenschwelle*)

According to Blumenberg, one can comprehend fully the transition from one period to another through the concept of epochal threshold (*Epochenschwelle*), albeit differentially and thus not directly. This new conception of epoch comes from an analysis of the linguistic meaning of the word "epoch." Going back over the history of the concept, from Antiquity to Historicism, Enlightenment, and the foundation of the philosophy of history, Blumenberg identifies two senses for the meaning of the word. In an initial stage, which lasted from the origins of thought to Enlightenment, *epoch* was an extraordinary event (from the Latin *extraordinarium,* made up of *extra,* "outside", and *ordo,* "order", that is "outside the order of things"), which was taken as the reference point to measure the temporal duration of the state of things. In this sense, the concept of epoch is still very closely linked to its astronomical meaning, according to which epoch (from the Greek, *epoche*) means the stopping of a movement, or more precisely, the point at which a movement inverts direction. In fact, in the technical language of ancient astronomy, *epoche* was the observation point of a star, in other words, its passing through the zenith, and in astrology, *epoche* was a position or constellation whose importance had been recognized in tradition. Univocally definable, the distances with reference to these points were used in chronological assessment. In this first sense, epochs are thus those points in the course of time that have been characterized by an out-of-the ordinary event, and which, as such, are taken as an absolute temporal reference (in the Latin sense of *ab-solutum,* "free", "independent of the rest"). Enlightenment introduces a variation in the meaning of the concept, which goes from the événement to the situation; this means that importance is no longer given to the actions but to the situations, or rather, according to what Historicism is going to radicalize, it is no longer the events but the characteristics of a period that make the epoch. Blumenberg contrasts these two meanings with a third: the epochal threshold. By this he means an imperceptible limit that is not clearly tied to any fact or any meaningful event.

In this manner, Blumenberg aims to overcome the gnoseological impasse that he claims is afflicting the previous two notions of epoch, which are totally dependent on substantialist premises. In other words, both meanings betray that expectation of meaning as regards reality and its historical progress that, as we have already seen, is unacceptable once the functional nature of the concepts and theories has been clarified. The only thing that the historian can therefore do, is undertake a differential study that is able to understand the epochal threshold, or rather, the traces that reveal that the previous conceptual configuration is in difficulty and that a new conceptual configuration is healing the rift. The conceptual function of the threshold image is to explain the situation in which one is no longer outside a place, but one has not yet entered a new one either; it is the point at which one can see the space one is coming from, and perceive the space one is entering, but in perspective, whilst embracing them fully and thoroughly. Differential analysis involves interrogating two testimonies that make it possible to perceive the epochal threshold. The presupposed condition for differential analysis to be historically valid is that the two testimonies can be compared because they ask similar questions (we have already seen that Blumenberg does not believe there is a canon of fixed questions, and that the questions and answers can appear on the horizon totally unexpectedly). It is only under this condition that differential analysis can make the epochal threshold clear, making accessible what must have happened to result in the incompatibility of their answers.

3.3 The origin of evil in the world

According to Blumenberg, of all the questions that have been debated throughout the centuries, there is one that helps one better understand the dynamic of the history of ideas and identify the epochal thresholds: the question regarding the origin of evil in the world. The strength of this question lies in the fact that it draws the historian's attention to the definition of the world, which is a fundamental philosophical term, and shows how, within the diverse conceptions of the world, relationships are defined between world, God, and man, which Blumenberg regards as the terms underlying the construction of the meaning of history.

Blumenberg identifies six response models. The first, Plato's *Timaeus,*[119] is the paradigm of the idea of the world as an *order* (*kosmos*); thanks to Aristotle, this idea was to dominate classical Greek thought. In Plato's tale of the formation of the cosmos, the problem of evil is of little importance in the philosophical system. In fact, ancient metaphysics has no need for a cosmogony because the world neither needs it nor is able to justify it: according to the demiurgic myth cosmos is everything that can be in accordance with the world of ideas, and the ancient metaphysics does not have to justify the cosmos because correspondence with

119 Plato, *Timaeus*, trans. R. G. Bury (Cambridge, MA: Harvard University Press, 1966), 108–111.

the world of ideas is guaranteed by the *persuasion* with which reason subjects necessity. The Demiurge is not omnipotent: the material he needs exists already, an unordered substrate of unknown cause, and it is by relying on the power of reason and its ability to convince that the world originates; that is, he orders the unordered substrate according to the model of the world of ideas. Blumenberg rightly draws the reader's attention to the fact that here we see in action, the "Greeks' belief in the power of speech and persuasion"[120] and how this is projected on to a cosmic plane. It is the Greek's faith in the power of discourse and persuasion that protects the guarantee of goodness of the work done by the Demiurge, and there is not the slightest doubt that the material might already have been corrupted by evil or that this might ruin the Demiurge's persuasion. Plato's demiurgic myth thus bequeathed tradition with an underlying ambiguity: the phenomenal world is a reproduction of ideas, but it is unable to reach its archetype. It is on this ambiguity that Neoplatonism (second model) focuses and, in the attempt to resolve it, translates the negative element of the demiurgic myth into concepts, making it an object of reflection, claiming that the phenomenal world is the mistake compared to the ideal model: *hyle*, the substrate the Demiurge needs to create the world, is of unknown origins and contains the seed of evil, in other words, the burden of the fact that there is *also* evil in the world rests on the inhomogeneity between archetype and material. Plotinus, who describes the origin of the world as the fall of the soul of the world into material, introduces the idea that the world originates from an act of disorder, starting with an ordered situation – the cosmos – which can be restored if the soul of the world inverts the process it is trapped in. Now, it is precisely this contemplation of the possibility of inverting this process that shows we have not yet reached gnostic dualism. In fact, in Gnosticism (third model), the Demiurge is the source of evil, the antagonist of the god of transcendent salvation, who has nothing to do with the creation of the world and therefore Gnosis does not need theodicy, because the good god is not compromised in the world, which is the labyrinth of the lost *pneuma.* The end of the world is the process that leads to definite salvation through the suppression of the illegitimate creation of the Demiurge. This is where the asymmetry lies compared to Neoplatonism: Neoplatonism foresees a symmetrical path to the prehistory of perdition for the redemption process, while Gnosticism does not foresee the restoration of the original state.[121] To stem this dangerous gnostic dualism, the Church had to dogmatize itself. The Middle Ages (from the origins to scholasticism: the fourth model) should therefore be seen as an attempt to

120 Blumenberg, *The Legitimacy*, 127.

121 Blumenberg is not interested in embracing the totality of the speculative variants of Gnosticism but rather in underlining that it was a challenge for both ancient tradition and Christianity, arguing with the former the perfection of the cosmos and with the latter the correlation between creation and salvation through the only God.

protect itself from the gnostic syndrome, reviving the world as a creation from the negativization of its demiurgic origins and saving its ancient dignity as a cosmos, by transferring it to the Christian system, a task that was made even more urgent as the much-awaited Parousia had not occurred. The world, which was proving to last much longer than expected, once again attracted questions regarding its origin and reliability. Since it appeared that redemption would be less spectacular than had been believed, metaphysical interest in the creation was reawakened and Christianity had to adapt to the rules of the game of the pre-existing world, which continued to exist; it had to prove its own ability in the discussion with the surrounding Hellenistic environment and its pressing questions about its position of the new doctrine regarding the old cosmos. The first and most complete attempt at trying to keep God the creator and God the Saviour together in a single system was thanks to Augustine. Although it had been expected that the salvation of man would have been a result of the destruction of the cosmos, Christianity's compromise with ancient metaphysics led to a new conservationism of the world, thanks to the introduction of the theological patrimony of the stoic formula of providence, according to which the world had been created for man. However, whilst explaining the duration of the world beyond the expectations of the Parousia, and its possible use as an anti-gnostic argument, the concept of providence still revived the discussion about the origins of evil in the world and removed any possibility of explanation by resorting to the material's pre-existing dualism. Evil thus became an element that was included in the creation from nothing (*creatio ex nihilo*). Once the gnostic response had been neutralized, man was then encumbered with the problem of the justification of God. It was for this reason that Augustine defined a new concept of freedom, with the aim of laying all the blame and responsibility for evil on man. For Blumenberg, the thematic question of *De libero arbitrio* is "the condition under which it was possible for the just God to punish man, on account of his failings, with the bad things in the world."[122] This theory allowed Augustine to interpret the defects in the world not as the original failure of its purpose in favour of man, but as modifying interventions by God in his work, with which he places nature at the service of justice towards man. In many ways Mediaeval Scholasticism goes back over Augustine's itinerary to exonerate God. At the end of the Middle Ages there was also a shift in the emphasis of the interpretation of man in the world and a different vision of the divine principle. According to Blumenberg, this was due to the nominalist current (fifth model). According to William of Ockham, an exponent of this current who appeared on the philosophical scene in the fourteenth century, reason is unable to offer justifications of truth that surpass sensory experience as reason's cognitive power is limited and conditioned by sensory experience. Oc-

122 Blumenberg, *The Legitimacy*, 133.

cam's differentiation is of great importance and marks a turning point in the relationship between reason and faith, which had been maintained in harmony until Anselm and Thomas. Nominalists believed that the cognitive power of reason cannot address the explanation of the supernatural. God becomes a hidden god who works above any ability of human knowledge, and what the human subject can know about the divine nature is only possible through the act of faith of Christian revelation. According to Blumenberg, the god of Nominalism has no *ratio creandi* whatsoever, in other words, no plausible explanation for the creation of the world. From such a vision of God to total and absolute liberty – the traces of which can be found in Descartes – it is just a small step. By contrasting faith and reason, one could say that this Ockhamist fideism encouraged the development of scientific thought, distinguishing it from that of metaphysics and theology. The rift that was created between theology and philosophy revealed the irrationality of the theological-metaphysical dogmas and their incompatibility with science. It might be more accurate to say that it was not so much Nominalism that encouraged the development of modern thought but rather the urgency, driven by the disappearance of the image of a god who intervened in the things of the world, to find new horizons of thought. The Middle Ages ended when in the core of its spiritual system it was no longer able to preserve the credibility of Creation as providence for man, and he was thus burdened with its affirmation. Human self-assertion (the sixth model) revealed man's eminent need for a new model of reality, having lost any cosmic advantage. This resulted in the particular importance that was given in this context to the concept of loss of order *(Ordnungsschwund)*. The crisis of late-mediaeval order, described as the autonomation of the sphere of human performance, resulted in man's construction of a counter-world that, detached from the model of the Greek cosmos and the Christian theological one, enabled him to stop the fall into nothingness. The need of the human subject to create a new order, or rather, a self-order was directly linked to a new vision of freedom, which had lost the characteristics Augustine had given it, and had become responsible for the condition of the world, as it was a need directed towards the future, not a past original sin. The human subject founds anthropodicy in antithesis to theodicy and evil in the world thus becomes simple aspects of effective reality. The metaphysical insecurity the human being finds himself thrown into, and the fear of nothingness force him to take charge of his existence (*Dasein*). The ensuing transformation of man's role from created creature to artificer of his own destiny also leads to changes in the concept of self-preservation (*Selbsterhaltung*): the latter essentially presents itself as transformation of the theology concept. With Newton's first law, the *perseverare in statu suo* is transformed into *statum suum mutare*, in other words, the physical laws of movement are embellished with the ability of transformation, which is fundamental for the development of the sciences and the entire philosophy of the Modern Age as a whole.[123] What the moderns claim, including Descartes, is that not only was the world created from nothing, starting from a temporal point zero, but it also has to defend itself against the effects of nothingness (it is no coincidence that Descartes talks of *création continuée*). *Conservatio* and *creatio* thus become two complementary aspects.

3.4 'Self-assertion' (*Selbstbehauptung*) and the first of the two key comparative analyses

In his comparative analysis of Epicureanism and Nominalism, Blumenberg asks why the ancient epochal crisis did not find its correspondence in self-assertion. In other words, he discusses the theory that Hellenism can be seen as a sort of impeded Modern Age, on the one hand by the irruption of Christianity, and on the other, by what is still a primitive and insufficient level of technology. Blumenberg wants to prove that this hermeneutic hypothesis is not valid, in as much as it is unable to perceive the different conception of the cosmos that dominates at the two historical moments, it is therefore not able to highlight the re-occupation of the theoretical places at the two historical moments. What Blumenberg wants to do, however, is to explain the process in which the metamorphosis of meaning does not simply represent a linear descent and a parental tie with the previous meanings, but above all expresses the need to adapt to the new constellations of reality.

The detailed comparative analysis of ancient atomism and nominalist voluntarism, which from Nicholas of Autrecourt on at least revealed its affinity with atomistic physics, highlights the fact that in late Antiquity and the late Middle Ages, heterogeneous attitudes towards the world were induced. It is true that there were different forms of man's turning away from the cosmos and the ideal of theory in Hellenistic philosophy, but the severity of the problem had remained hidden in the uninterrupted validity of the cosmic quality of reality. In fact, gnostic speculation is not an expression of a loss of order, but rather an expression of the overturning of the value of an order, that is, the ancient conception of the cosmos, which is becoming petrified. In other words, the world was in any case order, and that sufficed so that man would not need to perceive himself as self-asserted towards it. In fact, a characteristic of Epicureanism is the

123 Blumenberg explains elsewhere that this is not one of the many rational principles, but it is the actual beginning of the new rationality: Hans Blumenberg, "Selbsterhaltung und Beharrung. Zur Konstitution der neuzeitlichen Rationalität," in *Abhandlungen der Geistes- und Sozialwissenschaftlichen Klasse*, Jahrgang 1969, no. 11 (Mainz: Akademie der Wissenschaften und der Literatur, 1970), 4.

neutralization of the human reference to the cosmos, while atomistic physics had to establish the indifference of physical replies for the configuration of life in the world, that is, objectivization. The immanent aim of objectivization is to verify a hypothesis, while neutralization wants to eliminate uncertainties without, however, creating certainties. Basically, the epochal difference lies in the fact that Epicurus ignores the postulate of the dominion over nature because of its consideration of man's situation in the world; for both Bacon and Descartes, on the other hand, this postulate became the quintessence of the existential necessities foreseen for man. Epicurus did not regard making man *maitres et possesseurs de la nature* as a condition for the possibility of human existence in the world. What his desire for knowledge lacked, one could say, was technical implication – he wanted to be able to distance the phenomenon, and not produce it. The late-mediaeval man has no way out: neither towards the exterior, nor towards the interior: the world is devoid of order and God could be a malignant genius.

Towards the end of his study on the Modern Age, Blumenberg highlights the difficulties the Nominalists encountered. Their realistic theory of concepts, which tried to eliminate the substantialist and eidetic nuclei of reality, through logic had only managed to remove the difference between divine and human grandeur. In this manner, man had to continue to be forced to isolate himself from the world, and self-assert himself against it. The need for credibility and rational acceptability of the world leads the human subject to use the human instrument par excellence, reason, and to reawaken the theoretical curiosity that had been put to sleep by the Christian-mediaeval culture. The greatest difference between this moment and the earlier one is that the world has lost the order that characterized it, and now it is without a structure that can be referred to by man; as a result human freedom thus becomes responsibility towards a world that is available.

Since Creation loses credibility as providence, man is burdened with self-assertion (*Selbstbehauptung*). With self-assertion Blumenberg does not mean the pure biological preservation of the living being man with the means available to his nature; instead, he means a life programme that man subjects his own existence to in a historical situation and in which he traces how he intends to face the reality around him, seizing his own possibilities.

The places left free by providence and theology are reoccupied by self-assertion in the form of its most effective instrument: modern science. In this process the quantitative analysis of human performances and technical resources must also be interpreted. The destruction of faith in the structure of the world order had to mean an outstandingly pragmatic change in the conception of the world and man's relationship with the world. Furthermore, the growth of technical potential is not only the continuation, but neither is it just the acceleration of a process that embraces the entire history of humanity. The quantitative multiplication of human performances and technical resources can only be derived from a new quality of consciousness. In the growth of the technical sphere there is a will that consciously tackles the estranged reality, a will to conquer a new *humanity* in this reality. Man is now more interested in the lack of nature as it comprises the impulse for all his behaviour.

The other side of self-affirmation that is shown historically is that of curiosity. Whilst Aristotle believes there is correspondence between the possession of knowledge and happiness (*eudaimonia*), in *Confessions*[124] Augustine believes that curiosity is dangerous. In fact, according to Augustine, knowledge of the world and looking for salvation are anti-ethical concepts. In the Modern Age, there is a growing interest in human curiosity, mainly owing to the greater value attributed to human reason in the development of the natural sciences in the search for new foundations of the real. The research objective the new science of nature sets itself is not the metaphysical explanation of the enigma of the universe and the preservation of the truth of theological contents; instead, it is particularly interested in reoccupying this theological void at a purely anthropological level. Self-assertion has to be based on autonomous rationality or, to use Descartes' words, it represents self-justification (*Selbstbegründung*).

Blumenberg offers us two complementary aspects of science: on the one hand, it helps us exorcise the enigmatic character of nature, on the other, it reveals and confirms the mysterious nature of natural phenomena. With the Copernican revolution, which Blumenberg regards as the absolute metaphor of the Modern Age, the disenchantment of the world is clear. After Copernicus, man has become aware of his precarious and relative position in the universe and, if he wants to avoid being plunged into a void, he has to take reason as the only strong point, the only tool that allows human infiniteness to compensate the indifference and infinitude of the universe. Giordano Bruno marks this change in direction. Man must not abandon himself to *otium* and Lucretian-like to nature but has to be active in the world through work, the only instrument that can make him similar to a worldly god.

124 Augustine, *Conf.*, II, 13, in Augustine, *Confessions, Volume I: Books 1–8*, trans. Carolyn J.-B. Hammond (Cambridge, MA: Harvard University Press, 2014), 78–81; Augustine, *Conf.*, X, 55, in Augustine, *Confessions, Volume II*, 162–163; Augustine, *Conf.*, X, 57, in Augustine, *Confessions, Volume II*, 164–167.

Chapter 4: From metaphorology as an auxiliary discipline of the history of philosophy to metaphorology as a discipline of attention

> That smart sayings are derived from metaphor based on analogy and expressions that set things before the eyes has now been stated.
>
> But we must explain what we mean by "before the eyes," and what must be done to produce this. I mean that things are set before the eyes by words that signify activity.
>
> – Aristotle, *Art of Rhetoric*, III, 1411b, 10–11

In the previous chapter we saw that according to Hans Blumenberg, the transition from one historical period to another can be interpreted as the reconfiguration of the concept of order, which is the concept through which the relationship between man and the world is defined. We shall now focus on how Blumenberg suggests to study conceptual reconfigurations of the concept of order.

1. Metaphorology as an auxiliary discipline of the history of philosophy

Hans Blumenberg's first work, *Paradigmen zu einer Metaphorologie*,[125] focuses on the use of metaphors in philosophy. As regards content, a large part of the book is devoted to the presentation of a review of the reception of some metaphors throughout the history of thought, for example: the metaphor of light for the concept of truth, the metaphor of the naked truth for the philosophical and scientific truth, the organic and the mechanical metaphors for the compre-

125 Hans Blumenberg, "Paradigmen zu einer Metaphorologie," *Archiv für Begriffsgeschichte* 6, (1960): 7–142. Translated by Robert Savage as *Paradigms for a Metaphorology* (Ithaca, NY: Cornell University Press, 2010). Citations refer to the translation by Robert Savage. For the subjects dealt with in this chapter, I also considered: Hans Blumenberg, "Licht als Metapher der Wahrheit. Im Vorfeld der philosophischen Begriffsbildung," *Studium Generale* 10, (1957): 432–447; Hans Blumenberg, "Beobachtungen an Metapher," *Archiv für Begriffsgeschichte* 15, no. 2 (1971): 161–214; Hans Blumenberg, "Nachdenklichkeit," *Neue Zürcher Zeitung*, Zürich, November 21, 1980.

hension of the world, etc. These historical excursuses are accompanied by an introductory chapter on the underlying, philosophical motives of the book.

1.1 Metaphor, concept, and history

In the introduction to the *Paradigmen* Blumenberg asks us to imagine what would have happened if the Cartesian methodology programme had been implemented: what would have been the scenario if the four Cartesian method rules had always been respected?[126] If the clarity and accuracy of all the facts of the experience expressed in judgement had been fully implemented, we would find ourselves in a situation of perfect objectivity, which would correspond to "the perfection of a terminology designed to capture the presence and precision of the matter at hand in well-defined concepts."[127] There would no longer be anything undetermined and "logically 'provisional' (*logisch überholbar*)"[128] and the translated forms of the language would only be provisional forms, sooner or later to be replaced with logical forms.

This situation of perfect objectivity and logical-terminological perfection would not only result in the elimination of the historical studies of concepts, but of history itself. In fact, from a perspective of perfect logical-conceptual definition, the history of concepts is only of any "critical and destructive value (*einen kritisch-destruktiven Wert*)"[129] for the "failure of the actual presence (*Verfehlung der genauen Präsenz*)"[130] of reality. Therefore, from the perspective of the Cartesian methodology programme, the history of concepts is destined to disappear

126 "The first was never to accept anything as true that I did not incontrovertibly know to be so; that is to say, carefully to avoid both prejudice and premature conclusions; and to include nothing in my judgements other than that which presented itself to my mind so clearly and distinctly, that I would have no occasion to doubt it. The second was to divide all the difficulties under examination into as many parts as possible, and as many as were required to solve them in the best way. The third was to conduct my thoughts in a given order, beginning with the simplest and most easily understood objects, and gradually ascending, as it were step by step, to the knowledge of the most complex; and positing an order even on those which do not have a natural order of precedence. The last was to undertake such complete enumerations and such general surveys that I would be sure to have left nothing out," René Descartes, *A Discourse on the Method of Correctly Conducting One's Reason and Seeking Truth in the Sciences*, transl. Ian Maclean (Oxford: Oxford University Press, 2006), 17.

127 Blumenberg, *Paradigms*, 1.

128 Blumenberg, *Paradigms*, 2.

129 Blumenberg, *Paradigms*, 2.

130 Blumenberg, *Paradigms*, 2.

when the exact presence is achieved, which, according to Descartes, is bound to be reached.[131]

Nevertheless, although the sciences and philosophy reached a level of perfection with their highly accurate terminology, what is presented to us is the persistence of the historicity and the persistence of the use of figurative expressions even in highly abstract theoretical contexts. This persistence leads Blumenberg to pose "the fundamental question of the conditions under which metaphors can claim legitimacy in philosophical language."[132] Blumenberg sees two possibilities: either metaphors are the vestibule of conceptuality and, as such, reveal the incorrectness of the concept that has not yet been logically defined, or one could hypothesize that there are metaphors "that resist being converted back into authenticity and logicality,"[133] that is, absolute in the sense of independent of the concept and that, as such, are the first elements of the philosophical language. The function of absolute metaphors is the "concealment (*Verborgenheit*)"[134] of a concept's logical deficiency and, being absolute, their analysis would be determinant in the understanding of the history of thought; this is because we would thus find ourselves having to redefine the relationship between phantasy (*Phantasie*) and *logos* in the direction of a reassessment of phantasy. It would no longer be a container of images that can be drawn on while working on the definition of the concept, until its availability is used up; rather, it would be a "catalytic sphere from which the universe of concepts continually renews itself, without thereby concerting and exhausting this founding reserve."[135]

1.2 The Kantian origins of the problem of the absolute metaphor

To allow a better understanding of what the word 'metaphor' means, Blumenberg explains that he is reformulating the problem of symbols as Kant had formulated it in paragraph 59 of *Critique of Judgement.*

131 It was Giambattista Vico who realized that the implementation of the Cartesian method implied the elimination of history, and therefore opposed Cartesian logic with a logic of phantasy. Cartesian logic is founded on clarity and distinction, but according to Vico these characteristics are only reserved for the relationship that God has with his work, with what is the given for us. Man, on the other hand, only has the clarity of what he has produced: "the world of our images and artefacts, our conjectures and projections – in short, the universe of our 'imagination', in the new, productive sense of the term unknown to antiquity," Blumenberg, *Paradigms*, 2. Vico, according to Blumenberg, thus revived in philosophy the interpretation of the translated discourse of the metaphor, which was traditionally part of the teaching of rhetorical figures.

132 Blumenberg, *Paradigms*, 3.

133 Blumenberg, *Paradigms*, 3.

134 Blumenberg, *Paradigms*, 3.

135 Blumenberg, *Paradigms*, 4.

Kant calls the procedure of the *translation of reflection* on an object of intuition onto a totally different concept 'symbol', in other words, the procedure that explains how ideas (the concepts of reason) exhibit reality. Kant writes:

> The use of the word **symbolic** in contrast to the **intuitive** kind of representation has, of course, been accepted by recent logicians, but this is a distorted and incorrect use of the word: for the symbolic is merely a species of the intuitive. The latter, namely (the intuitive), can be divided into the **schematic** and the **symbolic** kinds of representation. Both are hypotyposes, i.e., presentations (*exhibitiones*): not mere **characterizations**, i.e., designations of the concepts by means of accompanying sensible signs, which contain nothing at all belonging to the intuition of the object, but only serve them, in accordance with the laws of association of the imagination, and hence in a subjective regard, as a means of reproduction; such things are either words, or visible (algebraic, even mimetic) signs, as mere expressions for concepts.
>
> All intuitions that are ascribed to concepts *a priori* are thus either **schemata** or **symbols**, the first of which contain direct, the second indirect presentations of the concept. The first do this demonstratively, the second by means of an analogy (for which empirical intuitions are also employed), in which the power of judgment performs a double task, first applying the concept to the object of a sensible intuition, and then, second, applying the mere rule of reflection on that intuition to an entirely different object, of which the first is only the symbol. Thus a monarchical state is represented by a body with a soul if it is ruled in accordance with laws internal to the people, but by a mere machine (like a handmill) if it is ruled by a single absolute will, but in both cases it is represented only **symbolically.** For between a despotic state and a handmill there is, of course, no similarity, but there is one between the rule for reflecting on both and their causality. This business has as yet been little discussed, much as it deserves a deeper investigation; but this is not the place to dwell on it. Our language is full of such indirect presentations, in accordance with an analogy, where the expression does not contain the actual schema for the concept but only a symbol for reflection. Examples are the words **ground** (support, basis), **depend** (be held from above), from which **flow** (instead of follow), **substance** (as Locke expresses it: the bearer of accidents), and innumerable other nonschematic but symbolic hypotyposes and expressions for concepts not by means of a direct intuition, but only in accordance with an analogy with it, i.e., the transportation of the reflection on one object of intuition to another, quite different concept, to which perhaps no intuition can ever directly correspond. If one may already call a mere kind of representation cognition (which is certainly permissible if it is a principle not of the theoretical determination of what an object is in itself, but of the practical determination of what the idea of it ought to be for us and for the purposive use of it), then all of our cognition of God is merely symbolic, and anyone who takes it, along with the properties of understanding, will, etc., which prove their objective reality only in beings within the world, as schematic, lapses into anthropomorphism, just as, if he leaves out everything intuitive, he lapses into deism, by which nothing at all, not even from a practical point of view, is cognized.[136]

136 Immanuel Kant, *Critique of the Power of Judgement*, trans. Paul Guyer and Eric Matthews (Cambridge: Cambridge University Press, 2000), 226–227.

Blumenberg also prefers to use the word 'metaphor' instead of 'symbol' to avoid creating any confusion with the logical meaning of the term and to make sure it is not burdened with other meanings. The overlapping of the problem of the symbol and that of the absolute metaphor can be recognized in the fact that Blumenberg, when speaking of absolute metaphors, does not speak of the *translation of meaning* of a word to another, but of the procedure of the *translation of the reflection.* In other words, here metaphor means the *mechanism* of the metaphoricity and not the translated expression of the literal one. Blumenberg is therefore interested in analysing the semantic problem of the metaphor, that is, the problem of the "mechanism bearing the transfer of meaning."[137]

1.3 Absolute metaphors have history (beyond the Kantian historical apriorism)

In short, we have seen that the absolute metaphor is the procedure of reflection, of which Blumenberg highlights the linguistic origin and irreducibility to the concept, that is, its absolute being, as it resists logical-conceptual reduction; in other words, when a metaphor is described as an *absolute metaphor*, one implies that it cannot be substituted by a concept. This does not mean, however, that an absolute metaphor cannot be substituted or corrected by another. In this sense, one can say that absolute metaphors have history and their history "brings to light the metakinetics of the historical horizons of meaning and ways of seeing within which concepts undergo their modifications,"[138] that is, absolute metaphors show how the different conceptual systems man uses to order reality are arranged. In fact, the questions that absolute metaphors answer are not: What world can we have? What are we waiting for? But rather: What is it we wanted to know? What is the world we believe we have? In other words, they are questions that Blumenberg calls "man's clandestine expectations in the face of reality"[139] and it is because of this unique function of retrieving the "substructure of thought" that metaphorology is closely linked to the history of concepts:

> (…) metaphorology seeks to burrow down to the substructure of thought, the underground, the nutrient solution of systematic crystallizations; but it also aims to show with what 'courage' the mind preempts itself in its images, and how its history is projected in the courage of its conjectures.[140]

137 Enzo Melandri, "Per una filosofia della metafora," in Hans Blumenberg, *Paradigmi per una metaforologia* (Bologna: Il Mulino, 1969), ix.

138 Blumenberg, *Paradigms*, 5.

139 "den clandestinen Erwartungen des menschen gegenüber der Wirklichkeit," Hans Blumenberg, *Die Lesbarkeit der Welt*, 2nd rev. ed. (Frankfurt am Main: Suhrkamp, 1983), 10.

140 Blumenberg, *Paradigms*, 5.

Blumenberg is not getting ready, however, to find a metaphorology as a classificatory science of absolute metaphors. He wants to lay the foundations for a metaphorological paradigm, a discipline with the preparatory task of demarcating the fields in which one is more likely to find absolute metaphors, or rather, procedures of translating reflection that are not constantly definable by resorting to concepts. In this sense the work of a paradigm is more radical than a history of metaphors because it focuses attention on the distortions of meaning in the history of concepts, and in history in general, making it possible to recognize *epochal thresholds.* More specifically, once an absolute metaphor has been identified, a metaphorological paradigm traces the historical lines of its development and, at the most important moments of this course, it studies the more particular uses, the ones that reveal the most radical distortions.[141]

141 Of help in clarifying this point is Enzo Melandri's reflection on the meaning of the book's title: Enzo Melandri, "Per una filosofia della metafora," introduction in *Paradigmi per una metaforologia* by Hans Blumenberg (Bologna: Il Mulino, 1969), vii,: *Paradigms for a Metaphorology* evokes the Kantian *Prolegomena zu einer jeden künftigen Metaphysik die als Wissenschaft wird auftreten können* (1783. English: *Prolegomena to any future Metaphysics that will be able to present itself as a Science*). The analogy between the titles is justified because, as seen earlier, Blumenberg makes a direct reference to Kant as a source of metaphorological research. However, to what extent is it possible to insist on this analogy and how far can one go? Should this implicit reference be interpreted as adhering to a research programme that would make the basic exposition of the fundamental principles and propositions of a doctrine precede the systematic exposition of that doctrine? But then, since in the entire *corpus* of Blumenberg's works there is no systematic exposition of metaphorology, can the *Paradigms* be regarded as the beginning of an ambitious project that was never completed? If one looks carefully, the analogy only concerns the form of the titles and not the content; on the contrary, the titles are complete opposites and in this sense a critical stance against critical philosophy is to be perceived. If one focuses on the inceptive meaning of 'for' in the title of Blumenberg's first work, certainly it alludes to a programmatic work that will be followed by the science of the metaphor. But paradigms, i. e. models, are discussed here, and not prolegomena, i. e. the exposition of a science's fundamental principles and propositions. Paradigms, as such, can potentially be replaced by others because paradigms do not lead to the original, to the *terminus a quo*; instead, prolegomena establish the *terminus a quo* of a doctrine that will be later set up. This is why Blumenberg's *Paradigms* are for a possible, unspecified metaphorology, but others would be potentially possible for investigating other paradigms; and Kant's *Prolegomena* are for any future metaphysics that wants to present itself as a science. And this is precisely what Blumenberg is trying to oppose. I would like to add other observations to Melandri's on the importance of the title that comes from an essay Blumenberg wrote in 1971: Hans Blumenberg, "Paradigma, grammatisch," *Archiv für Begriffsgeschichte* 15, (1971): 196, then in Hans Blumenberg, *Wirklichkeiten in denen wir leben* (Reclam, Stuttgart 1981), 157–162. Blumenberg reflects here on the concept "paradigm" that Thomas Kuhn introduced in the theory and history of science in his book *The Copernican Revolution: Planetary Astronomy in the Development of Western Thought* (Cambridge, MA: Harvard University Press, 1995), observing that: "One reads this text without, however, understanding anything other in the expression 'paradigm' than the meaning of 'example'," "Man liest diesen Text, ohne in dem Ausdruck 'Paradigma' etwas anderes als die Bedeutung 'Beispiel' wahrzunehmen," Hans Blumenberg, *Wirklichkeiten in*

First and foremost, metaphorology has to make the metaphorical implications of theories clear. For example, if one wanted to study the concept of truth from a strictly logical point of view, if one wanted to study that concept by making explicit the meaning of the given definitions, one would achieve little. In fact, Blumenberg says, the most common definition is the one that Scholasticism erroneously attributed to Isaac ben Salomon Israeli: "veritas est adaequatio rei et intellectus."[142] Although this formula allows very few modifications (basically two: either the *adaequatio* of the intellect to the object or of the object to the intellect), this limited latitude between the two positions (*Spielraum*) sufficed for all the philosophical systems working on the definition of the concept of truth. However, this definition – in either of the two meanings – never satisfies the question: what is the truth? So, anyone who wants to study the concept of truth should not limit themselves to a strictly logical point of view; they would be better off following the history of the metaphor associated with the problem of truth, that of light, because "the question explicates itself in a concealed plenitude never yet hazarded by any system."[143] The expression "concealed plenitude" refers to the fact that metaphors voice the attempt to reply to fundamental questions that appear to be naïve, pre-systematic and often ignored.

They are questions such as:

> To what extent does mankind partake of the whole of the truth? What situation do those who seek the truth find themselves in? Can they feel confident that what exists will freely reveals itself to them, or is knowledge to be acquired only through an act of violence, by

denen wir leben (Reclam, Stuttgart 1981), 158. However, continues Blumenberg, the expression "paradigm" can also be used in the sense of "grammatical example." And it is precisely with this meaning that Blumenberg is using it in the *Paradigms*. The absolute metaphors help in recognizing similar structures in reflections. But metaphors are linguistic examples and refer to similar linguistic structures. In fact, as seen earlier, Blumenberg's conception of the metaphor is directly derived from the conception of the symbol as Kant described it in § 59 of the third *Critique*. By renaming the translation procedure based on reflection with the word "metaphor", Blumenberg, however, obtains a twofold result: he divests the Kantian symbol of the logical tradition and places it in what Blumenberg recognized as its original philosophical field i. e. the reflection on the use of language. Indeed, by putting forward a metaphorical philosophy, Blumenberg concludes the first stage of his research on the study of the relationship philosophy–science; however, returning to the reflection on the use of language in philosophy, Blumenberg also begins to restore what he believes to be the original meaning of philosophy and its truth. In this initial stage, however, the critical aspect of philosophical expectations dominates over the constructive sense and the role of philosophy, which Blumenberg was to arrive at more explicitly in the 1980s, as we shall see at the end of this chapter.

142 For the historical reconstruction of this false attribution, see: Blumenberg, *Paradigms*, chapter 1, note 1, 7.

143 Blumenberg, *Paradigms*, 7. Hans Blumenberg had already tackled this subject in an essay several years earlier: "Licht als Metapher der Wahrheit. Im Vorfeld der philosophischen Begriffsbildung," *Studium Generale* 10, (1957): 432–447.

> outwitting the object, extorting information from it under duress, interrogating it on the rack? Is our share in truth meaningfully regulated by the economy of our needs, for example, or by our aptitude for superabundant happiness in accordance with the idea of a *visio beatificata?*[144]

The philosopher's language contains hints of how philosophy replied to these questions prior to judgement (that is, before formulating judgment), how philosophy regarded the relationship of man with the world and man with himself. Through metaphors, philosophical language expresses portrayal models that guide the most refined and abstract philosophical conceptions. In fact, the metaphor is not only to be found along the path from the metaphor to the concept, but also – and this is the result that is most affected by metaphorology – in the opposite direction, from the concept to the metaphor.[145]

Absolute metaphors are said to be answers to fundamental questions:

> Absolute metaphors 'answer' the supposedly naïve, in principle unanswerable questions whose relevance lies quite simply in the fact that they cannot be brushed aside, since we do not *pose* them ourselves but find them already *posed* in the ground of our existence.[146]

Regarding the original collocation of fundamental questions, a metaphorology can offer neither a method for the use of metaphors nor a method that allows us to solve the questions the metaphors are speaking about. The metaphor, according to metaphorology, is an essentially historical object whose truth is a pragmatic one. This means that the metaphor expresses truth to the extent that, speaking about the questions that cannot be answered but nor can they be left undecided, it decides, in other words, by producing a model that allows man to exist.

A closer look at this aspect of the matter is not included in the *Paradigmen*, and the 1960 work, once and for all, gives the reader: the definition of an auxiliary discipline of the history of philosophy, metaphorology; a problem that regards the meaning of philosophy whose resolution the newly-created discipline should also help achieve, and which is linked to the problem of the origin of absolute metaphors; finally, a task that was a legacy of Kant's third *Critique*, in other

144 Blumenberg, *Paradigms*, 7.

145 Here Blumenberg distances himself from Ernst Cassirer, who, together with Edmund Husserl, should be considered one of Blumenberg's authors of reference, as he himself stated when he was awarded the Kuno Fischer Preis: Hans Blumenberg, "Ernst Cassirers Gedenkend. Rede bei Entgegennahme des Kuno-Fischer Preises der Universität Heidelberg im Juli 1974," *Revue Internationale de Philosophie* 28, (1974): 456–463. For more about the subject of the myth and science in Cassirer, see: Ernst Cassirer, *An Essay on Man: An Introduction to a Philosophy of Human Culture* (New Haven, CT: Yale University Press, 1944; Hamburg: Felix, Meiner, 2006).

146 Blumenberg, *Paradigms*, 14.

words, finding the justification of the similarities between the rules that make the similarity between different things possible.

Before continuing with the presentation of Blumenberg's thought on the presence of metaphors in philosophical discourse, and before looking at how he deals with the questions left unanswered in the *Paradigmen*, I would like to outline the fundamental lines of this horizon of philosophical questions concerning the debate on metaphors to allow a better understanding of Blumenberg's stance.

2. Historical reconstruction of philosophical theories of the metaphor, with reference to Hans Blumenberg's metaphor theory

Although it has always been overshadowed by larger problems, that of the metaphor has been a constant in the history of philosophy and Western culture. In fact, the metaphor has not been the object of just one discipline: philosophy, rhetoric, and aesthetics have all had their share as have linguistics and psychology and, recently, following renewed interest, even disciplines such as epistemology and pedagogy have shown interest. Moreover, from the very moment that, as Umberto Eco pointed out, studying metaphors also means looking at "(and the list is incomplete) symbol, ideogram, model, archetype, dream, desire, delirium, rite, myth, magic, creativity, paradigm, icon, portrayal,"[147] even people who were not directly involved made their contribution to research.

2.1 Aristotle: Definition of the research space

Owing to the manifold points of view that have studied metaphors and the heterogeneity of the instruments used to do so, it is difficult to define the problem of metaphors univocally and offer a summary of the different solutions that have been put forward. If one is to define the general characteristics of the problem, I believe it is indispensable to look at the first extant treatise, that is Aristotle's, as it is impossible to discuss metaphors in Western tradition without

147 "(e la lista è incompleta) di: simbolo, ideogramma, modello, archetipo, sogno, desiderio, delirio, rito, mito, magia, creatività, paradigma, icona, rappresentazione": Umberto Eco, "Metafora e semiosi," in *Semiotica e filosofia del linguaggio* (Turin: Einaudi 1997), 142.

making either an implicit or explicit reference to *Poetics*[148] and *Rhetoric*,[149] to their contents and the history of their reception. Aristotle's treatise on the problem is certainly not exhaustive, but it does define the discussion area in which centuries of reflection on metaphors took place.

In *Poetics* and *Rhetoric* Aristotle discusses two different kinds of discourse (*logos*): rhetoric (*techne retorike*) is the art of everyday communication, the art of speaking in public; poetry (*techne poetike*) is the art of imitative communication, the art of poetry in the broader sense of creating a language that imitates reality. The contents of *Poetics* can be summarized in brief as follows: definition of poetry; classification of its forms; discussion of the best form of poetry, the tragedy, according to its history and its constituent elements; indications on how the best tragedy can be composed; discourse and its elements (the discussion of the metaphor belongs to this section); comparison of the epic genre with the tragic. The content of this work does obviously not differ very much from what one would expect: a treatise on poetry, its history, characteristics, and the element comprising it, first and foremost language.

The same cannot be said of *Rhetoric*. Although the content of the work is what one would expect – an explanation of the phenomenon of everyday communication with its three fundamental aspects: the sources for means of persuasion in public discourse, style (this is where metaphors are discussed) and the arrangement of the different parts of discourse – Aristotle's opinion on rhetoric clashes with our common understanding of it. In fact, according to Aristotle, rhetoric is not the art of decorating discourse, an unnecessary set of devices aimed at making discourse more pleasant. Aristotle says:

> (…) rhetoric is a sort of division of dialectic and resembles it, since neither of them is a science that deals with the nature of any definite subject, but they are merely faculties of furnishing arguments.[150]

What distinguishes rhetoric and dialectics are the faculties (*dynameis*) of each, which are the induction and the syllogism in dialectics, and the example and the enthymeme or dialectic syllogism in rhetoric. Therefore, in short, although ideally part of a broader discussion on discourse, rhetoric and poetics are considered distinct, while rhetoric and dialectics are similar. One could say that this is thanks to the alethic statute of the discourses that were studied: the discourses

148 Aristotle, Longinus, Demetrius, *Poetics. Longinus: On the Sublime. Demetrius: On Style*, trans. Stephen Halliwell, W. Hamilton Fyfe, Doreen C. Innes, W. Rhys Robert, rev. Donald A. Russell (Cambridge, MA: Harvard University Press, 1995).

149 Aristotle, *Art of Rhetoric*, trans. John Henry Freese, rev. Gisela Striker (Cambridge, MA: Harvard University Press, 2020).

150 Aristotle, *Rhe.*, A, 1356a, 4–6, in Aristotle, *Art of Rhetoric*, 18–19.

developed in poetics are ones that *imitate* reality; while those of rhetoric and dialectics concern reality – everyday life in the former, and science in the latter.

Summarizing Aristotle's discussion of metaphors in the way it is presented in *Poetics* and *Rhetoric*, one can perceive these three themes, which have defined the range of the discussion of metaphors up to today: definition of the metaphor and elucidatory examples[151] from poetic and everyday language; study and evaluation of the heuristic value of the metaphor;[152] finally, judgement on the use of metaphors in philosophy.[153]

2.2 A history of the reception of *Poetics* and *Rhetoric*

If we now look at the history of how Aristotle's two works were received, we can understand how interest towards the problem of the metaphor changed over the centuries. In fact, whilst Aristotle's treatment of the metaphor remained canonical in rhetorical tradition, through Cicero and Quintilian, with just minor changes, what did change significantly is the relationship between rhetoric, logic

151 "A metaphor is the application of a word that belongs to another thing: either from genus to species, species to genus, species to species, or by analogy. By 'from genus to species' I mean, e.g., 'my ship stands here': mooring is a kind of standing. Species to genus: 'ten thousand noble deeds has Odysseus accomplished'; ten thousand is many, and the poet has used it here instead of 'many'. Species to species: e.g. 'drawing off the life with bronze,' and 'cutting with slender-edged bronze'; here he has used 'drawing off' for 'cutting' and *vice versa*, as both are kinds of removing. I call 'by analogy' cases were *b* is to *a* and *d* is to *c:* one will then speak of *d* instead of *b*, or *b* instead of *d*. Sometimes people add that to which the replaced term is related. I mean, e.g., the wine bowl is to Dionysus as the shield to Ares: so one will call the wine bowl 'Dionysus' shield,' and the shield 'Ares' wine bowl.' Or old age is to life as evening to day: so one will call evening 'the day's old age,' or, like Empedocles, call old age 'the evening of life' or 'life's sunset.' In some cases of analogy no current term exists, but the same form of expression will still be used. For instance, to release seed is to 'sow,' while the sun's release of fire lacks a name; but the latter stands to the sun as odes sowing to the seed, hence the phrase 'sowing his divine fire.' This type of metaphor can further be used predicating the borrowed term while denying one of its attributes: suppose one were to call the shield not 'Ares' wine bowl' but 'a wineless wine bowl'," Aristotle, *Poet.*, 1457b, 7–32, in Aristotle, *Poetics*, 104–107.

152 Aristotle, *Rh.*, III, 1410b, 14–17, in Aristotle, *Art of Rhetoric*, 396–397; Aristotle explains that the heuristic value of metaphors should be attributed mainly to the fourth kind of metaphor – analogy – because it "sets things before the eyes", representing an object in action: Aristotle, *Rh.*, III, 1411b, 20 and following, in Aristotle, *Art of Rhetoric*, 402–403.

153 "It is important to use aptly each of the features mentioned, including double nouns and loan words; but much the greatest asset is a capacity for metaphor. This alone cannot be acquired from another and is a sign of natural gifts: because to use metaphor well is to discern similarities," *Poet.*, 1459 a, 4–8, in Aristotle, *Poetics*, 114–115. Aristotle underlines that the use of the metaphor is a sign of good cognitive activity, also in Aristotle, *Rh.*, III, 1412a, 6–7, in Aristotle, *Art of Rhetoric*, 408–409.

(or philosophy) and poetics. An outline of the history of this relationship equals an outline of the history of reflection on the metaphor.

After Aristotle the tie between rhetoric and dialectics already became looser, taking the path that led to a "poetical totalization of rhetoric",[154] in other words, towards the affirmation of the indivisibility of poetics and rhetoric and therefore the annihilation of the latter in the former. Several fundamental vicissitudes in the history of Western culture provide trail marks along this course. For example, in the Middle Ages Ovid was considered as the first to postulate a relationship between poetry and the art of oratory. However, another two testimonies that date back to the Greek-Latin world are much more important and explicit. One is the change that Dionysius of Halicarnassus made to the constitution of rhetoric in *De compositione verborum*, in which the enthymematic is abandoned so that only the rhythm of the phrases is considered. The second comes from Tacitus in *Dialogus de oratoribus:* the historian traces the causes of the decadence of eloquence back to Domitian's imposition of silence in the *forum.* By doing so, Tacitus declares, eloquence deviates towards an independent art, poetry. Things do not change in the Middle Ages: even though rhetoric is included in the disciplines of the *trivium*, which, together with the *quadrivium* define the ideal of mediaeval culture, its function is supplementary. Rhetoric is the inessential art of decorating the essential and is recognized in its essentiality through dialectics and expressed suitably with a correct use of grammar. As the Middle Ages came to an end, so did its cultural idea of rhetoric. By now, freed from dialectics once and for all, rhetoric was to follow the development of literature, which was also no longer dependent on philosophy. From this moment on, philosophy was to continue with dialectics alone, guided by a new value that was to perfect its definition throughout the entire Modern Age: evidence. Language was also to follow this value, and this was the same as recommending that philosophers abstained from using metaphors.

Restricting the focus now to the studies of metaphors carried out in the twentieth century, with the aid of the interpretative grid based on Aristotle, I shall try to highlight how consideration of the problem changed, and which aspects research focused on. I do not intend to look at the various solutions that were put forward in detail but will only look at those works or authors who determined the general course in these years and who created the paradigms that research on metaphors was to be based on.

154 Roland Barthes, "L'ancienne rhétorique," *Communications* 16, (1970): 172–223.

2.3 The twentieth century: "The age of metaphoromania"

In the twentieth century interest in the metaphor went from being secondary, overshadowed by larger problems, and became the main interest in most philosophical research.[155] This change was directly due to the re-evaluation of rhetoric, where the metaphor was considered a figure *par excellence*, and the so-called linguistic shift that positioned language as the main object of philosophy. The first, extremely important contribution to research on metaphors came from Max Black who, with his works,[156] introduced into analytical philosophy the concept that rejects the position of a metaphor as a decoration or as a comparison and promoted the idea that the metaphor has an irreducible meaning and a particular cognitive content.

According to M.L. Johnson, the 1960s and 1980s will go down in history as "the age of metaphoromania".[157] In fact, it was precisely in this period that studies were published that are now considered classics, for example: Paul Ricœur, *La Métaphore Vive*[158] and the book edited by Andrew Ortony, *Metaphor and Thought.*[159]

1980 saw the publication of another important volume that marked a further change in perspective. Written by a linguist and a philosopher, George Lakoff and Mark Johnson, *Metaphors We Live By*[160] arose from the authors' interest in "how people understand their language and their experience."[161] Based on linguistic evidence, Lakoff and Johnson formulated the following thesis: contrary to what

155 This is also evidenced by the fact that scholars studying metaphors at that time could draw on several tools that comprised a reference base shared by all metaphorologists. In particular, an English journal devoted to metaphors, their theory, and history: *Metaphor and Symbolic Activity. A Quarterly Journal*, eds. Howard R. Pollio, Lawrence Erlbaum Associates Inc. Publish.; another journal, in French, devoted to the problems and history of imagination, frequently published several issues on the metaphor, regarding it as a subfield, at times a replacement for imagination: *Cahiers de l'imaginaire*, published under the guidance of Gilbert Durand and Michel Maffesoli by the publisher Privat in Toulouse. Other equally indispensable instruments included the following bibliographies: Warren A. Shibles, *Metaphor: An Annotated Bibliography and History* (Whitewater, WI: Language Press, 1971); Jean-Pierre van Noppen, *Metaphor: A Bibliography of post-1970 Publications* (Amsterdam: John Benjamins, 1985); Jean-Pierre van Noppen and Edith Hols, eds., *Metaphor II: A Classified Bibliography of Publications from 1985 to 1990* (Amsterdam: John Benjamins, 1990.

156 See above all Max Black, *Models and Metaphor* (Ithaca, NY: Cornell University Press, 1962).

157 Mark Johnson, ed., *Philosophical Perspective on Metaphor* (Chicago, IL: Minnesota University Press, 1981).

158 Paul Ricœur, *La métaphore vive* (Paris : Seuil, 1975).

159 Andrew Ortony, *Metaphor and Thought* (Cambridge: Cambridge University Press, 1979).

160 George Lakoff and Mark Johnson, *Metaphors We Live By* (Chicago: University of Chicago Press, 1980).

161 Lakoff and Johnson, *Metaphors We Live By*, ix.

many people think about metaphors, that is, that they are merely an instrument to embellish language, a rhetorical device, in short, an expedient of the extra-ordinary language and not the common language:

> (…) metaphor is pervasive in everyday life, not just in language but in thought and action. Our ordinary conceptual system, in terms of which we both think and act, is fundamentally metaphorical in nature[162]

The entire book is a lengthy analysis of metaphorical expressions that are used in everyday language and in specialized fields, mainly in the scientific and philosophical fields, with the aim of demonstrating the pervasiveness of their thesis.

If one takes M. Black and Lakoff and Johnson's works as paradigmatic, it is possible to say[163] that in America it is difficult to trace all essays prior to the year 1980 back to a global perspective and, on the contrary, research is still extremely heterogeneous. The questions raised by Black in 1962 can, however, be summarized, that is:

> "How do we recognize a case of metaphor?" "Are they any criteria for the detection of metaphors?" "Can metaphors be translated into literal expressions?" "Is metaphor properly regarded as a decoration upon 'plain sense'?" "What are the relations between metaphor and simile?" "In what sense, if any, is a metaphor 'creative'?" "What is the point of using a metaphor?" (…) The list is not a tidy one, and several of the questions overlap in fairly obvious ways. But I hope they will sufficiently illustrate the type of inquiry that is intended.[164]

The publication of Lakoff and Johnson's book (1980) marked a change in the research and became a paradigm for the research to follow. Testimony to this is, for example, an anthology published in 1985, edited by Paprotté and Dirven, *The Ubiquity of Metaphor.*[165] It is these two editors who underline the change in paradigm: not only the metaphor, which has been wrenched away from the domain of rhetoric, has become the object of diverse disciplines, but the questions surrounding it have also changed. The questions now are: if one can recognize a metaphorical expression, it requires a recognition strategy that is fundamentally different to the clarification of a literal affirmation; metaphorical skill is developed in the same way as a linguistic skill in general; there is a correlation between a subject's mnemonic faculty and their metaphorical skill; can metaphorical meaning or the degree of metaphorical understanding be measured? It is this ubiquity of metaphorical processes that the book tries to illustrate in the

162 Lakoff and Johnson, *Metaphors We Live By*, 3.

163 I am following the chronological division adopted by van Noppen in the aforementioned article but am specifying it more clearly.

164 Max Black, *Models and Metaphor* (Ithaca, NY: Cornell University Press, 1962): 41–42.

165 Wolf Paprotté and René Dirven, eds., *The Ubiquity of Metaphor: Metaphor in Language and Thought* (Amsterdam: John Benjamins, 1985).

language system, in the use of language, and in psycholinguistic processes. The essays in the first part adhere closely to Lakoff and Johnson's thesis: the metaphor is a mental construction that is based on experience and determined culturally: conventional metaphors and dead metaphors are very important for the intuitions that they give us in conceptual processes and that allow the development of mental portrayals in a large number of semantic fields; the metaphor is not a marginal linguistic phenomenon, on the contrary, it constitutes the basic use of language while the literal use is derived from it. The second part of the anthology explores how the metaphor can function as a mechanism that systematically explains a large number of lexical-syntactical or morphological processes. The third, lengthiest part and the most susceptible to developments deals with the role metaphors play in comprehension. It is the greater number of contributions on this aspect of research that indicates the change in perspective that has occurred.

After 1985 the main question becomes: what can humanity *do* with the results of the research on metaphors that has been conducted in recent decades? Now that the metaphor has been promoted from its status as a decoration to that of a fundamental category that allows man to structure and understand the reality he is living and moving in, now that many of its mechanisms have been identified and described, the problem presents itself in the comparisons of the practical use that can be made of these intuitions.[166] Such a question has resulted in, for example, countless studies on the use of metaphors in politics, theology and religion. But conferences have also been organized on the subject: "what can one do with metaphors?"

However, in America, in addition to the enthusiasm shown towards metaphors, there are also people who, using the most refined analytical contemporary theories, appear to have also questioned the actual possibility of the metaphor, as it was described and studied in that period. It suffices to mention Donald Davidson's essay "What metaphors mean."[167] According to Davidson, "metaphors mean what the words, in their most literal interpretation, mean."[168] This hypothesis is justified during a concise criticism of the most widespread conceptions of the metaphor – Richards', Black's, Freud's,[169] Lakoff's, to name but a

166 Jean-Pierre van Noppen, "More Books on Metaphor," *Revue Belge de philologie et d'histoire* 66, no. 3 (1988): 632.

167 Donald Davidson, *Inquiries into Truth and Interpretation* (Oxford: Oxford University Press, 1985).

168 Davidson, *Inquiries into Truth and Interpretation*, 245.

169 Sigmund Freud discussed the phenomenon of the metaphor in a work dated 1905, devoted to the relationship existing between jokes and the unconscious: Sigmund Freud, *Der Witz und seine Beziehung zum Unbewussten.* This work is to be regarded as a provisional arrival point for studies on unconscious dynamism. The study, started in 1895 with *Entwurf einer Psychologie* and continued in the seventh chapter of *Die Traumdeutung* (1899), was to be

few of the most representative. The essay therefore also offers a critical introduction to the contemporary debate, particularly in the English language.

In Europe the debate on metaphors was not as lively as in the Anglo-Saxon countries. Philosophers who took part included Ricœur and Derrida, who were the ones who enjoyed the greatest international renown. These studies on metaphors represent a chapter of their philosophical activity and it was a chapter they could write together. In fact, they produced a philosophical comparison that was developed in the following texts: in 1971 Derrida published *La mythologie blanche. La métaphore dans le texte philosophique*, Ricœur commented it in the eighth study of *La mètaphore vive* (1975); Derrida's reply then arrived in 1978, at a conference held in Geneva.[170] What were the two philosophers discussing? The role of the metaphor in the language of philosophy, starting with a common phenomenological-hermeneutic background.

2.4 Hans Blumenberg and the revival of the Aristotelian discussion framework

This was therefore how the main paradigms and main lines that characterized research on the metaphor developed in the past century, and are probably still current today. If one only looks at the problems that were dealt with, one can see that the questions were still those raised by Aristotle: What is a metaphor? What role does it have in knowledge? What weight does it have in philosophical discourse? This revival of all the Aristotelian themes was certainly encouraged by the reassessment of everyday language and the studies carried out in analytical and epistemological fields.

Hans Blumenberg tackles the problem of the metaphor by starting with the question of the use of metaphors in philosophical discourse. The questions he begins with are: Are metaphors used in philosophical discourse? What role do they play? Or rather, are they accessories – and therefore replaceable or even eliminable – or do they lay foundations and are therefore indispensable and inevitable? In short, do metaphors in philosophical discourse make it or betray it?

revived in 1915 with metapsychological contributions, in 1920 with *Jenseits des Lustprinzips* and in 1922 with *Das Ich und das Es.* According to the hypothesis underlying the thesis on dreams and jokes – but also on metaphors and on all the figurative uses of language – they are of the greatest significance in men's lives when considered within a quantitative and dynamic conception of the psychic apparatus. It was after Freud's research that the problem of the metaphor also became a problem.

170 Jacques Derrida, "La mythologie blanche. La métaphore dans le texte philosophique," in Jacques Derrida, *Marges de la philosophie* (Paris: Les Editions de Minuit, 1972): 247ff.; Paul Ricœur, *La mètaphore vive* (Paris : Seuil, 1975) ; Jacques Derrida, "Le retrait de la métaphore," in Jacques Derrida, *Psyché. Inventions de l'autre* (Paris: Galilée, 1987–1988): 63–93.

Can one do without using metaphors in philosophical discourse? Can one decide not to use metaphors? Tackled from this perspective, the problem is particularly interesting because it allows one to reflect, yet again, on the sense and meaning of philosophy, but from a specific position. In fact, we have already seen how opposition to the use of the metaphor in philosophy is part of a philosophical tradition that goes back to the Greek-Roman period and has its most complete form in the Modern Age. Still, this tradition essentially goes against a characteristic of the beginnings of philosophy.-How can this renewed interest in metaphors in philosophy therefore be interpreted? As an attempt to return to the origins? An attempt to recover a sense of philosophy that has been lost? But if so, which sense? These are the questions Hans Blumenberg seems to be answering in his formulation of the historical-philosophical programme of a metaphorology whose origins, not by chance, lie in Kant's third *Critique.*

3. Metaphorology as a discipline of attention

In 1980 Blumenberg wrote an article entitled *Nachdenklichkeit*[171] for the *Neue Zürcher Zeitung*, in which he reflected on what philosophy is, and how it originated. In this article Blumenberg returned once again to the Kantian question that the Königsberg philosopher himself had left unanswered, that is, the question of what makes reasoning in analogies on heterogeneous experiences possible.[172]

3.1 Stimulus-reaction or stimulus-dilation

Blumenberg's article dated 1980 starts with a comparison with the functionalist and organic explanation of life, according to which every living being reacts according to a stimulus-reaction scheme to the reality surrounding it. According to Blumenberg, man does not respond to the stimuli from the world of life in the same way as other living beings, in other words, following the stimulus-reaction scheme, because man is the being that hesitates. As seen earlier, Blumenberg perceives man as the biologically most unsuitable living being, because he lacks the ability to respond to the stimuli of reality, which is, on the other hand, an element in an animal's response to its habitat (*Umwelt*). This is also why Blumenberg believes that the world concept (*Welt*) is one of the philosophically most

171 Hans Blumenberg, "Nachdenklichkeit," *Neue Zürcher Zeitung*, Zürich, November 21, 1980.
172 In the quotation here on page 94 Kant says: "This business has as yet been little discussed, much as it deserves a deeper investigation; but this is not the place to dwell on it."

relevant concepts, because it tells us what man expects from his relationship with reality. In fact, man is able to counter-balance his possible disadvantage compared to other living beings, and compared to life itself, because a great number of possible actions (of responses and not reactions) to a stimulus, to a prompt, result in what we call experience, which is the human response in which not only signals are perceived, but things, and one learns to wait for what is still to become manifest.

3.2 The rise of philosophy from 'pensiveness' (*Nachdenklichkeit*)

Blumenberg hypothesizes that hesitation was the first step towards civilization, that is, towards that system of questions and answers that have the function of compensating for humans' biological inadequacy.[173] Blumenberg says that we have an idea of thinking about what creates the shortest link "between two points, between a problem and its solution, between a need and its being satisfied, between interests and their consent to them."[174] Those who are pensive, on the other hand, are not expected to produce results: "Pensiveness includes an experience of freedom, and even more freedom of rambling."[175] However, no form of sociality can allow its members to ignore the functionalism and actual dialogical strategies, including philosophy, that do not allow one to remain pensive, and it is from this perspective that they need to be understood.

If, on the one hand, philosophy is to be understood as the discipline that tackled these problems methodically, at the extreme it is also the demonstration of the impossibility of having final answers. If regulated thought appears to be the furthest thing possible from pensiveness, many philosophical exponents are against this separation, such as, for example, Socrates and Kant. Therefore, although philosophy is not reducible to pensiveness, "one cannot deny its origins from this and above all its wish to be at its service."[176]

Blumenberg offers one of Aesop's fables as an example of pensiveness, one of the things Socrates devoted himself to whilst in prison:

> A poor man was carrying a load of wood on his shoulders. After a while he was feeling faint, so he sat down by the side of the road. Putting aside his burden, he bitterly called out to Death, summoning Death with the words 'O him!' Death immediately showed up and said to the man, 'Why have you summoned me?' The man said, 'Oh, just to have you

173 Although life requires utility, it has granted "to its favourites the experience of freedom from the objective. And this brings into being every civilisation," Blumenberg, "Nachdenklichkeit."
174 Blumenberg, "Nachdenklichkeit."
175 Blumenberg, "Nachdenklichkeit."
176 Blumenberg, "Nachdenklichkeit."

help me pick this burden up off the ground!' (The fable shows that everyone clings to life, even if they suffer from affliction and oppression)[177]

All of Aesop's fables end with a sentence that explains what the fable is teaching (the *epimythion* or 'moral of the story'). Humanists and philologists had noticed the disproportion between these sentences and the stories they belong to, and there has always been an excess of meaning on either one side or the other. According to Blumenberg, the pensiveness provoked by the fable depends on the pensiveness that is displayed in the actual fable:

> The old man in the tale is not a 'thinker' who has changed his mind about the scarce value of life between throwing away his load, and the arrival of death; he is someone who learns that it is only in hesitation that one benefits from the profit that this brings. The old man threw away his unbearable burden because in the end he decided he wanted to await death, and having thrown away his burden grants him deferral, he draws a deep breath and looks at the world once again, understanding what the price would be if he were to free himself of his burden once and for all. Whilst he is lost in reflection, the death he called approaches; and it seems that the old man is granted that deferral that he had acquired with his fatigue of life. The tale does not say anything about what was going through the old man's head to move death to help him carry on walking with his burden, almost as if that had been the reason he had been summoned. However, it is precisely what the tale does not tell us that the tale grants us a space to be pensive.[178]

As this fable so clearly shows, pensiveness is a pause in the functionalistic scheme and the philosopher has to:

> preserve if not to renew some of that pensiveness, of its origin from the lifeworld. This is why it must not be bound to any particular aspects regarding its kind of utility. Its tie with the lifeworld would be destroyed if the right to question a philosopher were restricted by the normativity of the replies or also just the constriction of asking questions according to the possible answers and their disciplines.[179]

177 "The Poor Man and Death," in *Aesop's Fables*, trans. Laura Gibbs (Oxford: Oxford University Press, 2002), 223.

178 Blumenberg, "Nachdenklichkeit."

179 Blumenberg, "Nachdenklichkeit." Blumenberg continues as follows: "Philosophy merely represents a more general result in each culture: that of the insuppressible nature of its elementary needs and problems through its hypothetical overcoming. Culture is also respecting problems we cannot find a solution to and that make us reflect and leave us pensive."

3.3 A phenomenological-anthropological reply to Kant

When Blumenberg wrote the article on *Nachdenklichkeit* a considerable amount of time had elapsed since the metaphorology project as it had been formulated in *Paradigms;* furthermore, from a phenomenological perspective the anthropological question, which had formed the background of *Legitimacy* and had found its correct philosophical formulation in the Kantian problem of the symbol, now occupied an important place in his reflections.[180]

I think that a comparison between *Paradigms* and *Nachdenklichkeit* might facilitate understanding since the idea of the absolute metaphor also leads us to reflect on pensiveness, because the pensiveness of man also emerges in absolute metaphors and their history.[181] We have seen this extensively when we discussed the loss of order (*Ordnungsschwund*), epoch in its diverse meanings, and the logical inadequacy of the concept: every time the historical movement becomes clear at a conceptual level, there is a redefinition of the *order* in the countless fields it is to be found in.

Therefore, in my analysis of Blumenberg I feel it is necessary to underline this phenomenological characteristic of metaphorology as a discipline of attention, in other words, in the sense of a discipline that once again draws attention to the pensiveness that precedes and accompanies every conceptual formation, thus allowing one to understand something more about the history of concepts. When absolute metaphors are being sought and questioned, one is not searching for an original meaning; attention is drawn phenomenologically to an aspect of history and conceptual formation that is, for historical-cultural reasons, considered marginal but can, in fact plumb very deep meanings.[182]

180 It was no coincidence that amongst the previously unpublished works that were published posthumously was the essay on man, in its most complete form for printing, entitled *Beschreibung des Menschen:* Hans Blumenberg, *Beschreibung des Menschen*, ed. Manfred Sommer (Frankfurt am Main: Suhrkamp, 2006).

181 We could perhaps even go so far as to define *Nachdenklichkeit* as the form that the absolute metaphor assumes when the historical problem becomes a philosophical-phenomenological problem.

182 "Dienst an der Schärfung der Wahrnehmungsfähigkeit im weitesten Sinn ist das, was die Philosophie gemein hat und was sie gemein macht mit allen 'positive' Disziplinen. Nur daß allein sie kein anderes Verfahren hat, ihre 'Phänomene' zu konservieren, als sie zu beschreiben. (…) Deshalb wird es eine Phänomenologie der Geschichte geben, zu der einige Anläufe in den wenigen Arbeitsproben dieses Bändchen bemerkbar sein sollten," Hans Blumenberg, *Wirklichkeiten in denen wir leben* (Stuttgart: Reclam, 1981) 6, "What philosophy has in common and makes it similar to other 'positive' branches of knowledge is the contribution it gives to the improvement of the perception – 'perception' here has a broad meaning. The only difference to the other positive disciplines is that philosophy keeps its 'phenomena' by describing them. (…) Therefore, there can be a phenomenology of history and I aim to explain some aspects of it in the following essays."

There is a great affinity between this conception of the history of concepts and Paolo Rossi's explanation of the history of ideas with the concept of "intellectual fossils."[183] In particular, the idea that the history of ideas also has to confront experiences that detract linearity from the historical process, and are certainly less coherent with the genealogical expectations of the historian of ideas; while unable to offer total enlightenment, they are, however, able to delve deeper and deeper into historical understanding, establishing connections and implications that show us the historical complexity, and the complexity and wealth of reality.

This lengthy excursus on Hans Blumenberg and metaphorology ends the methodological part of the thesis, whose objective was to introduce and justify the proposal to study the metaphor of inner writing as an absolute metaphor for memory. In other words, in conceptual formation the leading paradigm of both mnemonics and theories of memory is the metaphor of inner writing.

Among the many ways of studying the role of metaphors in the history of ideas,[184] I chose the historical-phenomenological approach of Hans Blumenberg's metaphorology, which consists in drawing attention to the connections between themes and phenomena that reoccur throughout the history of philosophy. The reason for this choice is mainly theoretical: among the authors who reflected upon metaphors in the last century, it is Blumenberg who regains the Aristotelian character of philosophy as a "discipline of attention," which seems to me of great value nowadays.

In my research the reoccurrences which I would like attention to focus on regard how reflection on natural memory and artificial memory was formulated throughout the history of philosophy. Starting in the following chapter I would like to attempt a limited interpretation and analysis with the aim of testing a hermeneutic hypothesis: the metaphor of inner writing is the absolute metaphor for mnemonics and theories of memory. This is prompted by one of Hans Blumenberg's works, this time *Die Lesbarkeit der Welt*, because it was whilst reflecting on this study by Blumenberg that I formulated the hypothesis on the metaphor of inner writing as an absolute metaphor of memory. I will not apply the research lines that Blumenberg applies in the *Paradigmen*; in particular, I will not carry out a differential analysis because the aim of my research is not to demonstrate an epochal transition, but how an absolute metaphor guides the reformation of philosophical problems.

183 See here, pp. 32–33.

184 On other approaches to the study of metaphors in historical research, see for instance: Benjamin Specht, ed., *Epoche und Metapher: Systematik und Geschichte Kultureller Bildlichkeit* (Berlin: De Gruyter, 2014); Eckard Rolf, ed., *Metapherntheorien: Typologie-Darstellung-Bibliographie* (Berlin: De Gruyter, 2005).

Chapter 5: On Blumenberg's interpretation of Giordano Bruno

1. Giordano Bruno, philosopher of Copernicanism

Blumenberg discusses Bruno in four different works, in which his analysis of the main problem of Nolanus' philosophy plays a central role in the interpretation of the Modern Age. These works are: *Die Legitimität der Neuzeit*,[185] *Die kopernikanische Wende*,[186] *Die Genesis der kopernikanischen Welt*,[187] and *Die Lesbarkeit der Welt*.[188]

For the themes dealt with in this chapter, in addition to the three main works referenced in the following notes, I also consulted: Hans Blumenberg, "Der kopernikanische Umsturz und die Weltstellung des Menschen. Eine Studie zum Zusammenhang von Naturwissenschaft und Geistesgeschichte," *Studium Generale* 8, (1955): 637–648; Hans Blumenberg, "Einleitung," in Nicolaus von Cues, *Die Kunst der Vermutung*, ed. Hans Blumenberg (Bremen: Dieterich, 1957), 7–69; Hans Blumenberg, "Kosmos und System. Aus der Genesis der Koperikanischen Welt," *Studium Generale* 10, (1957): 61–80; Hans Blumenberg, "Die Vorbereitung der Neuzeit," *Philosophische Rundschau* 9, (1962): 81–133; Hans Blumenberg, "Kopernikus im Selbstverständnis der Neuzeit," in Akademie der Wissenschaften und der Literatur in Mainz, *Abhandlungen der geistes- und sozialwissenschaftlichen Klasse, Jahrgang 1964*, no. 5 (1965): 339–368; Hans Blumenberg, "Nachruf auf Erich Rothacker," in *Jahrbuch der Akademie der Wissenschaften und der Literatur in Mainz* (Mainz: Akademie der Wissenschaften und der Literatur, 1966), 70–76; Hans Blumenberg, "Nachbemerkung zum Bericht über das Archiv für Begriffsgeschichte," in *Jahrbuch der Akademie der Wissenschaften und der Literatur in Mainz* (Mainz: Akademie der Wissenschaften und der Literatur, 1967), 79–80; Hans Blumenberg, "Das Universum eines Ketzers," introduction in Giordano Bruno, *Das Aschermittwochsmahl*, trans. Ferdinand Fellmann (Frankfurt am Main: Insel, 1969), 9–51; Hans Blumenberg, "Kopernikus und das Pathos der Vernunft. Das Denken der Neuzeit im Zeichen der kopernikanischen Wende," *Evangelische Kommentare* 6, (1973): 460–465; Hans Blumenberg, "Versuch zu einer immanenten Geschichte der kopernikanischen Theorie," *Studia Copernicana*, no. 16 (1978): 473–486.

185 Hans Blumenberg, *Die Legitimität der Neuzeit* (Frankfurt am Main: Suhrkamp, 1966; 2nd rev. ed. Frankfurt am Main: Suhrkamp, 1988). Translated by Robert M. Wallace as *The Legitimacy of the Modern Age*, (Cambridge, MA: MIT Press, 1985). Citations refer to the translation of Rober M. Wallace.

186 Hans Blumenberg, *Die kopernikanische Wende* (Frankfurt am Main: Suhrkamp, 1965).

187 Hans Blumenberg, *Die Genesis der kopernikanischen Welt* (Frankfurt am Main: Suhrkamp, 1975).

Blumenberg's interpretation of Bruno can be listed with those that see a philosophical translation of Copernican thought in Nolanus' philosophy; that is, an attempt to resolve philosophical problems using conceptual instruments that come from a different set of questions. According to this interpretation, Bruno's mnemonics is the expression of a cultural climate rather than the result of independent reflection i. e., it belongs to the history of the effects of Copernican thought.[189] This is not a reason for Blumenberg to minimize the importance of Giordano Bruno's work, however. On the contrary, he acknowledges that it played a key role in understanding the transition from the Middle Ages to the Modern Age. What Blumenberg does not do is acknowledge that Bruno had any *autonomy* in the development of themes and problems.[190] One can criticize this interpretation for continuing to adhere to an enlightened vision of the Modern Age as a period of empirical-scientific rationality and, therefore, as a period that sees Copernicanism as the most influential, representative, and paradigmatic consequence of the Copernican revolution.[191]

These concerns aside, however, I believe that Blumenberg offers instruments that allow new research perspectives which do not necessarily lead to the total understanding of modern thought, as Blumenberg himself wanted to do, but which present other aspects or at the very least develop them. Indeed, if one understands metaphorology as a discipline of attention, one must also surmise that the metaphorological studies are not conclusive and that every scholar can perceive aspects of absolute metaphors and highlight them to plumb the depths of historical phenomena. And this is what I shall start with in this chapter: I shall

188 Hans Blumenberg *Die Lesbarkeit der Welt* (Frankfurt am Main: Suhrkamp, 1981; 2nd edition revised, Frankfurt am Main: Suhrkamp, 1983). Citations refer to the second edition.

189 According to Thomas S. Kuhn, *The Copernican revolution: Planetary astronomy in the development of Western thought* (Cambridge, MA: Harvard University Press, 1995).

190 I use the expression 'autonomy' in Blumenberg's sense of 'legitimate.'

191 This interpretation certainly has to be seen in relation to the Kantian and Neo-Kantian tradition that Hans Blumenberg referred to. At one of the few points where he refers to himself and his own research, Blumenberg mentions Ernst Cassirer as an inevitable reference point for any historian of modern thought: Hans Blumenberg, "Ernst Cassirers Gedenkend. Rede bei Entgegennahme des Kuno-Fischer Preises der Universität Heidelberg im Juli 1974," *Revue Internationale de Philosophie* 28, (1974): 456–463, later in *Wirklichkeiten in denen wir leben* (Stuttgart: Reclam, 1981), 163–172. Even if they start from different premises and with different interpretative aims, there is no doubt that in Cassirer's analysis of modern thought Bruno acts as a cornerstone for the further development of thought when it tends towards Kantian rationalism and his Copernican philosophical shift. See: Ernst Cassirer, *Das Erkenntnisproblem in der Philosophie und Wissenschaft der neuren Zeit: Erster Band*, in Ernst Cassirer, *Gesammelte Werke. Hamburger Ausgabe*, ed. Birgit Recki (Hamburg: Felix Meiner, 1999), 225–261; Ernst Cassirer, *Individuum und Kosmos in der Philosophie der Renaissance* (Leipzig: G.B. Teubner, 1927; Hamburg: Felix Meiner, 2002). Another author with whom Blumenberg not only shares the same interpretative perspective but also the exploration of many other subject is Thomas S. Kuhn, *The Copernican revolution.*

present a general outline of Blumenberg's interpretation of Bruno, drawing attention to an aspect of the absolute metaphor of the world as a book that Blumenberg did not develop, but that I believe is both fruitful and fundamental for the understanding of mnemonics and Bruno's philosophy.

1.1 The second of two comparative model analyses: Nicholas of Cusa and Giordano Bruno

The interpretation of Giordano Bruno's thought plays a very important role in the structure of reasoning against the theorem of secularization in *Die Legitimität.* This is because Nolanus is one of the two authors who were the subject of the differential analysis used to exemplify the concept of epochal threshold and it was with this concept that Blumenberg completed the critique of historical substantialism that the historical-interpretative use of the secularization category was to be based on. We have seen[192] that the epochal threshold is an imperceptible limit that is not tied in any obvious manner to any fact or meaningful event and that a differential study makes it possible to track a threshold that can be ascertained as one that has not yet been reached, or as one that has already been crossed. To identify the epochal threshold, one must therefore question at least two views: one that still finds itself on this side of the threshold, and the other that has already left it behind. The two views can be compared in as much as they ask homologous questions, and differential analysis makes accessible what must have occurred to make them incompatible.

Epicurean and nominalist comparative analysis was directed at exemplifying the hermeneutic principle, according to which, when the function of a concept changes within a philosophical system, one cannot speak of similarities with previous historical phenomena. On the other hand, the comparative analysis of Nicholas of Cusa and Giordano Bruno[193] illustrates the other principle, according to which anyone speaking of an epochal shift has to show that what was produced was irreversible.

Blumenberg interprets Nicholas of Cusa as making an extreme attempt to save the stability of knowledge in the Middle Ages by arranging it systematically. The

192 See here, Chapter 2, pp. 82–83.

193 Blumenberg, *The Legitimacy*, Part 4: "Aspects of the Epochal Threshold: The Cusan and the Nolan", 457–596. Bruno's interpretation here is also repeated in his two books on the Copernican revolution and the Copernican world: Hans Blumenberg, *Die Genesis der kopernikanischen Welt* (Frankfurt am Main: Suhrkamp, 1975); Hans Blumenberg, *Die kopernikanische Wende* (Frankfurt am Main: Suhrkamp, 1965). Blumenberg refers to *Die Legitimität* in both texts as the main reference for his understanding of Bruno's philosophy and therefore I shall limit my presentation to this part of *Die Legitimität.*

soundest proof of this lies in the systematic endeavour of his work, which no longer has the serial unity of Scholasticism texts. The three exponents of mediaeval reality (God, the universe and man) are not placed one above the other but are rather joined one to the other in such essential interdependency that the mutation of any element also affects the others. Nicholas of Cusa concentrates his efforts on defining the objective interdependence of theology, anthropology, and cosmology to avoid the critical auto-dissolution of the Middle Ages that, owing to its vacillation between anthropocentrism and theocentricism, is incapable of keeping the three elements together.

In fact, on the one hand mediaeval anthropocentrism is to be understood as a consequence of the concern about justifying the biblical God in history and beyond its eschatological nullity, by translating God into a rule of the world and of the correlation between nature, history and man, which was fully developed in the scholastic system of pure rationality. On the other hand, theocentricism is the product of the dissolution of scholastic rationality owing to the excessive amplification of the transcendence of its God. The first motive maintains the unity of the metaphysical triangle, made up of theology, anthropology, and cosmology, while the second tears it down. Blumenberg believes, therefore, that Nicholas of Cusa tries to force the anthropocentric and theocentric elements into a single structure, increasing the transcendence of God whilst also bringing both man and the cosmos closer to this same characteristic.

According to Blumenberg, in certain ways Nicholas of Cusa anticipates Bruno's philosophy: adhering to Nominalism and the recognition of the authentic dignity of the human system of understanding of reality; the destruction of the scholastic cosmos in overlapping levels and the negation of the separation between the supralunar and sublunar world; the enrichment of the world object owing to the idea of a new metaphysical dignity that makes it questionable. These are all themes that Bruno will go on to develop, but that can no longer be interpreted as themes emanating from the last stage of the Middle Ages.

According to Blumenberg, what is unique about Bruno's position is his philosophical rethinking of Copernican cosmology, in which he finds the justification for his anti-Trinitarianism and his refusal to believe in the incarnation. It is in these theological problems that Blumenberg identifies the nucleus of reflections at the origin of Nolanus' philosophical research. The instrument used to radicalize Nicholas of Cusa's thought was none other than Copernican cosmology. According to Copernican cosmology, the cosmos was no longer the static universe of the ancients, which could lead one to surmise something like the supernatural. It was only in the Copernican infinite universe that one could think of something like incarnation. By adopting Copernicus' ideas of scientific theory in philosophy, Bruno places himself entirely outside the Middle Ages, even though he had not yet arrived at the fundamental formula of the Modern Age; in other words, the idea of progress and self-assertion, owing to his adhesion to the pagan conception of cyclic time and therefore against the Copernican vision of time as progressive.

What I would like to do, however, is try a different approach and show that it is through the studies of mnemonics and, more specifically, through the formulation and entirely new understanding of the absolute metaphor of the world as a book that Bruno reaches a reconfiguration of the concept of order, that is, the concept that dictates the relationship between man and the world, which is to result in his reworking of the concepts of nature, language and practice, in a way that is no longer mediaeval.

2. The metaphor of the world as a book

Blumenberg's interpretation of Giordano Bruno as a Copernican philosopher is also offered in a metaphorological perspective in *Die Lesbarkeit der Welt.* Published almost twenty years after *Die Legitimität*, the work is dedicated to the absolute metaphor of the world as a book, which Blumenberg interprets as the metaphor for the "experimentalism of everything"[194] or rather, for modern empiricism.

2.1 Ernst R. Curtius, Erich Rothacker, Hans Blumenberg: Three approaches to the study of the metaphor of the book

In reconstructing the genesis of his research on the metaphor of the world as a book,[195] Blumenberg shows how it is influenced by the first study on the subject by Ernst R. Curtius,[196] through the figure of Erich Rothacker. A proponent of a terminological encyclopaedia of culture science, Rothacker was not only one of the founders of *Begriffsgeschichte*, but also the founder of the *Archiv für Begriffsgesschichte* (1955), in which *Paradigmen zu einer Metaphorologie* was published for the first time in 1960. Blumenberg's reconstruction is very useful for better understanding *Die Lesbarkeit*, and clearly demonstrates its derivation from the *Paradigmen.*

In 1942, Eric Rothacker, one of the editors of the *Deutsche Vierteljahresschrift*, had published Ernst R. Curtius' study on the metaphor of the world as a book and

194 Blumenberg, *Die Lesbarkeit der Welt*, 9–16.
195 Blumenberg, *Die Lesbarkeit der Welt*, 12–15.
196 E. R. Curtius, "Schrift- und Buchmetaphorik in der Weltliteratur," *Deutsche Vierteljahresschrift* 20, no. 4, (1942): 359–411.

writing, which can be regarded as the originator of later studies. Curtius began with Goethe's reflections on the metaphor as a sign of the productivity of language and the role of fantasy in thought[197] and, sharing the poet's hopes, he laid the foundation for a historical study on the metaphors of world literature. Curtius' project started with the metaphors of the book and writing because he believed that they were the best explanation for language productivity, that is, the fact that metaphors have a "close 'life relationship' (*Lebensbezug*) with man or that allow 'the interaction of all things' (das Wechselleben der *Weltgegenstände*)."[198] Aimed at identifying the moment in which the book was ascribed a sacred value, this study resulted in a detailed collection of uses of the metaphor of the book from ancient Greece to Shakespeare.

Perhaps because he was influenced by Curtius' work and set out to criticize the results of his research, in 1950[199] Erich Rothacker outlined a research plan in which he foresaw the publication of his research results on the book of nature (*das Buch der Natur*) in 1956.

In 1958 Blumenberg presented an analysis of metaphorology to a commission of the Deutsche Forschungsgemeinschaft for research on *Begriffsgeschichte*, presided over by Hans Georg Gadamer and in the presence of Rothacker. On this occasion Blumenberg used the comparison between the metaphors of writing, of reading, and of the book, with the implicated metaphors of organism and mechanism, to explain what metaphorical research consists of.[200] He did not, however, make any reference to Rothacker's research as the book he had announced in 1950 as pending had not yet been published and Blumenberg was convinced that the project had been abandoned. In addition, Blumenberg was even more convinced since Rothacker did not intervene during the commission sitting. For the same reason, when Blumenberg gave Rothacker's funeral oration in 1966 he did not mention the meeting about their research on Curtius; the book was still not published in the period between the presentation of the metaphorology project and Rothacker's death. With the intention of going back to the project he had outlined in the 1960s, in the 1978–1979 winter semester Blu-

197 Johann Wolfgang von Goethe, "Noten und Abhandlungen," in *West-Östlicher Divan. 2. Noten und Abhandlungen* (Berlin: Akademie, 1952).

198 Curtius, "Schrift- und Buchmetaphorik in der Weltliteratur," 361. The in-text quotation are from Goethe, "Noten und Abhandlungen."

199 Eric Rothacker, *Mensch und Geschichte. Studien zur Anthropologie und Wissenschaftsgeschichte* (Bonn: Athenäum, 1950), see the autobiographical text at the end of it.

200 Blumenberg, *Die Lesbarkeit der Welt*, 12–13. The subject had already been explored in Hans Blumenberg, "Paradigmen zu einer Metaphorologie," *Archiv für Begriffsgeschichte* 6, (1960): 7–142. Translated by Robert Savage as *Paradigms for a Metaphorology* (Ithaca, NY: Cornell University Press, 2010). Citations refer to the translation of Robert Savage. On the comparison between mechanistic metaphor and the metaphor of the book see, Blumenberg, *Paradigms*, chap. 6, 62–76.

menberg held a series of lectures on metaphorology and once again he used the metaphors of writing and the book as his examples. This time, however, he went further; not wanting to leave the question of the relationship between his research and Rothacker's open to any criticism regarding posthumous papers, he stated explicitly that Rothacker's manuscript did not exist and that the scholar had likely never started the project for a monograph on the metaphor of the book of nature. It was not until 1979 that Blumenberg realized he had made a mistake, when Wilhelm Perpeet published some of Rothacker's work for the first time, "Materialien und Grundsätzliches zur Metapherngeschichte" (Materials and Fundamental Considerations for a History of the Metaphor), entitled *Das Buch der Natur.*[201]

This reconstruction of the origins of *Die Lesbarkeit* helps us to understand two things: first of all, that *Die Lesbarkeit* originates in the *Paradigmen*, thus revealing a continuity in Blumenberg's philosophical reflections that very often scholars do not acknowledge; secondly, it also furthers our understanding of the more theoretical part of Blumenberg's work on the metaphor of the world as a book, which otherwise, once again, might seem merely to be a collection of philosophical anecdotes about a literary *topos*. In fact, in *Die Lesbarkeit* Blumenberg does more than simply reconstruct the origins of his work and acknowledge his mistake. He adopts Rothacker's criticism of Curtius and, using Rothacker's concept of significance (*Bedeutsamkeit*), distances himself from both the latter and Curtius by reviving one of the fundamental theses of the *Paradigmen*, that is, that of the pragmatic value of the metaphors, which as we have seen also means that absolute metaphors have a history. In other words, they are not 'absolute' in the sense that they are historical a priori, but in the sense that concepts cannot replace them in their paradigmatic function.

Let us now look at this passage in detail. Rothacker and Blumenberg's criticism of Curtius[202] lies in the fact that although he did select his material very carefully and studied numerous sources meticulously, offering an extensive collection of examples, what did not emerge from Rothacker's study was that he defined the significance (*Bedeutsamkeit*) of the experience of the book of nature. Rothacker used the "principle of significance" (*Satz der Bedeutsamkeit*)[203] for the

201 Eric Rothacker, *Das Buch der Natur: Materialien und Grundsätzliches zur Metapherngeschichte*, ed. Wilhelm Perpeet (Bonn: Bouvier, 1979).

202 Eugenio Garin criticized Curtius for the same reason: "Alcune osservazioni sul *libro* come simbolo," in *Umanesimo e simbolismo*, ed. Enrico Castelli (Padua: CEDAM, 1958), 91–102. Whilst arguing for the importance of the theme of the book as a symbol, which is "at the centre of a complex web of conceptions and disputes: and encompasses, in its various meanings, the variation of a vision of the world and knowledge", p. 91, Garin criticizes Curtius for not having contextualized the countless examples he gathered, so that the meaning of many is not understood.

203 Eric Rothacker, *Zur Genealogie des menschlichen Bewusstseins* (Bonn: Bouvier, 1966), 44–48.

fact that the experience of the world of life is never the experience of a homogenous and undifferentiated whole, but on the contrary, it is an experience in which the human interest toward the world comes out. In Blumenberg's terms we could say that Curtius' research did not allow the paradigmatic function of the metaphor of the book to emerge (so far Blumenberg's opinion, although based on diverse arguments, agrees with Rothacker's). On the other hand, in the research project for the book of nature Rothacker said he wanted to demonstrate that "from the literary metaphorics of the book one can explain the monumental philosophical task entitled 'The world as a hermeneutical problem (*Welt als hermeneutisches Problem*)', and that it is possible to solve it."[204]

Rothacker had therefore analysed the problem of the historical significance or function of the metaphor of the book, but Blumenberg believed that not even he had managed to produce more than a mere collection of examples. This was because he had not reconstructed the history of metaphors from a functionalistic perspective and thus, had not understood that the paradigm of legibility is the paradigm of the Modern Age for the experimentability of the world, and not an apriorist historical paradigm that is able to respond to the problem of the world, in the ahistorical sense. Blumenberg, therefore, distances himself from both Curtius' topic, criticizing the total indifference that the value of the material he collected suffers, and Rothacker's hermeneutic perspective, because he does not believe that the world as a hermeneutic problem can be solved once and for all; nor does he believe that a single problem of the world that is portrayed identically throughout the course of history has never existed.

2.2 The absolute metaphor of the world as a book: A metaphor for the experimentability of everything

The starting point for Blumenberg's study on the metaphor of the world as a book is the malaise of contemporary civilization denounced by the *Kulturkritik*. Blumenberg sees the denunciation of a loss of meaning that is expressed in the discomfort of contemporary civilization as an expression of the disappointed expectations that is difficult to trace, because they correspond to the expectations with which man related to the reality that stimulated him. It is the historian's task to find out where these expectations may be hidden and where they could still occur. In other words, the concept that should be questioned is, once again, the concept of world and to understand contemporary malaise one must ask oneself:

204 Blumenberg, *Die Lesbarkeit der Welt*, 15.

"What kind of world did they believe they could have?"[205] For Blumenberg this is always the most useful question when studying man's expectations of reality.

The field in which one can study the expectations of modern man is the metaphor of the world as a book of nature, that is, as a paradigm of the testability of everything, or rather, of modern empiricism. This absolute metaphor describes man's desire for a meaningful world and:

> the desire that the world reveals itself to be just as accessible as it is in the manner of mere perception and even the precise predictability of its phenomena; that in the state of aggregation of legibility it can open up with a donation of meaning as a totality of nature, life and history, certainly not a natural and spontaneous need like that of magic – of acquiring power over uncontrolled strength. From this point of view it is only comparable to that other unique desire of an immediate identity, in other words, that the god himself reveals himself to be edible, since at the same time nothing remains and that he is entirely incorporated: incarnation as a ritual.[206]

In other words, the paradigm of the legibility of the world suggests that the idea of carrying out experiments on the world is not obvious, "it is not a natural need,"[207] that is, it is not always available and does not even depend on technical availability.[208] In fact, as Curtius' extensive study also shows, the metaphor of the book is not the paradigm of the testability of everything from the very beginning of its history. Indeed, whilst on the one hand it is true that experience of the world in the same way as experience of the book implies the dissemination of the book (and therefore an advanced degree of production and fruition) and widespread literacy, on the other hand it is necessary that "the experience of the book is made autonomous in its own experience of totality"[209] because it makes itself the paradigm of the testability of everything. This is where Blumenberg corrects Rothacker's concept of significance: to guarantee the historical significance of a metaphor, above all one must show that "it would not be plausible in every period."[210]

---

205 Blumenberg, *Die Lesbarkeit der Welt*, 10. In this passage Blumenberg reformulates Kant's questions in the first *Critique* about what we can know in terms of "what we believe we can know."

206 Blumenberg, *Die Lesbarkeit der Welt*, 10.

207 Blumenberg effectively insists that: "Only those who believe that the theoretical empirics of the Modern Age is roughly the 'most natural thing in the world' – an immediate relationship with the things that only had to be discovered and that was finally allowed – may take as rhetorically redundant the fact that this offer occurs in the language of rivality with the book, of overcoming all preceding legibilities," Blumenberg, *Die Lesbarkeit der Welt*, 11.

208 See here, Chapter 3, pp. 83–87: late antiquity as the first modern age that failed owing to the lack of technology.

209 Blumenberg, *Die Lesbarkeit der Welt*, 10–11.

210 Blumenberg, *Die Lesbarkeit der Welt*, 22.

The interpretative scheme that Blumenberg applies to the absolute metaphor of the world as a book is the same one that we have seen in *Die Legitimität.* The metaphor of the world as a book becomes an absolute metaphor when a second attempt at overcoming the Gnosis is made; that is, in the transition from the Middle Ages to the Modern Age. In Blumenberg's view, Curtius' thesis, according to which the book becomes an (absolute) metaphor of the world with the rise of Christianity, because Christianity is the religion of the book, cannot be supported. This is because before the meeting with Gnosticism, nature does not have the same value as it does when Christianity has to defend itself against it: the Greek cosmos is not the Christian world at the beginning of the Middle Ages, and this is not the Christian world at the end of the Middle Ages. It is true, however, that if Plato's cosmogony and the Greek concept of cosmos developed here is compared with the biblical *creatio ex nihilo* and the Christian world, from the very start this lent itself to being understood as a book while the former did not. In fact, the Platonic cosmos is the Platonic cosmos of ideas and in the world of phenomena images are perceived that, through "their simplification in a profile, to what makes it possible to recognize them,"[211] create concepts. Furthermore, one does not speak in cosmogony; while the biblical creation occurs through the word that commands what has to be created from nothing. But the historical revelation of God in the diverse sacred books is against the idea that God has already declared himself in nature in a manner that is both comprehensible and sufficient. Only when nature, the product of creation, is developed in its redemptive function, is the first step taken towards a revival of nature, which is no longer (only) deception, prison, and labyrinth. This has not yet brought us to see nature as a book, but at least a positivity of nature has been retrieved, inserting it in the redemption process of man. It is only with Pelagianism, that is, it is only when nature absorbs the qualities of the divine that it can become anti-Christian; and Giordano Bruno and Spinoza represent the height of this thinking because they are the most illustrious exponents of the pantheism promoted by the new Copernican conception of the cosmos.[212]

3. A critique of Blumenberg's interpretation of Bruno

We have seen that Blumenberg's interpretation of Bruno plays a key role in both *Die Legitimität* and *Die Lesbarkeit*; although in his latter analysis Blumenberg only grants Bruno one single sentence, but one of greater hermeneutic weight than many exemplifications that illustrate the thesis of the book. It is worth

211 Blumenberg, *Die Lesbarkeit der Welt*, 22.
212 Blumenberg, *Die Lesbarkeit der Welt*, 35.

summarizing what we have discussed so far. In *Die Legitimität* Bruno is one of the two philosophers who exemplifies the concept of the epochal threshold (and thus has a central function in the criticism of the historical substantialism of the secularization theorem) and, by interpreting his theological-philosophical thesis as part of the history of the effects of Copernicanism, Blumenberg demonstrates the signs of the transition from the Middle Ages to the Modern Age. In *Die Lesbarkeit*, on the other hand, Bruno is the first modern author who lays down the philosophical basis of empiricism, because he offers a philosophical translation of Copernicus' infinite astronomical universe into the philosophical infinite-pantheist universe. In doing so, he thus expands the interpretation of the medieval metaphor of the world as a book of God to an absolute metaphor of the testability of everything by modern man, emphasizing the aspect of the reading of the book.[213]

The overall interpretation of Bruno that Blumenberg offers us certainly has the merit of underlining the impact of the effects of Copernicanism, understood as scientific theory, in the history of philosophy in the early Modern Age. It also, however, revives the interpretation of Bruno as a philosophical vulgarizer of Copernicus, that makes one lose sight of, and I believe this is the central aspect that deserves criticism, the autonomy of the path that Nolanus followed to reach his formulation of a gnoseology that in his conclusions agrees with Copernicanism, understood now as the cultural atmosphere, that is, as a horizon of meaning that is rearranging itself.

Blumenberg analyses the metaphor of the world as a book from a Copernican perspective. Proof of this is the fact that Blumenberg interprets this metaphor only as a metaphor of the *legibility of the world* and neglects the moment of writing in the world. The aspect of metaphorics regarding the writing of the world had been, however, very important in mediaeval thinking because it was one of the arguments against *curiositas*. In fact, in the mediaeval formulation of the metaphor of the world as a book, God is both the subject of writing and subject of reading of the book of nature and of the book of history, while man is the passive object of both books. Blumenberg perceives the paradigm change as taking place at the threshold of the Modern Age, that is, when the moment of reading the book

213 Bruno's philosophy thus also plays a central role in Blumenberg's interpretation of the Modern Age as an independent rational period in which self-assertion is one of its most important characteristics. This reveals both Blumenberg's debt to Cassirer, but also what he disagrees with. At the centre of Cassirer's interpretation of the Modern Age is Giordano Bruno's philosophy since his philosophical interpretation of Copernicanism introduces categories into philosophy that will lead to rationalism and Kantism; Blumenberg, on the other hand, above all describes the consequences that Bruno's Copernicanism have on the man-world relationship and thus, on the development of the self-assertion category in history.

is no longer a characteristic of God but is also attributed to humanity and concentrates on the new experience of world that foresees that this is also legible to humanity.

Blumenberg is certainly interested in this aspect of metaphorics because, leaving aside the criticism of historical substantialism, he also interprets the Modern Age from the perspective of empirical rationality and the issue that represents this aspect of the Modern Age best is the Copernicus question and the history of its effects. In the Middle Ages, however, and even up to Bruno, the metaphor of the world as a book reached its philosophical supremacy because it emphasized that it had been God who had written the book of the world and only he could do it. This created an image of the distance between God and man. This metaphor thus had its philosophical supremacy because, as Blumenberg has rightly shown, it helped portray the terms of the man-world-God relationship from a theological perspective.

One example suffices to help us understand how the perception of the man-world-God relationship changed through the metaphor of the world as a book. Galileo Galilei's statement, when he said that the world is written in mathematical characters, and this means that everything that is written can be understood by anyone who knows this language and without the need for the intermediation of the Scriptures:

> Philosophy is written in this grand book, the universe, which stands continually open to our gaze. But the book cannot be understood unless one first learns to comprehend the language and read the letters in which it is composed. It is written in the language of mathematics, and its characters are triangles, circles, and other geometrical figures without which it is humanly impossible to understand a single word of it; without these, one wanders about in a dark labyrinth.[214]

This is truly thc momcnt in which thc mctaphor of thc world as a book reveals itself as a metaphor of modern empiricism because Galileo's words presuppose the conviction of the existence of a unitary conception of the reading of the world and its rules, and a unitary conception that can be shared and reproduced with time. And it is precisely these characteristics that are to define modern experimentalism: with the same instruments and the same conditions, the experiments carried out on nature yield the same results, which can be interpreted in the same way, and are thus reproducible, that is, if the conditions are the same, valid and repeatable with time.

By studying the history of the metaphor of the world as a book, I believe that it is possible to demonstrate that the idea that the writing of the world is done in comprehensible characters and can be reproduced by man permeated the

214 Galileo Galilei, *The Assayer*, in *Discoveries and Opinions of Galileo*, trans. with an introduction and notes by Stillman Drake (New York: Anchor Book, 1957), 237–238.

mnemonic sciences and is not an effect of Copernicanism. To do this, however, it is necessary to draw attention to the fact that there are two sides to the metaphor of the world as a book: one is that of reading, the other is that of writing. It is true that throughout the history of the absolute metaphor the aspect of reading is prominent, because it explains the relationship between man and world from a Christian theological perspective, and it is therefore a passive relationship in as much as it is God who writes the book of nature (even Galileo Galilei was convinced of this). There is, however, a field in which the active aspect of the metaphor of the book, that of writing, is favoured. The field is that of theories of memory and mnemonics in the sixteenth century and the key exponent and person most conscious of this understanding of the metaphor of the world as a book and memory is Giordano Bruno.

4. Metaphors for memory and mnemonics

I shall now return to the texts I analysed in Chapter one, defining the sources of the mnemonic arts, because I would like to demonstrate the role that the metaphor of inner writing has in illustrating rules for the creation of artificial memory. The aim of this study is therefore to demonstrate that the metaphor of inner writing is an absolute metaphor, that is, the leading paradigm in the conceptual formation of artificial memory and it is the element of the interpretation that guides and furthers our understanding. Furthermore, I shall demonstrate that the other metaphors that are usually a generic reference to memory are technically metaphors for natural memory and can be traced back to the moment of reading the book. To conclude, combining the two theses, I believe that: the metaphor of the world as a book, with its two aspects of reading and writing, has guided the conceptual formation of the philosophical and scientific understanding of memory (both natural and artificial memory); in particular, the metaphor of writing is an operative metaphor that is necessary to explain artificial memory, while the other metaphors are metaphors for natural memory and illustrate its retentive function.

The starting point for this presentation is therefore the following observation. Metaphors for memory are oriented towards two semantic fields: the metaphor of seal-writing and the metaphor of the ark-stomach. The first group of metaphors describes artificial memory while the second describes natural memory.

4.1 Metaphors for natural memory

Metaphors for natural memory are those that highlight the retentive function of memory, its function as a container. They are metaphors such as that of the ark and the stomach.

For Cicero memory is *thesaurus:*

> Now let me turn to the treasure-house of the ideas supplied by Invention, to the guardian of all the parts of rhetoric, the Memory.[215]

And Quintilian also defines it as follows:

> It is with good reason that it has been called the Treasury of Eloquence.[216]

But he also sees memory as the stomach:

> And so not only should children (as I recommended) learn as much as possible by heart from the beginning, but students of any age who are concerned to improve their memory by study should be willing to swallow the initially wearisome business of repeating over and over again what they have written or read, and as it were chewing over the same old food.[217]

There is a minimal, but significant difference between the two metaphors. While the metaphor of memory as an ark expresses only the retentive function, and therefore the passive function of natural memory, the metaphor of memory as a stomach also expresses the possibility that natural memory reworks the facts of the experience it contains and transforms them into something else, thus also symbolizing an active function of natural memory. It is no coincidence that it is Quintilian who accompanies this reflection on the two memories with this double image. We have seen that unlike Cicero, Quintilian was not convinced of the use of artificial memory and claimed that natural memory was able to privilege those characteristics that were to be reproduced and perfected in artificial memory.

From the level of conceptual formation, the two metaphors result in different implications and guide the definition of the concept of *memory.* If I think of natural memory (Aristotle's *mneme*, I mean) as an ark, I will have to explain the soul's ability to retrieve what is deposited in memory by introducing another

215 "Nunc ad thesaurum inventorum atque ad omnium partium rhetoricae custodem, memoriam, transeamus," *Rhet. Her.*, III, xvi, 28, in [Cicero], *Rhetorica ad Herennium*, trans. Harry Caplan (Cambridge, MA: Harvard University Press, 1954), 204–205.

216 "neque inmerito thesaurus hic eloquentiae dicitur," *Inst.*, XI, ii, 1, in Quintilian, *The Orator's Education, Volume V: Books 11–12*, ed. and trans. Donald A. Russell (Cambridge, MA: Harvard University Press, 2002), 58–59.

217 "Quare et pueri statim, ut praecepi, quam plurima ediscant, et quaecumque aetas operam iuvandae studio memoriae dabit devoret initio taedium illud et scripta et lecta saepius revoluendi et quasi eundem cibum remandendi," *Inst.*, XI, ii, 41, in Quintilian, *The Orator's Education*, 234–235.

element (for example *anamnesis*, remaining with the Aristotelian model for the functioning of memory). If, on the other hand, I think of natural memory as a stomach, whilst preserving the idea of memory as a container of facts of sensory experience, I am using an image that is *also* already operative, thus making the search for another element or function of memory to complete the concept I have been given of the metaphor as superfluous.

4.2 Metaphors for artificial memory

Whilst metaphors for natural memory illustrate its retentive function, metaphors for artificial memory highlight the function of memory, in other words, the ability to summon the images deposited in natural memory. Two metaphors for artificial memory are the wax upon which a seal impresses a distinctive shape, and writing, understood first and foremost as a system of portrayal and only then as an instrument that transmits linguistic meaning. Since the gesture of impressing a distinctive shape on a wax tablet is one of the first experiences of writing, we can say that metaphors for artificial memory belong to the same semantic field as writing.

The author of *Rhetorica ad Herennium* uses the metaphor of writing on wax tablets to explain the important moment in the construction of the memory system, which is the formation of the *loci*. We have seen that the selection of the *loci* is very important because a well-constructed system of *loci* can be used more than once to remember different things. In fact, the author explains, the images in the *loci* can be removed when they are no longer needed and can be replaced with other ones, just like when we are writing on a wax tablet and cancel what we have written so we can use the tablet again:

> Those who know the letters of the alphabet can thereby write out what is dictated to them and read aloud what they have written. Likewise, those who have learned mnemonics can set in backgrounds what they have heard, and from these backgrounds deliver it by memory. For the backgrounds are very much like wax tablets or papyrus, the images like the letters, the arrangement and disposition of the images like the script, and the delivery is like reading.[218]

and:

218 "Quemadmodums igitur qui litteras sciunt possunt id quod dictatur eis scribere, et recitare quod scripserunt, item qui mnemonica didicerunt possunt quod audierunt in locis conlocare et ex his memoriter pronuntiare. Nam loci cerae aut chartae simillimi sunt, imagines litteris, dispositio et conlocatio imaginum scripturae, pronuntiatio lectioni," *Rhet. Her.*, III, xvii, 30, in [Cicero], *Rhetorica ad Herennium*, 208–209.

> We shall need to study with special care the backgrounds we have adopted so that they may cling lastingly in our memory, for the images, like letters, are effaced when we make no use of them, but the backgrounds, like wax tablets, should abide.[219]

In his treatise on *ars memoriae* in *De oratore* Cicero also refers repeatedly to the metaphor:

> It has been sagaciously discerned by Simonides or else discovered by some other person, that the most complete pictures are formed in our minds of the things that have been conveyed to them and imprinted on them by the senses, but that the keenest of all our senses is the sense of sight, and that consequently perceptions received by the ears or by reflexion can be most easily retained in the mind if they are also conveyed to our minds by the mediation of the eyes, with the result that things not seen and not lying in the field of visual discernment are earmarked by a sort of outline and image and shape so that we keep hold of as it were by an act of sight things that we scarcely embrace by an act of thought. But these forms and bodies, like all the things that come under our view require an abode, inasmuch as a material object without a locality is inconceivable.[220]

Cicero, however, also draws attention to the figurative aspect of the metaphor, creating a parallel between *scriptura* and *pictura* that, as we shall see, is to be very important in Giordano Bruno's mnemotechnics:

> the ability to use these will be supplied by practice, which engenders habit, and by marking off similar words with an inversion and alteration of their cases or a transference from species to genus, and by representing a whole concept by the image of a single word, on the system and method of a consummate painter distinguishing the positions of objects by modifying their shapes.[221]

219 "Locos quos sumpserimus egregie commeditari oportebit, ut perpetuo nobis haerere possint; nam imagines, sicuti litterae, delentur ubi nihil utimur; loci, tamquam cera, remanere debent," *Rhet. Her.*, III, xvii, 31, in [Cicero], *Rhetorica ad Herennium*, 210–211.

220 "Vidit enim hoc prudenter sive Simonides sive alius quis invenit, ea maxime animis effingi nostris quae essent a sensu tradita atque impressa; acerrimum autem ex omnibus nostris sensibus esse sensum videndi; quare facillime animo teneri posse ea quae perciperentur auribus aut cogitatione si etiam commendatione oculorum animis traderentur; ut res caecas et ab aspectus iudicio remotas conformatio quaedam et imago et figura ita notaret ut ea quae cogitando complecti vix possemus intuendo quasi teneremus. His autem formis atque corporibus, sicut omnibus quae sub aspectum veniunt sede opus est, etenim corpus intellegi sine loco non potest," *De or.*, II, lxxxviii, 357–358, in Cicero, *On the Orator: Books 1–2*, trans. E. W. Sutton and H. Rackham (Cambridge, MA: Harvard University Press, 1942), 468–469.

221 "quam facultatem et exercitatio dabit, ex qua consuetudo gignitur, et similium verborum conversa et immutata casibus aut traducta ex parte ad genus notatio et unius verbi imagine totius sententiae informatio pictoris cuiusdam summi ratione et modo formarum varietate locos distinguentis," *De or.*, II, lxxxviii, 358, in Cicero, *On the Orator: Books 1–2*, 468–469.

> with the result that the arrangement of the localities will preserve the order of the facts, and the images of the facts will designate the facts themselves, and we shall employ the localities and images respectively as a wax writing tablet and the letters written on it.[222]

> But what business is it of mine to specify the value to a speaker and the usefulness and effectiveness of memory? (…) of giving such close attention to the instructions of your client and to the speech of the opponent you have to answer that they may seem not to just pour what they say into your ears but to imprint it on your mind?[223]

> Nor is it true, as unscientific people assert, that memory is crushed beneath a weight of images and even what might have been retained by nature unassisted is obscured; for I have myself met eminent people with almost superhuman powers of memory, Charmadas at Athens and Metrodorus of Scepsis in Asia, who is said to be still living, each of whom used to say that he wrote down things he wanted to remember in certain 'localities' in his possession by means of images, just as if he were inscribing letters on wax. It follows that this practice cannot be used to draw out the memory if no memory has been given to us by nature, but it can undoubtedly summon it come forth if it is in hiding.[224]

Quintilian also addresses the two aspects of the metaphor, describing first the figurative and then the semantic:

> By Images I mean the aids we use to mark what we have to learn by heart; as Cicero says, we use the Sites as our wax tablet, the Symbols as our letters.[225]

> I say nothing of the fact that there are some words which cannot be represented by any Symbols, for example Conjunctions. For suppose that, like shorthand writers, we have definite Images for all these things ad (of course) infinite Sites for them (…).[226]

---

222 "sic fore ut ordine rerum locorum orto conservaret, res hautem ipsas rerum effigies notaret, atque ut locis pro cera, simulacris pro litteris uteremur," *De or.*, II, lxxxvi, 354, in Cicero, *On the Orator: Books 1–2*, 466–467.

223 "Qui sit autem oratori memoriae fructus, quanta utilitas, quanta vis, quid me attinet dicere? (…) ita audire vel eum unde discas vel eum cui respondum sit ut illi non infundere in aures tuas orationem sed in animo videantur inscribere?", *De or.*, II, lxxxvi, 355, in Cicero, *On the Orator: Books 1–2*, 466–467.

224 "Neque verum est quod ab inertibus dicitur, opprimi memoriam imaginum pondere et obscura etiam id quod per se natura tenere potuisset; vidi enim ego summos homines et divina prope memoria, Athenis Charmadam, in Asia, quem vivere hodie aiunt, Scepsium Metrodorum, quorum uterque tanquam litteris in cera sic se aiebat imaginibus in eis locis quo haberet quae meminisse vellet perscribere. Quare hac exercitatione non eruenda memoria est si est nulla naturalis, sed certe si latet evocanda est," *De or.*, II, lxxxviii, 360, Cicero, *On the Orator: Books 1–2*, 470–473.

225 "Imagines voco quibus ea quae ediscenda sunt notamus ut, quo modo Cicero dicit, locis pro cera, simulacris pro litteris utamur," *Inst.*, XI, ii, 21, in Quintilian, *The Orator's Education, Volume V: Books 11–12*, ed. and trans. Donald A. Russell (Cambridge, MA: Harvard University Press, 2002), 68–69.

226 "Mittoquod quaedam nullis simulacris significari possunt, ut certe coniunctiones. Habeamus enim sane, ut qui notis scribunt, certas imagines omnium et loca scilicet infinita (…)" *Inst.*, XI, ii, 25, in Quintilian, *The Orator's Education, Volume V: Books 11–12*, 70–71.

> Something that every student will find useful is to learn by heart from the same tablets on which he wrote the speech. He thus pursues his memory along a trail, as it were, and sees in his mind's eye not only the pages but almost the actual lines: and so, when he speaks, he is almost in the position of a person reading aloud And if we come to an erasure or some addition and alteration, these are a sort of signal, the sight of which prevents us from going wrong.[227]

> I do not think I need to dwell on the question of what produces Memory. Many hold, however, that certain traces are impressed upon the mind, in the way that the mark of a signet persists in the wax.[228]

> This exploit of Simonides seems to have led to the observation that memory can be assisted if localities are impressed upon the mind. Everyone will believe this from his own experience.[229]

Let us now return to our medieval sources of mnemonics and see what happens to the metaphors of memory. Of particular importance is Albertus Magnus' position as regards the tradition concerning the use of metaphors in writing because it clearly shows how their role in mnemotechnical or philosophical texts is not merely rhetorical, but instead clearly perceived as part of the interpretation with the function of clarifying and furthering mnemonic rules and precepts. Albertus Magnus criticizes the metaphor of inner writing because he believes it implies that one must use a limited number of images, as is the case with letters; instead, countless images must be used:

> (18) One then also studies the rules Tullius gives for the images to be deposited in the places he spoke of. In fact, Tullius says, "the places are very similar to wax tablets or sheets of paper, and the images similar to letters, the arrangement or place of the images similar to writing, and pronunciation to reading." But this does not appear to be true. In fact, there are few letters if the elements are counted, and depending on the order in which they are arranged, they are able to express everything that has to be pronounced,

227 "Illud neminem non iuvabit, isdem quibus scripserit ceris ediscere. Sequitur enim vestigiis quibusdam memoriam et velut oculis intuetur non paginas modo sed versus prope ispos, estque cum dicit similis legenti. Iam vero si litura aut adiectio aliqua atque mutatio interveniat, signa sunt quaedam quae intuentes deerrare non possumus," *Inst.*, XI, ii, 32, in Quintilian, *The Orator's Education, Volume V: Books 11–12*, 74–75. Here the metaphor of writing is not being used for the artificial memory, but according to Quintilian, the practice of writing and reading are useful in themselves to reinforce the natural memory.

228 "Non arbitror autem mihi in hoc inmorandum, quid sit quod memoriam faciat, quamquam plerique inprimi quaedam vestigia animo, velut in ceris anulorum signa seruentur, existimant," *Inst.*, XI, ii, 4, in Quintilian, *The Orator's Education, Volume V: Books 11–12*, 60–61.

229 "Ex hoc Simonidis facto notatum videtur, iuvari memoriam signatis animo sedibus, idque credet suo quisque experimento," *Inst.*, XI, ii, 17, in Quintilian, *The Orator's Education, Volume V: Books 11–12*, 66–67.

as Democritus said was the case in the comedies and tragedies; on the other hand, countless images are required otherwise reality cannot be suitably expressed.[230]

(21) (...) This also shows quite clearly that, to acquire artificial memory, application is necessary in the images and in the objects and in the words, and furthermore that the images are rare and noteworthy; and it therefore appears that there are no determinant images, which we can use to remember everything or occurrence, as we do with letters to express everything or fact in writing.[231]

I believe that this criticism is of great importance to my argument because it shows the fundamental value that his metaphor had in the understanding of the mnemonic arts and its philosophical principles. Thomas of Aquinas, on the other hand, evokes the analogy used in *Rhetorica ad Herennium* and does not criticize the implications as Albertus Magnus had done:

Third, a person should put his care and concern into the things he wants to memorize, because the more deeply stamped they are on the mind the less likely are they to disappear. And so Cicero remarks that taking trouble keeps the shapes of images intact.[232]

5. The metaphor of inner writing as an absolute metaphor

The aforementioned examples illustrate the thesis according to which the *metaphor of inner writing* is the one that allows one to penetrate the understanding of the *ars memoriae* more fruitfully. In fact, ever since Plato, philosophy had entrusted the understanding and description of memory to the metaphor of

230 "(18) Ulterius etiam quaeritur de praeceptis, quae dat Tullius de imaginibus collocandis in locis dictis. Dicit enim Tullius, quod 'loci cerae aut cartae simillimi sunt, imagines litteris, dispositio vel collocatio imaginum scripturae, pronuntiatio autem lectioni'. Hoc enim non videtur. Litterae enim paucae sunt secundum numerum elementorum et secundum diversas ordinationes exprimunt, quidquid venire debet in locutionem, sicut dicebat Democritus in comoediis et tragoediis accidere, sed imagines oportet multas habere valde vel non expriment rem in proprio genere," Albertus Magnus, *De bono*, IV, qu. 2, art. 2, 18, 475, in Albertus Magnus, *Opera omnia: Tomus 28: De bono*, ed. Heinrich Kühle, Carl Feckes, Bernhard Geyer, and Wilhelm Kübel (Monasterii Westfalorum in aedibus Aschendorff, 1951), 248a–248b.

231 "Ex his omnibus patet ad memoriam artificialem exigi stadium in imaginibus et negotiis et verbis et etiam insuper, ut sint imagines rarae et isnignes, et ita videtur, quod non sint determinatea imagines, quibus utamur ad omnia memorando, sicut utimus litteris ad omnia significando per scriptum," Alberto Magno, *De bono*, IV, qu. 2, art. 2, 21, 476, in Albertus Magnus, *Opera omnia: Tomus 28: De bono*, 249a.

232 "Tertio oportet ut homo sollicitudinem apponat, et affectum adhibeat ad ea quae vult rememorari: quia quando aliquid magis fuerit impressum animo, tanto minus elabitur. Unde et Tullius dicit quod *sollicitudo conservat integras simulacrorum figuras* [*Rhet ad Heren.* III, 19]," Thomas Aquinas, *Summa theologiae. Volume 36: Prudence (2a2æ. 47–56)*, ed. Thomas Gilby (Cambridge: Blackfriars, 1974), 62–63.

inner writing, and the analogical tie between the functioning of writing and the understanding of memory is still very close and topical today.[233]

In the analysis I will carry out in the following two chapters I will not interrogate two authors, that is, I will not carry out a comparative analysis, but will limit myself to an analysis that deals with what Blumenberg calls the "translation (*Übertragung*)":

> Faced with an artificial structure of speculative statements, the interpretation will only 'dawn' on us once we have succeeded in entering into the author's imaginative horizon and reconstructing his 'translation'.[234]

The "translation" is what Blumenberg defines as "background metaphorics (*Hintergrundmetaphorik*)"[235] in the same passage

> Metaphorics can also be in play where exclusively terminological propositions appear, but where these cannot be understood in their higher-order semantic unity without taking into account the guiding idea from which they are induced and 'read off'.[236]

My decision to proceed in this way rather than with differential analysis is motivated by the fact that Giordano Bruno is obviously aware of the role that the metaphor of inner writing as a background metaphorics has, not only in the understanding of the mnemonic arts and memory, but also in his contribution to its improvement, as this programmatic extract from *De umbris idearum* shows:

> It is said that it is from these same foundation and in the same succession that the art that guides the hand proceeds. Hence – going back to the aspect that concerns our study – in ancient antiquity they used knives to write on the bark of tree. This was followed by the age of letters engraved with a chisel on stone; then came papyrus with black sepia ink. Then came the parchments that were marked more clearly using artificial ink. Then paper and the encaustic technique; finally letters were imprinted with a press, using an immensely more efficient technique. From knives to nibs, from nibs to sponges, from sponges to inkwells, from inkwells to pens, one finally arrived at – and this is what I mean – letters melted in lead. We believe that the same thing happened for the techniques of inner writing, from the period in which this form of human activity was started for the very first time by the poet Simonides or by another author: in fact, by

233 It suffices to think of how biologists explain DNA: the genetic memory of every living being is the genetic code. In other words, the information is in DNA like the words of a code. It also might be that the increasing understanding of how DNA functions, and which has led from the genetic to the epigenetic, can be understood as a chapter in the development of the history of the metaphor of writing. Once again, as in the sixteenth century, the shift from genetic to epigenetic was produced by a redefinition of the order of the relation that introduces the metaphor: whilst in genetics the moment of reading the code is favoured, in epigenetics attention is drawn to what happens when the code is being written, and, once again, one lingered on man's active role – this time in the "writing" of the genetic code.

234 Blumenberg, *Paradigms*, 62.

235 Blumenberg, *Paradigms*, 62.

236 Blumenberg, *Paradigms*, 62.

> adopting places and images instead of paper and letters of the alphabet, and replacing the work of the writer and quill with the activity of fantasy and the cogitative faculty, they contrived to write the images of the things to be remembered in an inner book. Which and how many innovations we have been able to add to their work, will be judged by those who set about comparing our treatises with their works.[237]

In the following chapter I shall present Giordano Bruno's mnemonics, making sure to offer a concrete demonstration of what he affirmed regarding his contribution to the improvement of the art, like the perfection of the technique of writing in printing with mobile characters.

237 "Hinc et eadem serie progressum facere dicitur ars quam manus ducit. Ideo – ut ad propositum intentionis nostrae spectat – cultris in arborum corticibus prior scripsisse perhibetur vetustas. Cui successit aetas in lapidibus celte excavatis inscribens; quam sequuta est papyrus sepiarum succis exarata. Inde pergamenaer membranae atramento artificioso magis intinctae. Proinde charta et inchaustum, praeloque premendae in usum longe omnium patissimum literae. A cultris, inquam, ad stilos, a stilis ad spongia, a spongiis ad calamos, a calamis ad pennsa, a pennis ad fusilia tandem elementa perventum. Haud secus in iis, quae ad scripturam pertinere videntur internam, contigisse arbitrarum, dum ab antiquo humanum studium sive a melico Simonide sive ab alio sumpserit exordium; qui <usu?> locorum et imaginum proportionalium chartae atque scripturae, actuque phantasiae et cogitativae locum scriptoris et calami subeuntibus, species/rerum memorandarum in interno libro inscribere studuerunt. Quorum industriae quid et quantum addiderimus, ipsorum, qui haec nostra cum illorum monumentis conferre potuerunt, esto iudicium" Giordano Bruno, *De umbris idearum*, Pars prima, xv–xvi, in *Opere mnemotecniche: Tomo I*, eds. Marco Matteoli, Rita Sturlese, and Nicoletta Tirinnanzi (Milan: Adelphi, 2009), 134–135.

Chapter 6: "Ad internam scripturam, et non vulgares per memoriam operationes explicates"

Perge liber. Neque enim ingoras eundem solem, eamdemque Artem
– Giordano Bruno, *De umbris idearum*, *Dialogus praelibatorius*

I shall now illustrate how Giordano Bruno's *ars memoriae* fits in the tradition of the mnemonic arts. With the presentation of Bruno's *ars memoriae* and reference to the technique as it is explained in the *De umbris idearum*,[238] I shall demonstrate both the consistency of the *ars* and the novelty it introduced into the mnemonics tradition. Furthermore, with the analysis of the role of the metaphor of inner writing in the *De umbris*, I shall show how these two features of Bruno's *ars memoriae* – consistency and novelty – are clarified further by the particular weight that Bruno gives to the analogy between memory and writing; as we have seen, this analogy not only has a lengthy history in the tradition of mnemonics, but it also plays a key role in the explanation of its rules and principles.

Highlighting these two features of Bruno's *ars* from a metaphorological perspective allows me to explain the third aspect, that is, its excess as regards tradition. It is precisely this third aspect that lets us understand how Giordano Bruno's mnemonic works communicate philosophically with some of the central themes of Bruno's philosophy.

In the expressions "consistency", "novelty" and "excess" I therefore synthesize the following thesis: 1. Bruno has no intention of either amending the precepts of mnemonics or of placing himself outside this tradition; 2. On the contrary, Bruno perceives his *ars memoriae* as the soundest answer to the question of the precepts and the principles of mnemonics that were proposed by the numerous critics of mnemonics; 3. Bruno sees this clarification as an epochal task; 4. by carrying out this task and, more specifically, endowing mnemonics with a metaphysics that underlines its principles and thus makes them more comprehensible by inserting them in a broader gnoseological framework, Bruno gives his

238 Giordano Bruno, *De umbris idearum*, in *Opere mnemotecniche: Tomo I*, eds. Marco Matteoli, Rita Sturlese, and Nicoletta Tirinnanzi (Milan: Adelphi, 2004). All subsequent citations refer to this edition.

ars memoriae a feature of excess as regards tradition, because the *ars memoriae* will no longer be conceived as an *ars* amongst the others, but instead as a unique *ars*. In other words, the technical level of the *ars memoriae* will not only coincide with the gnoseological but also with the metaphysical one.

1. Giordano Bruno's *ars memoriae* (1): Consistency, novelty, and excess as regards the tradition of the mnemonic arts

In Giordano Bruno's *ars memoriae* there are significant elements of continuity with the mnemonics tradition, both regarding its precepts and the principles it refers to. What makes Bruno's mnemonics different is the introduction of two technical novelties: on the one hand, a terminological reform of the elements with which the artificial memory system is constructed, that is *locus* and *imago*, called by Bruno *subiectum* and *adiectum* or *forma*; and on the other hand, the introduction of a new element in addition to these two, the *organum*.

As far as the first novelty is concerned, it might seem to be a simple linguistic exercise because all the characteristic features and rules of *locus* and *imago* in mnemonic tradition are transferred to *subiectum* and *adiectum* in Bruno's mnemonics. The lexical novelties that Bruno introduces are the result of a profound rethinking of the modalities in which mnemonic places and mnemonic images are combined together to create the artificial system of memory, as can be seen clearly when the *organum* is introduced and its applications are shown. Furthermore, it is with the terminological reform of the fundamental elements of mnemonics that Bruno lays the foundation for the second novelty i.e., the introduction of a third element, the *organum*, which is the element that makes it possible to explain how the soul can evoke what is stored in the system of places and images that has been created combining different *subiecta* and *adiecta*. Therefore, the innovation that Bruno has entrusted with his contribution to perfecting the *ars memoriae* is an improved technical explanation of how the soul goes from the construction of an artificial memory system to retrieving the data it has stored there.[239]

239 "Unde nobis ita successisse presumimus, ut quidquid ab antiquioribus hac de re fuit consideratum, praeceptum et ordinatum – quatenus per eorum scripta, quae ad nostras devenere manus, extat explicatum –, non sit conveniens pars inventionis nostrae, quae est inventio supra modum praegnans, cui appropriatus est liber *Clavis magnae*," Giordano Bruno, *De umbris idearum, Ars memoriae Iordani Bruni*, Pars prima, xvi, 140–141, "This is why we believe we have brought the technique to such a degree of perfection that everything has been theorized, prescribed and ordered by the most ancient authors – at least as far as we know from the documents at our disposal – and cannot be legitimately accepted as part of our method: indeed, it was a highly fruitful discovery to which the book *Clavis Magna* is

Bruno understands that much of the criticism directed at mnemonics regards its artificial feature, as we have seen already evidenced in the most ancient source of rhetoric, the anonymous treatise *Rhetorica ad Herennium.*[240] The heart of the criticism is that mnemonics does not act directly on natural memory, but through the construction of an artificial *ordo* (*ordo idearum*), whose validity and correspondence with the *ordo rerum* is never explained. Thus, it has always been unclear how the transition from one level of reality to another takes place, and what guarantees the correctness of this transition. In other words, it has never been explained, either from a technical nor from a philosophical perspective, how it is possible to recognize the things or words that are to be evoked in the images stored in the artificial places of memory once the sensory stimulus has already produced the mental image. The epochal contribution that Bruno is preparing for the development of mnemonics is to show how it is possible that the two levels of reality – the *ordo idearum* and the *ordo rerum* – correspond.

The first step of his strategy is to establish the correspondence and internal consistence of the orders within artificial memory, that is, between the *ordo locorum* and the *ordo imaginum.* The aim of Bruno's new terminology is to criticize mnemonic tradition for not having explained the fundamental connection between the order of the places and the order of the images in the artificial memory system.[241] Bruno clarifies this important relationship between the two elements by replacing the old terminology with terms that explicate the semantic reference to the concept of the relationship: the *subiectum* is where the

dedicated." One must not let oneself be deceived by the peremptoriness with which Bruno presents the importance of the novelties he introduced to mnemonics. As we shall see, Bruno has to make sure the novelties he introduces are in line with tradition to demonstrate their innovative power; it is also true, however, that if Bruno's *ars memoriae* is regarded as the fulfilment of mnemonic tradition, the latter is preserved by transforming it, and it is the product of this transformation that I call the excess of Bruno's *ars memoriae* in the mnemonic tradition.

240 See here, Chapter one, pp. 36–42.

241 "Ex adnexionis defectu accidit infirmitas illa, qua utentibus arte multoties collocata species non occurrit; non tamen ex hoc capite rem ipsam perpendisse videntur praedecessores nostri. Hic est qui interim visus sensum refringit magis quam lumen excellentius, densior obscuritas, magna celebritas, distantia dispergens et id genus alia, quae locis, quibus uti consueverunt, solent accidere. Hinc, veluti percussi canes lapidem mordentes vel baculum, verum discriminis huius authorem minime percipientes, alium incusant," Giordano Bruno, *De umbris idearum, Ars memoriae Iordani Bruni*, Pars prima, xvi, 140–141, "An error in how such a connection is established [the connection between the objects and images for the objects] results in the defect that those using the art are unable to remember an image that has been stored more than once. But the authors before us do not appear to have taken the problem into consideration from this perspective. And this is the error that can temporarily blur the sense of sight more than a light of images that is too close up or too distant, so they are dispersed, and all the other incidents one comes up against when using mnemonic places. As a result, like beaten dogs biting a stone or stick, they accuse someone else, without realising who is really to blame."

adiectum is placed, but it is also what the *adiectum* is predicated on, and the latter can only be in relation to something on which it is placed or predicated, in other words, its *subiectum*. The importance of this terminological novelty will become more evident with the introduction of the *organum* or *scrutiny* i. e., the instrument that allows the soul, through the cogitative function, to order the mnemonic images, referring them correctly to the things they represent. Through scrutiny, operating semiotically in a similar way to that in which each sign is given a meaning in language and writing, the cogitative function can carry out the transition from the *ordo idearum* to the *ordo rerum*.

The second step, which explains what guarantees the correctness of the transition from the *ordo idearum* to the *ordo rerum*, consists in basing the *ars* on a kind of a "Platonic metaphysics"[242] that can justify the correspondence not only from a gnoseological perspective but also from an ontological one. However, with this second step, with this attempt to embed the justification even further from a sounder theoretical perspective, Bruno twists the *ars memoriae* until it assumes a position that is excessive as regards the mnemonic tradition. In fact, Bruno not only transform mnemonics from a theory of memory within a philosophy of nature but pushes mnemonics until it coincides with the same philosophy of nature, thus implementing that revolution of the mediaeval order that we saw Cusano initiate.

Let us now look more closely at how Bruno carried out this convergence of the *ars memoriae* and the theory of memory.

2. Giordano Bruno's *ars memoriae* (2): Consistency and novelty as regards the tradition of the mnemonic arts

2.1 The *subiecta*

The first significant difference compared to the mnemonic tradition, therefore, lies in the redefinition of the fundamental terms of the *ars memoriae*. Bruno speaks of "substrate" (*subiectum*) instead of "place" (*locus*) and of "added image" (*adiectum* or *forma*) instead of "image" (*imago*).

242 "Istam eruditorum pauci intelligant, intelligentibus autem omnibus usu veniat; sitque quam omnes, sive rudes sive eruditi, facile scire et exercere possint, quamque sine doctore, tantum in metaphysicis et doctrinis Platonicorum bene versati, possint intelligere," Giordano Bruno, *De umbris idearum, Dialogus Praelibatorius*, 34–35, "Let us admit it. Instead, this art can only be understood by few polymaths: it can still be practised by anyone who understands it; and thus, in addition, everyone, whether learned or not, will easily be able to recognize and apply it, even without the aid of a teacher, as long as they are good judges of Platonic metaphysics."

Redefining the elements of mnemonics, Bruno gives them each two definitions, one operative and the other theoretical. The operative definition can easily be inserted into the course of the tradition, also without explaining the theoretical novelties it entails; it can, therefore, be quickly understood and used in mnemonic practice. The theoretical definition refers to the one explained in *Clavis Magna*[243] and is more difficult for those who are only interested in having a more efficient set of rules to learn the *ars memoriae*, without going into its theoretical significance in detail. By proposing two definitions, Bruno is still trying to keep memory's two levels of interpretation separate, the technical part on the one hand, and the theoretical part on the other.

In the first definition of *subiectum*, Bruno does not appear to stray too far from the traditional definition:

> The first substrate is therefore an artificial extension, or rather a pre-arranged bosom in the fantastic fantasy, occupied by the figures of the receptacles that have arrived through the windows of the soul, distinguished into different parts, able to understand all the seen and heard realities according to their order, and to keep them in accordance with the wish of the soul.[244]

We recognize all the elements of the classical definition of *locus: locus* or *subiectum* is an artificial space (*technica extensio*) that reaches the soul through sensory perception (*ex animae fenestris influxere*) and is made up of the images of real places, which can, in turn, contain everything that has been seen or heard in the same order they occurred.

In the second definition, however, referring to his detailed explanation in *Clavis Magna*, Bruno defines the *subiectum* as "fantastic chaos" (*phantasticum chaos*). Fantastic chaos is a highly plastic material that can take on countless forms, like a "clouds buffeted by external winds, which, depending on the variety and intensity of the impulses received, can receive infinite figures of all kinds.[245]

If we now go back to the first definition in light of the second, one understands that Bruno is already introducing an emphasis that marks a conceptual divergence with tradition when he says that the artificial memory system is in the

243 For a reconstruction of the relationship between the *De umbris idearum* and the *Clavis magna*, see here, note 67, pp. 57–58.

244 "Primum ergo subiectum est technica extensio, sive sinus in phantastica facultate ordinatus, ex speciebus receptaculorum consitus, quae ex animae fenestris influxere, diversis distinctum partibus, visa omnia atque audita suo recipiens ordine et ad animae libitum reti/nens," Giordano Bruno, *De umbris idearum, Ars memoriae Iordani Bruni, Secunda pars, De subiectis, I*, 148–149.

245 "nubes ab externis impulsa ventis, quae pro impulsum differentiis atque rationibus infinitas omnesque subire valet specierum figuras," Giordano Bruno, *De umbris idearum, Ars memoriae Iordani Bruni, Secunda pars, De subiectis, I*, 148–149.

fantastic faculty: the *subiectum* is *sinus in phantastica facultate ordinatus.*[246] The novelty lies in the fact that, identifying the site of the artificial memory system in the fantastic faculty means that the faculty of memory is no longer understood as something passive, but as something that is able to operate on images in what is a potentially infinite manner. However, this potentiality is *ordered*, it is stemmed and governed by the *organum,* by scrutiny, which is the way in which the cogitative faculty takes part in the formation of the artificial memory system and, therefore, in the formation of memory.

If we are to understand the conceptual divergence from tradition, it is necessary to clarify that here Bruno's controversial target is the conception of the *locus* according to the most important treatises in the Renaissance. The authors of the mnemonic treatises had proposed countless explanations and numerous recommendations for the choice of the most suitable places to be used as memory systems. They could be either real places or structures taken from literature,[247] but they always had to have a direct, tangible reference to reality. If we think of the guiding image for the conceptual formulation of these mnemonic *loci*, it is clear that it was the metaphor of the ark: artificial memory was thus perceived as being made up of a receptacle in which images of the things that were later to be re-summoned to memory were placed.[248]

The idea of memory as a receptacle, as a container, imposed significant limits on the application of the technique: the form of the container was defined and

246 This novelty had been announced in advance in the first part of *Ars memoriae Iordani Bruni:* "Nobis autem cum datum est illam invenisse et / perfecisse, nec locis materialibus – verificatis scilicet per sensus exteriores – ultra non indiguimus, nec ordini locorum memorandum ordinem adstrinximus, sed puro phantasiae architecto innixi, ordini rerum memorandarum locorum ordinem adligavimus," Giordano Bruno, *De umbris idearum*, *Ars memoriae Iordani Bruni*, *Pars prima*, XVI, 140–141, "But since we have been allowed to discover and perfect that technique, we no longer had any need of material places – that is, places that have been verified by the external senses – neither have we had to connect the order of the concepts to be memorized to the order of the places; relying purely on the pure architecture of fantasy, we have made the order of the places dependent on the order of the things to be remembered."

247 Like, for example, the shops along a road in a city or like the Inferno and Paradise, see figs. 5, 6 and 7.

248 In Johannes Romberch's famous illustration of *Congestorium artificiose memorie* (fig. 1), also revived by Cosma Rosselli in *Thesaurus artificiosae memoriae* (figs. 2, 3), we can see the collocation of the functions of the soul in the skull. In this depiction memory occupies the last place. This depiction is in perfect accordance with the concept of natural memory as an ark, as a thesaurus, that is, as a place where the facts of sensory experience that have been elaborated by the other faculties of the soul are deposited. With regard to this depiction, I cite the list of cogitative faculties from Giordano Bruno, *De monade, numero et figura:* "Novem sunt cognoscitivae potentiae in homine: VISS, AUDITUS, GUSTUS, TACTUS, OLFACTUS, PHANTASIA, COGITATIO, MEMORIA, RATIO," in Jordani Bruni Nolani, *Opera latine conscripta. Publicis sumptibus edita*, I, II, Recensebat F. Fiorentino (Neapoli: Morano: 1884), 455.

established once and for all, because it was taken from reality and transported to natural memory. This not only meant that the mnemonist had to pay great attention to the choice of the most suitable place to store what was to be remembered, but also to make sure it was suitable for any possible developments of the system. An example should help clarify this. If I want to memorize the seven cardinal virtues, I will have to choose, for instance, a house with an equal or greater number of rooms. A number of rooms equal to the number of cardinal virtues guarantees the memorization of what I want to send to memory now; however, if I know that in the future other elements will be added to this memory system (I could decide, for example, to look in more detail at the conception of the seven theological virtues in the twelfth, thirteenth and fourteenth century), it would be better to have a larger *locus* from the very start, so that there is room for subsequent knowledge. In fact, restructuring a memory system after its initial creation could lead to errors or present difficulties for memory of the kind that one tries to avoid with the rules for the composition of the *loci.*[249] This difficulty comes from the fact that the mnemonic *locus,* in the form it is understood in the artificial memory systems that are guided by the image of memory as an ark, is a place that is already thoroughly defined.

The first definition of *subiectum*, which Bruno presents as the one that is most respectful of tradition, already suggests a possible solution, with the modification of the image-guide for the formulation of the concept of "receptacle" or *locus.* The *subiectum* is a container (*sinus*) but it is governed (*ordinatus*) by the fantastic faculty. What this actually means is explained in the second definition, which states how the *sinus* is to be understood: the receptacle of artificial memory is a fantastic primordial material (*chaos*).[250] The *subiectum* is therefore not only retentive, as it was defined in Renaissance mnemonic treatises, but it preserves by working on what is to be remembered,[251] and the extent of its action is due to it being a material that is without order and form.

249 See here, Chapter one, pp. 34–47.

250 This evokes Plato's *Timaeus* and an analogy between the Demiurge and the soul that forges the memory system. Both are working with material that has not been ordered and what they do is shape this material, transforming it from *chaos* to order (*kosmos*), following the model of the world of ideas. One should bear in mind both this evocation and the analogy, Bruno suggests, because it allows us to better understand the transition from the gnoseological justification of the correspondence between *ordo idearum* and *ordo rerum* to its ontological justification.

251 As confirmation of the productivity of the primordial fantastic material, Bruno explains that the *subiectum* is made up of material parts that can be seen, as the fantastic faculty only works on images: "quatenus eadem suo ordine phantastica facultas valeat contemplari, vel ipsis utens tanquam partibus atque principiis, in monstra novasque innumeras metamorphoses digerere et digestas velut orbi adfixas intueri," Giordano Bruno, *De umbris idearum*, *Ars memoriae Iordani Bruni, Secunda pars, De subiectis, II,* 150–151, "because the fantastic faculty – according to its own order – can either contemplate them as they are or, using them

It is interesting to look more closely at what Bruno is trying to do here because it is a method that we find in all his works. Bruno does not want to reform the mnemonic tradition so radically that it is transformed or distorted. On the contrary, he believes that his task is to realize this tradition, implementing it to the full.[252] In fact, if one reads and compares the two definitions of *subiectum*, one understands that at first Bruno continued to define the *subiectum*, working on the guiding idea of a container; but one also perceives that by defining the *locus* as *subiectum*, and thus giving a central role to fantasy in the memorization process, the guiding image of memory as a container – in the sense of an ark or stomach – is no longer sufficiently effective for Bruno to reach the objective he had set himself. Next, Bruno needed an image for the container that is as indeterminate as possible so that fantasy can elaborate (order) it as it likes, albeit under the control of reason (the cogitative faculty). Indeed, it is only in this fashion, only by working simultaneously on both the images and the places housing them that one can construct a memory system that is so totally coherent and consistent that it can also guarantee the retrieval of what has been deposited there.[253]

---

as parts and principles, arrange them into extraordinary configurations and countless metamorphoses, and contemplate them in this arrangement, almost as if they were affixed to a circle." Bruno refers to *Clavis magna* for the interpretation of the *subiecta* that have no material characteristics. These were deemed to be *subiecta* that were schematically or geometrically constructed, like, for example the seals of the "square encyclical" and "circular encylical" of the *Explicatio*. See Giordano Bruno, *Opere mnemotecniche: Tomo II*, ed. Marco Matteoli, Rita Sturlese, and Nicoletta Tirinnanzi (Milan: Adelphi, 2009), 88–89 and 141–142; but also the comment in Giordano Bruno, *Opere mnemotecniche: Tomo I*, eds. Marco MatteolI, Rita Sturlese, Nicoletta Tirinnanzi (Milan: Adelphi, 2004), 481.

252 The theme of Mercury can be implicitly perceived here, with which Bruno explained this epochal meaning of his contribution to the history of the mnemonic arts and the history of philosophy in general. Like Mercury, the messenger of the gods, who knows divine will and whose task is to communicate it to men, Bruno sees himself as a messenger of truth, forced to journey from one place to another, confronting those who are not ready to accept his message. On this subject see: Michele Ciliberto, *La ruota del tempo: Interpretazione di Giordano Bruno* (Rome: Editori Riuniti, 1986); Michele Ciliberto, *Umbra profunda: Studi su Giordano Bruno* (Rome: Edizioni di Storia e di Letteratura, 1999), 160–161; Michele Ciliberto, *L'occhio di Atteone: Nuovi studi su Giordano Bruno* (Rome: Edizioni di Storia e di Letteratura, 2002), 17–18; Michele Ciliberto, *Pensare per contrari: Disincanto e utopia nel Rinascimento* (Rome: Edizioni di Storia e di Letteratura, 2005).

253 In the following paragraph we shall see the image guiding the new conceptual formulation that Bruno is proposing. Here I would like to underline the internal dynamism in Bruno's text, because it is an aspect that makes his method of philosophical work on concepts and theories stand out. I am referring to the fact that Bruno's thought has never been completely espoused in a theory that can be defined or explained systematically. Reading Bruno's work, each time one has the impression one is entering an alchemical laboratory just when the alchemist is trying to give material a new form. The alchemist never really knows what form the material will take, because it develops independently in his hands and he has no choice but to follow its transformations, pursuing them and trying to take them into account, but at the end of the process what he finds in his hands is always unexpected.

As I shall show in the rest of the chapter, the guiding image that Bruno has in his mind is clearly that of a sheet of paper upon which the printer printed characters which have the characteristic of being images that represent letters. I ask the reader to bear this image in mind throughout the remaining explanation of the technical aspects of Bruno's *ars memoriae.*[254]

2.2 The *adiecta* or *formae*

In his interpretation of the *adiecta* or *formae*[255] Bruno also starts with two definitions, one that is easier to implement and of more immediate use because it is based on that of the *imagines*, and one that refers to *clavis universalis*, and is therefore more difficult and aimed at those who wish to understand the deep reasons of the *ars.*

As we have already seen for the *subiecta*, apart from linguistic novelties, in the first definition we also find all the traditional elements that determine the *imagines:*

> We define added image of form – limited to the genre of this treatise – each element that is given to a physical, artificial or fantastic substrate to express or mean something thanks to the diligent artifices of the cogitative faculty, presenting or outlining figures, marking with characters, or indicating, as is the case in painting and writing.[256]

According to Bruno, the aspect that should be stressed is that the image is *added* to the *subiectum*, thus meaning that the *subiectum* and *adiectum* cannot be

254 I shall complete the explanation of the *subiecta* with a note about their rules that, as I mentioned earlier, are the traditional ones, in accordance with mnemonics in Renaissance literature. For example, the basic model of mnemotechnic architecture is given by the measurements of the human body with raised, open arms, as recommended, for example, by Johannes Romberch: Giordano Bruno, *Cantus Circaeus, Caput II: De conditionibus subiectorum, § 2*, in Giordano Bruno, *Opere mnemotecniche: Tomo I*, ed. Marco Matteoli, Rita Sturlese, and Nicoletta Tirinnanzi (Milan: Adelphi, 2004), 674–675. For the portrayal of this rule in Romberch, see fig. 4; each successive space is constructed proportionally to this module, so that the distances are respected to allow real movement in the interior. Furthermore, there must also be a proportion between the *subiecta* and the intermediary spaces, so that the internal eye is not fatigued; for the same reason, the *subiecta* have to be clearly separated in space, but not too distant from one another.

255 Bruno specifies here that the term *form* is used to mean "restricted to mnemotechnics." It is true, however, that there is also an analogy with the *form* of the physical world. This aspect will be dealt with in the following chapter.

256 "Adiectum vero seu forma in genere isto definitur subiecto sive physico sive technico sive phantastico appositum, ad aliquid per solertem cogitationis apparatum, presentando, effigiendo, notando vel indicando ad picturae scripturaeque similitudinem, exprimendum vel significandum," Giordano Bruno, *De umbris idearum, Ars memoriae Iordani Bruni, Secunda Pars*, 166–169.

indifferent to one another, if one wants to guarantee memorization, but there has to be some sort of relationship of reciprocal involvement.

The definition of the *Clavis Magna* concentrates even more effectively on the intrinsic belonging of *adiectum* and *subiectum*, because here the *adiectum* or *forma* (form) define the order of the portrayals in the substrate. The *forma* acts under the guidance of the fantastic chaos, that is, the *subiectum*, to write everything that has to be said with language. Primordial chaos can therefore be formed and ordered, and then reordered infinitely and by anyone:

> However, the form – as far as can be seen from the origins of *Clavis Magna*, is the order of the portrayals that can be object of thought, established and made visible, arranged in accordance with a series of statues, or rather, in a micro-cosmos, or rather, in general, inside any other architectural structure, to write or depict internally – under the guidance of the fantastic chaos, susceptible to every metamorphosis – all of which can be expressed through language. We present an image, now with the intention of illustrating it, but because it is useful to observe it as an example here, as well.[257]

It is therefore in the fantastic faculty that the semiotic process which structures the artificial memory system takes place: the *subiectum* is like a white sheet of paper upon which one places the *adiecta*, which represent things in reality. In the same way that words represent things, it is in the fantastic faculty that the semiotic correspondence between internal images and the objects of external reality[258] takes place. What guarantees the correctness of the semiotic process,

257 "Forma vero, ut ex radicibus *Clavis magnae* elicitur, est deppromptus et explicatus ordo cogitabilium specierum, in statuas vel microcosmon vel in aliam generaliter architecturam dispositus, ad quo<d>libet dicibile interius notandum vel figurandum ex ductu phantastici chaos metamorphoses omnes admittentis. Cuius typum non tanquam hic declarandum, sed ut et hic inspiciendum apponimus," Giordano Bruno, *De umbris idearum*, *Ars memoriae Iordani Bruni*, Secunda pars, 168–169. The figure, which is commented in the following paragraph, has been lost. It is interesting, however, because what Bruno suggests is perfectly in line with a philosophy of images: observing an image helps understand something complicated, like a definition of the *Clavis magna*.

258 When Bruno goes on to define the rules of the composition of the *adiecta*, he still preserves the precise reference to the mnemonic precepts in this section. The difference to previous tradition is Bruno's aim of underlining the nexus of reciprocity between *subiectum* and *adiectum*, from prescription, according to which, for example, the dimensions of the *adiecta* have to be proportional to the volume of man and follow natural relationships. The images have to be spectacular because they need to awaken the fantasy, even if it is the cogitative faculty that is guiding the entire process and opens up access to memory through the senses and fantasy. Furthermore, if attention is to be maintained, the *adiecta* have to carry out an action on the *subiecta*, or in their interior, or they have to be the object of an action by the *subiecta* or in their interior. Avoiding uniformity of the *adiecta* used and seeking a difference in the interior of the same *subiectum*, without using the same *adiecta*, also helps maintain attention. Finally, one can use the same *adiecta* in the same memory system, but it is better that they are very far from one another and that they carry out different actions on different *subiecta*. This is because one must try as much as possible to apply the principle that the *subiectum-adiectum* relationship is univocal and essential.

however, and therefore the correspondence between *ordo rerum* and *ordo idearum* in artificial memory?

2.3 The *organum*

The other great innovation that Bruno introduces to mnemonics tradition is that of a new element, the *organum*, which explains how the soul creates the *ars*; that is, how the facts in the *subiecta* and in the *adiecta* can be retrieved. Bruno believes that clarifying the instrument that the soul uses to create the *ars* can help overcome all the criticism directed at it, most of which regards its effectiveness and practical features. A perfect knowledge of the *ars* is only possible if one also understands the essence of the instrument through which "the form is transmitted from the agent to the substrate,"[259] its characteristics and the method used to acquire it.

If one is to know and understand the essence of the *organum*, one must have knowledge of all the stages comprising reminiscence and memory and establish which of these stages corresponds to the *organum:*

> Nine elements converge to make reminiscences and memory possible. The preliminary intention, in virtue of which one of the external or internal senses carries on following the impulse of an external object. The stimulus impressed on the imagination, when the sense, touched in this fashion, immediately or indirectly awakens the imagination. The impulsive reaction that drives the imagination to investigate. The conscious act with which the imagination immediately begins its study. The scrutiny with which the imagination searches, understanding. The imagination, or rather the memorable species. The content of the image, or rather the peculiar character in virtue of which it can become the specific object of memory, separating itself from all the others. The portrayal of that content, in such a way, as is natural, that content makes itself present. Finally, judgement, through which one understand that such is the content of that image.[260]

259 "ab agente in subiectum formae vehiculum," Giordano Bruno, *De umbris idearum*, *Ars memoriae Iordani Bruni*, Secunda pars, I, 180–181.

260 "Novem concurrunt ad rememorationem faciendam et memoriam. Intentio antecedens, qua primum aliquis sensus extrinsecus vel intrinsecus fit in actu ex hoc, quod movetur ab obiecto. Provocatio imaginationis, ubi sensus commotus iam mediate vel immediate expergefacit imaginationem. Imaginationis motus passivus, quo pellitur ad investigandum. Imaginationis activus motus, quo iam investigat. Scrutinium, quo intendens imaginatio investigat. Imago, utpote species memorabilis. Intentio imaginis, nempe ratio qua memorabilis efficitur in praesentiarum, aliis exclusis. Praesentatio illius intentionis, quod scilicet intentio illa praesens efficiatur. Et iudicatio, qua apprehenditur eam esse intentionem illius imaginis," Giordano Bruno, *De umbris idearum*, *Ars memoriae Iordani Bruni*, Secunda Pars, II, 182–183.

Calling to mind Averroës' comment about Aristotle's *De Memoria et Reminiscentia,* Bruno both partially follows and modifies it, dividing the reminiscence process into nine stages. The starting point is the desire and will to activate a memory (I want to remember the landline number of a friend in Berlin) followed by the activation of the fantasy by a stimulus (the prefix for landline numbers in Berlin is "030") and the start of fantasy's search amongst the various memories (all the telephone numbers that have been memorized). The cogitative faculty now searches consciously, using scrutiny (selecting the German landline numbers with the prefix "030"). Through scrutiny, the cogitative faculty identifies an image, which is the one that contains the meaning one wants to remember (I gradually exclude the telephone numbers of other friends in Berlin) and I characterize it as a significant unit; it will be reason's task to establish whether the attribution of this meaning to the image is correct (the friend's number I was looking for was a permutation of the figures of his wife's date of birth, who was born on the same day I was).

The *organum* with which the soul creates the *ars* is *scrutiny.* According to Bruno, it corresponds to the moment in which the cogitative faculty is searching and distinguishing, like a stick in a pile of acorns looking for a chestnut. In this image, the pile of acorns is the fantastic fantasy, and the stick is *scrutiny*, which is the instrument reason uses, knowing how to reconstruct the process that led to the attribution of chestnuts to several acorns. In fact, *scrutiny* alone is not sufficient to explain how the soul associates the thing to the *adiectum.* The instrument has to be employed by reason, which knows how to recognize a *significant relationship* such as the one between meaning and significant.[261]

261 "In the light of these considerations, he remembers that to achieve its own objective, this art does not avail itself of other means other than those of sensible realities, formed, shaped, contracted to a specific time and place, as is the case – we demonstrated it in the first volume of *Clavis magnae* – also for all the other artificial works of the soul. However, with this the intention is not to claim that all things must be used as images, since many of the things to be remembered are not susceptible to fantastic portrayal, neither can they be reproduced in the form of effigies or presented allusively with a similar technique: terms such as ousia, hypostasis, mind and other similar concepts belong to this genre. Instead, all things have to be used as signs of significant reality, images of imaginable reality. Furthermore, one must not forget that images are no less tied to signs that signs are connected to images," "Istis consideratis, memento huic arti media alia usu venire non posse ad suum finem consequendum quam sensibilia, formata, figurata, tempori locoque contracta, quemadmodum et in omnibus aliis technicis animae operibus accidere in primo volumine *Clavis magnae* fuit expressum. Nihilo tamen minus non uti intelligitur omnibus tanquam imaginibus, siquidem multa, quorum debet esse memoria, imaginabilia non sunt neque effigiabilia neque simili quodam insinuabilia, cuiusmodi sunt termini usia, ypostasis, mens, caeteraque id genus, sed ut signis significabilium, imaginibus imaginabilium. Et cum hoc illud non est mente praetereundum, quod non minus sunt alligatae signis imagines, quam signa imaginibus sunt adnexa," Giordano Bruno, *De umbris idearum, Ars memoriae Iordani Bruni,* Pars prima, xv, 138–141.

2.4 A technique of inner writing for images: The metaphor of inner writing as a leading paradigm of conceptual formulation

A new conceptual paradigm, that of inner writing, emerged in the analysis of the three technical novelties introduced by Giordano Bruno in *ars memoriae.* More specifically, we saw how Bruno's treatise went from the absolute metaphor of the ark to that of inner writing.

Let us turn now to the metaphor of inner writing and let me underline my thesis i. e., Giordano Bruno's mnemonic works best represent the philosophical awareness of the relation between the development of writing techniques and the development of memory theories. In this part I will explain why the inner writing metaphor is an absolute metaphor in Bruno and to illustrate it I will take three examples.

We have seen that the inner writing metaphor has a very long history in mnemonics. Already the anonymous author of the *Rhetorica ad Herennium* and Cicero in the *De oratore* used this metaphor to illustrate the basic rules of the *ars memoriae.* If you want to remember a speech you are going to give, first you have to choose an image that represents the concept or the word that you intend to keep in mind, and secondly you have to lay out this picture in a location, but this process must be done by following the order of the words of your speech. Only by respecting this order can you be certain that, when you have to recall your speech, every object laid out and organized in that order will restore the word that you had originally put in. Both Cicero and the anonymous author say that this memorizing technique is similar to what happens when we write: we draw signs in a certain order, and we allocate a meaning to each sign that we will be able to recall later when we read that text.

At this point, at the beginning of this metaphor's history, it was not yet an absolute metaphor, because it was used as a means of *comparison* to explain something. It is true that without the writing metaphor it would have been difficult to understand and to use this technique, but it would not have been impossible. The metaphor had begun to shape the conceptual understanding of memory but had not yet become a substitute for the concept itself as it would in Bruno.

An example of this can be found in the frontispiece of the *De umbris idearum,* which is the first book Bruno published on the *ars memoriae.* The title and subtitle show that Bruno uses "inner writing" as an absolute metaphor and not as a metaphor, as a comparison. Bruno writes:

> The shadows of ideas, in which is implied the art of searching, invention, judging, ordaining, and connecting and that are explained for the 'inner writing' and extraordinary mnemonics.[262]

It is evident here that the expression "inner writing" is used in a technical sense: it is not a metaphor, a comparison, but it is a kind of proper name.

The second example is paragraph XI of the part titled "Ars memoriae" in *De umbris idearum.*[263] It is quite a long quotation, but we will hear in Bruno's own words how he understands the value of his contribution to the history of the art of memory, and we will see that this value can only be understood in reference to the connection between the development of writing techniques and the "inner writing" technique. I need to summarize two statements that Bruno provides at the beginning of it, because we will need them when we come to drawing our conclusions: there is only one principle that explains everything and we can call it "*nature*", and the work of hand belongs to this principle too, which means that by working with hands nature is expressing itself. And now let us recall here how Bruno speaks about his contribution to the tradition of the art of memory:

> It is said that it is from these same foundation and in the same succession that the art that guides the hand proceeds. Hence – going back to the aspect that concerns our study – in ancient antiquity they used knives to write on the bark of tree. This was followed by the age of letters engraved with a chisel on stone; then came papyrus with black sepia ink. Then came the parchments that were marked more clearly using artificial ink. Then paper and the encaustic technique; finally letters were imprinted with a press, using an immensely more efficient technique. From knives to nibs, from nibs to sponges, from sponges to inkwells, from inkwells to pens, one finally arrived at – and this is what I mean – letters melted in lead. We believe that the same thing happened for the techniques of inner writing, from the period in which this form of human activity was started for the very first time by the poet Simonides or by another author: in fact, by adopting places and images instead of paper and letters of the alphabet, and replacing the work of the writer and quill with the activity of fantasy and the cogitative faculty, they contrived to write the images of the things to be remembered in an inner book. Which and how many innovations we have been able to add to their work, will be judged by those who set about comparing our treatises with their works.[264]

---

262 "De umbris idearum./ Implicantibus artem, Quaerendi, In-/veniendi, Iudicandi, Ordinandi,/ et Applicandi:/ Ad internam scripturam, et non vulgares/ per memoriam operationes explicatis./" Giordano Bruno, *De umbris idearum*, 2–3.

263 Giordano Bruno, *De umbris idearum*, *Ars memoriae Iordani Bruni*, Pars prima, xv–xvi, 134–135.

264 "Hinc et eadem serie progressum facere dicitur ars quam manu<s> ducit. Ideo – ut ad propositum intentionis nostrae spectat – cultris in arborum corticibus prior scripsisse perhibetur vetustas. Cui successit aetas in lapidibus celte excavatis inscribens; quam sequuta est papyrus sepiarum succis exarata. Inde pergamenaer membranae atramento artificioso magis intinctae. Proinde charta et inchaustum, praeloque premendae in usum longe omnium patissimum literae. A cultris, inquam, ad stilos, a stilis ad spongia, a spongiis ad

Bruno concludes by saying that the reader should judge for himself whether his achievements in the *ars memoriae* are equal in importance to the invention of the printing press. What Bruno says about the relations between the development of writing techniques and the development of "inner writing" techniques is clear, but what is very significant here is that he knows his mnemonics will change the way we configure the *book of memory*. We have seen that the absolute metaphor of the *book of nature* defined the order in which man, nature, and God were related, and the *book of memory* was seen as a *speculum*, a mirror of that of nature. Bruno understands that stressing the importance of the work of the hand and understanding a memory as "a printed inner writing" would transform the idea of order engraved in the book of memory, and therefore in the book of nature: the relation would no longer be passive, but active and productive.

This will be made clear in the third example, which is taken from the *Explicatio triginta sigillorum*.[265] In this work Bruno gives a selection of images that can be used as mnemonic pictures, but he also analogically describes his contribution in the art of memory. The images go from very natural and material ones to the more symbolic and abstract. What he does is to describe the passage that goes from the metaphor of the book of nature to the one of inner writing, the first being a passive metaphor and the second being an operative one. He achieves this thanks to the metamorphosis of two Llullian images: the tree of knowledge and the steps. In fact, if we list the first ten images, they are: the field, the sky, the chain, the tree, the forest, the steps, the grafter, the farmer, the tablet, the typesetter. The first seven images are the disassembling of the two Llullian images. Starting from the eighth image, Bruno changes the configuration of the understanding of the idea of order, introducing an operative action: the grafter cuts and grafts the tree that no longer gives fruit to create a productive tree. But what the grafter does is like what we do when we write on the bark of the tree with a knife. In the same analogical way, the farmer ploughs the earth and signs or leaves a mark on it, as if it were writing on a wax tablet. Hence from the tablet to the table of the typesetter.

These examples support what I have claimed so far: one, inner writing is an absolute metaphor in Giordano Bruno's mnemonics, because it leads and shapes

calamos, a calamis ad pennsa, a pennis ad fusilia tandem elementa perventum. Haud secus in iis, quae ad scripturam pertinere videntur internam, contigisse arbitrarum, dum ab antiquo humanum studium sive a melico Simonide sive ab alio sumpserit exordium; qui <usu?> locorum et imaginum proportionalium chartae atque scripturae, actuque phantasiae et cogitativae locum scriptoris et calami subeuntibus, species / rerum memorandarum in interno libro inscribere studuerunt. Quorum industriae quid et quantum addiderimus, ipsorum, qui haec nostra cum illorum monumentis conferre potuerunt, esto iudicium," Giordano Bruno, *De umbris idearum*, Pars prima, xv–xvi, 134–135.

265 Giordano Bruno, *Explicatio triginta sigillorum*, in Giordano Bruno, *Opere mnemotecniche: Tomo II*, eds. Marco Matteoli, Rita Sturlese, and Nicoletta Tirinnanzi (Milan: Adelphi, 2009).

the conceptual understanding of the *ars memoriae*; two, using this absolute metaphor, Bruno changes the meaning of the concept of order from a passive meaning to an operative one.

3. Giordano Bruno's *ars memoriae* (3): An excess in the wake of the tradition of the mnemonic arts

Summarising what has been said so far, Bruno's *ars memoriae* originates from the attempt to make the mnemonic technique more intelligible by explaining the most obscure point of each treatise: in artificial memory, how does the soul associate the image in the mnemonic *locus* to the thing or word it represents? The first step that Bruno takes in this direction is a redefinition of *locus* and *imago* to show (or at least to let one sense through this terminological re-definition) their essential connection; that is, the fact that from the very beginning they are chosen in a one-to-one relationship. The second step consists of the identification of the different stages in the memory process that correspond to the instrument with which the soul orders the artificial memory system. I stressed that in this redefinition stage of the *ars memoriae* Bruno is using a conceptual paradigm that has a long history in mnemonics, that of inner writing but that, unlike the tradition, which concentrates more on the passive-receptive aspect of the metaphor of the book, he privileges the operative aspect.

I explained earlier that, from a strictly technical point of view, Bruno makes functional changes to the classical structure of mnemonics, with the sole aim of making it easier and more practical to use. In this sense I believe that Bruno's *ars memoriae* is consistent with the course of mnemonic tradition: Bruno is not working on its destruction or radical reformation; he only wants to provide strong arguments that make mnemonic critics re-examine their positions. What I intend to explain on the following pages is that, by following this objective, the form Bruno gives to his *ars memoriae* results in it representing an *excess* in the same course of the tradition. The excess is a gnoseology that is based on the idea that there is only one *ars* of which the *ars memoriae* is a phenomenal expression. This gnoseological approach has a strong impact on the philosophical works in which Bruno further develops his reflection on the *ordo*, going on to the ontological justification of the correspondence between *ordo rerum* and *ordo idearum*, thus completing the theoretical-philosophical justification of the mnemonic arts in the system of knowledge.

3.1 Criticism of *ars memoriae*

Giordano Bruno began his study of the mnemonic arts early on, when he was already studying in Naples but perhaps before he entered the convent of San Domenico Maggiore.[266] If one bears in mind the importance of the mnemonic tradition in Dominican circles, one could even hypothesize that his actual decision to enter the convent was motivated by the possibility of practising the techniques which help someone become an accomplished speaker. We must therefore bear in mind that the Dominican friar Giordano Bruno studied in an environment in which mnemonics played an important role, above all in regards to his ethical treatise.[267] We must also bear in mind that, however, if it is true that it was the Augustinian friar Theophilus Vairanus who introduced him to Llull's works, Bruno must have also had prior extensive preparation in the Franciscan mnemonic tradition.[268] Furthermore, Bruno's literary production is testimony to an interest that, although it changed over the years, remained constant during his lifetime, so much so that his fame as a philosophy teacher equalled his renown as a mnemonics teacher. This can be seen in the famous passage from the *Costituti Veneti:*

> Such renown did I acquire that King Henry III summoned me one day, wanting to know whether the memory I had and what I professed was natural or magical art; my reply gave him satisfaction; and with what I told him and made him also experience, he admitted it was not magical arts, but science. And after this I had a book on memory published with the title *De Umbris Idearum*, which I dedicated to His Majesty; and on this occasion I was made extraordinary, waged lecturer; and I went on to read in that city, as I have already said, perhaps five years.[269]

---

266 Likely it was the Augustinian friar Teophilus Vairanus who introduced Bruno to Llull's work: Michele Ciliberto, *Introduzione a Giordano Bruno* (Rome: Laterza, 2000), 7. See also: Saverio Ricci, *Giordano Bruno nell'Europa del Cinquecento* (Rome: Salerno Editrice, 2000).

267 See here, Chapter one, pp. 50–53.

268 This hypothesis is also supported by the importance of the figure of Theophilus Vairanus in Bruno's studies. It was Theophilus Vairanus who introduced him to Neo-Platonism and Augustine, which was to prove to be of fundamental importance for Bruno's views in relation to the Trinitarian dogma, the term 'person' and the conception of memory. For more about the importance of Theophilus Vairanus in relation to Bruno's conception of the Trinitarian dogma and the term 'person' and, more generally, Vairanus' philosophical influence on Bruno, see: Michele Ciliberto, *Introduzione a Giordano Bruno* (Rome: Laterza, 2000), 7.

269 Luigi Firpo, *Il processo di Giordano Bruno* (Rome: Salerno Editrice, 1993), 161–162: "Acquistai nome tale che il re Henrico terzo mi fece chiamare un giorno, ricercandomi se la memoria che havevo et che professava era naturale o pur per arte magica; al quale diedi soddisfattione; et con quello che li dissi et feci provare a lui medesmo, conobbe che non era per arte magica ma per scienzia. Et doppo questo feci stampar un libro de memoria sotto il titolo *De umbris idearum*, il qual dedicai a Sua Maestà; et con questa occasione mi fece lettor straordinario et provisionato; et seguitai in quella città a legger, come ho detto, forsi cinqu'anni." For an analysis of Bruno's experience in Paris in the European context of the

It was in Paris that Giordano Bruno's work as a teacher of *ars memoriae* acquired particular importance and it should be considered in the context of lively debate on the utility of *ars*, as can be seen from the writing of *De umbris idearum*, which followed his successful cycle of lessons on the mnemonic arts.

The numerous characters with imaginary names that Bruno introduced in the "Dialogus Praelibatorius" reveal the vivacity of a debate that Bruno embraced, so much so that he made it the centre of the first work that he printed in Paris. The people he was indirectly replying to with the publication of *De umbris idearum* were men of letters, grammarians, theologians, physicians, and legal experts. These were all people who, owing to their professional experience or studies, had been taught the mnemonic arts and judged them negatively.

The criticisms directed at the technique to reinforce natural memory by creating an artificial memory were the usual ones: firstly, the impossibility of assessing the real fruits of mnemonics and the conviction that natural memory can be reinforced only by a wealthy lifestyle or medication; but also the observation that the study of mnemonic classics had yielded no fruits and that, if it had been otherwise, all scholars would have been students of mnemonics, too; and the conviction that it is only useful for those who were born with a good memory, or the conviction that all these rules and images are only an unnecessary burden on memory.

In the first part of *Ars memoriae Iordani Bruni* in *De umbris idearum*, Bruno explains the reason why his *ars memoriae* is an innovation in mnemotechnic tradition and why this novelty places it on a higher level than the other mnemonic arts. The originality lies in explaining the Platonic metaphysics upon which the *ars* is founded. Making explicit and dwelling on the theoretical premises of the *ars* make it possible to place mnemonics in a much broader context than the simple theory for reinforcing natural memory: in fact, the *ars memoriae* belongs to what Bruno calls that *unique science* that Bruno compares to the sun.

3.2 A unique *ars:* Metaphor of the shadow and metaphor of inner writing

The metaphor of the unique sun, which the book is asked to reveal by opening itself, is certainly a reference to the Copernican conception of the universe, but only marginally. Bruno does not reduce his philosophical understanding of reality to the philosophy of nature that originates from the Copernican revolution; instead, he understands that the conceptual meaning of Copernicanism can be

sixteenth century, see: Saverio Ricci, *Giordano Bruno nell'Europa del Cinquecento* (Rome: Salerno Editrice, 2000), 141–177.

expressed philosophically, as an expression of a unique principle that pervades each level of reality.

In other words, at this stage, instead of placing his philosophical conception in the bosom of Copernicanism, Bruno shows that two ancient absolute metaphors, that of light and that of the world as a book, are still operative in Copernicanism. Carrying out another epochal conceptual leap, what Bruno does is decline them operatively and no longer passively – a move that can already be seen in the decision not to speak of a "unique philosophy" but rather a "unique *ars*" where *ars* is the expression of nature's productivity.

Bruno begins the introductory section of *De umbris idearum* on the mnemonic arts in what appears to be a traditional fashion: mnemotechnics can stimulate a dull nature or direct it, correct it, or support it. This is possible (and here is the twist that Bruno makes in the *ars memoriae*) because it emulates the same diligence of perfect nature. The soul can understand the *ars* because, on the one hand the *ars memoriae* is an expression of the unique *ars* in which nature expresses itself and, on the other, because man understands himself metaphysically as a shadow of ideas. This is the twofold metaphysical foundation of Bruno's mnemonics.

The Platonic metaphysics that Bruno refers to for a more detailed understanding of the *ars memoriae* is a metaphysics of the shadow. The concept of *umbra*, which is one of the central motifs in Giordano Bruno's philosophical reflection, refers to the Platonic and Neoplatonic tradition and the absolute metaphor of light as the metaphor of truth.[270] As Nicoletta Tirinnanzi[271] explained in such detail, whilst in these traditions shadow had a negative connotation, underlining the limits of the human condition, which is an umbral one compared to the divine, which is comparable to light, Bruno is able to reassess the strong points in the umbral nature of the human condition. Nolanus exalts the positivity of *esse in umbra* with an interpretation of the biblical image of Shulamite sitting in the shadow of her beloved. Shulamite is in perfect condition, not because she has risen above the natural *umbra*, but because she sees the shadow as a place of absolute stability since it is the shadow of her beloved. One therefore sees that for Bruno the concept of *umbra* is one of *medium* that not only allows an exchange at various levels of reality, but also one that guides reasoning over the limit and the communication between divinity, men, and nature.[272]

270 See Hans Blumenberg, "Licht als Metapher der Wahrheit. Im Vorfeld der philosophischen Begriffsbildung," *Studium Generale* 10, (1957): 432–447.

271 Nicoletta Tirinnanzi, *Umbra naturae: L'immaginazione da Ficino a Bruno* (Rome: Edizioni di Storia e Letteratura, 2000).

272 Tirinnanzi, *Umbra naturae*, 215.

The faculty that allows this communication between diverse levels of reality, which can combine the *umbrae naturae* in new, endless ways, is the *phantasia.*[273] By virtue of its analogy with nature, the fantastic faculty is not only able to combine the external *umbrae* with the internal ones, but it is also able to elaborate them as infinitely as the productivity of nature. *Phantasia* and nature are expressions of that unique principle creator that pervades the universe and manifests itself in the infinite production of aggregates.

The unique *ars* that the metaphor of the sun refers to in the opening of *De umbris idearum* is therefore the infinite productive activity of the principle creator of the universe. The *ars memoriae* is, therefore, not just a mere manifestation of the unique *ars*, but is the manifestation that represents it analogically more accurately, because the artificial is constructed in the *phantasia, umbra naturae emulatrix.* In fact, we have seen that Bruno places the artificial memory system in the *sinu phantastico*[274] and not in natural memory.

This is what I have called the excess of Bruno's *ars memoriae.* The problem Bruno is tackling is a technical one: justifying the correspondence between *ordo idearum* and *ordo rerum,* to convince the critics of mnemotechnics of the validity of the use of an artificial memory system. Bruno's first move is to identify the metaphor of inner writing as a more effective conceptual paradigm than that of the ark and thus guide it towards solving the problem. In fact, by using the metaphor of inner writing, Bruno is able to explain that whatever is deposited in artificial memory can be used to recall the facts of the sensory experience in the memory because when constructing the artificial memory, the soul uses an *ars* that is based on the same semiotic principles of writing.[275] His second step consists of the ontological justification of the *ars memoriae*, by explaining how it is part of the unique *ars* that is represented by the metaphor of the sun, giving to the book of the world the fruits of its production.

What the first and second step of this defence of mnemonics[276] have in common is the metaphor of inner writing. The metaphor of inner writing belongs to a family of writing metaphors that also includes that of the world as a book (the metaphor of the world as a book is an example of the metaphor of writing). Now, if it is true that the world is the book in which God, the principle creator, writes

273 In *Acrotismus Camoeracensis* Bruno says that fantastic activity is *umbra naturae emulatrix:* "Non enim plus debet habere imaginatio naturalis, vel naturaliter posse debet, quam natura: quinimo quid aliud crediderim esse imaginativam potentiam, praeterquam naturae umbram aemulatricem?", in Jordani Bruni Nolani, *Opera latine conscripta. Publicis sumptibus edita*, I, I, Recensebat F. Fiorentino, 117 (Neapoli: Morano, 1879).

274 See here, p. 139.

275 I am referring to the introduction of the *organum* as a constitutive element of the mnemonic system and the redefinition of *locus* and *imago.* See here, pp. 145–146.

276 Which shows its excess compared to mnemonics because it exceeds the limits of the mnemonic and gnoseological technique, shifting the discussion horizon to ontology.

(metaphor of the world as a book), and according to Bruno it is also true that artificial memory is the book in which man writes (inner writing metaphor), the co-existence and the analogical correspondence between the two metaphors is guaranteed in Bruno's philosophy by the fact that both are expression of an infinite productive force that, in man, is placed in the *phantasia*, *umbra naturae emulatrix*.[277]

Offering a summary and concluding this analysis of the use of the metaphor of inner writing in Giordano Bruno's *ars memoriae*, I would like to go back to my initial hypothesis: the metaphor of writing, which has a lengthy history in the tradition of mnemonics, was given the function of a paradigm in the configuration of Bruno's mnemonics. In fact, we have seen that it was none other than Bruno who placed both the comprehension of the history of mnemonics and the comprehension of the innovation that he is attempting to introduce in it in the wake of the history of the development of the technique of writing. Bruno believes that mnemonics is *scriptura interna* and his contribution to its development has the same epochal value as the invention of mobile character printing.

The analysis of several key passages in the early works on mnemonics is sufficient to demonstrate that this analogy is an operative one, and one that Bruno uses to let himself be guided, not only in the redefinition of the terminology and the precepts of mnemonics, but also to give the *ars memoriae* an ontological foundation. Bruno exploits the familiarity of the metaphor of the world as a book with the metaphor of writing to rethink the relationship between man, nature, and God, thus managing to give the *praxis* a positive value that goes beyond the finite condition of man. The transition from the gnoseological to the ontological level is made possible by the interweaving of the themes of the metaphor of inner writing with those of the metaphor of shadow, laying the foundations for the philosophical elaboration of the notions of order, nature, language, and creativity.

277 From this perspective the initial image of the "Dialogo prelibatorio," *De umbris idearum*, 17–18, with the exhortation to the book to advance, to open and to reveal the unique sun, that is the only productive principle of the universe, is not an exhortation to the book of nature i. e. to God to reveal itself, but to the book of man i. e. to man itself to embrace the understanding of the universe.

Concluding remarks

> Less than a year after I entered medical school in 1952, the structure of DNA was being elucidated. (...) How did the Viennese past leave its lasting traces in the nerve cells of my brain? How was the complex three-dimensional space of the apartment where I steered my toy car woven into my brain's internal representation of the spatial world around me?
>
> – Eric R. Kandel, *In Search of memory: The Emergence of a New Science of Mind*

> The recent discoveries about neuroplasticity make the essence of the intellect more visible, its steps and boundaries easier to mark. They tell us that the tools man has used to support or extend his nervous system (...) have shaped the physical structure of the human mind.
>
> – Nicholas Carr, *The Shallows: What the Internet Is Doing to Our Brains*

1. I decided to explore Giordano Bruno's *ars memoriae* beginning with my personal experience of reading an e-book, because it puts us in a similar situation to the one Bruno, but also many other mnemonists, found themselves in. On the one hand, training the memory through the use of mnemonic precepts entailed making a theoretical effort to understand the mechanics of memory, in order to master the functions of retention and recall, and on the other hand, engendered a more or less conscious reflection on the experience of reading and writing, since the entire tradition of the *ars memoriae* is based on the image of the soul that reads and writes.

This aspect of the history of the ideas about the comprehension of memory presents us with a subject that I deliberately left in the background as I preferred to concentrate here on the methodological aspects of the history of the mnemonic arts and memory theories. The subject is that of the impact of the use of instruments in the understanding of the relationship between man and the world: the instruments we use redefine our relationship with the world, our understanding of it and, according to the neurosciences, even our brain is modified based on which instruments we use.

This also applies to our understanding of memory and, of all the instruments we use, it is particularly true of reading and writing, both of which are activities that are connected to the collection and production of highly singular phenomena that go by the name of *information* and, more generically, *meanings*.

Hence, after studying the history of mnemonics it seems to be evident that there is a conceptual link between the reading and writing experience, and information storage techniques (mnemonics) and memory theories. What I aimed to establish is not only that the history of mnemonics cannot be understood if it is not seen in relation to the history of memory theories, and if one does not show that both fields of study fuelled one another reciprocally, but the same can also be said of the conceptual formation of memory theories. In other words, when we fail to establish relations between the history of memory theories and mnemonic systems we overlook some connections that are fundamental for the modern and contemporary development of philosophical and scientific theories that deal with memory and its understanding.

How we understand the phenomenon of memory, however, both from the mnemonic and theoretical point of view, may only be grasped if we constantly refer to the analogy with writing in its various forms. This premise has been true up to the present, even in the modern scientific theories of memory, as Eric Kandel, the Nobel laureate neuropsychiatrist who investigated the physiological basis of memory storage, shows at the beginning of his autobiographical essay, when he wonders about how memory traces are deposited in his brain's nerve cells. In a certain way, there is so little difference between Kandel's and Aristotle's questions concerning sensations, which are similar to the imprint of a signet ring in wax.

Now that I have restated my hermeneutical hypothesis, I would like to conclude by highlighting some features of the discussion and suggest some possible ways in which this research could develop.

2. How far Bruno went in his philosophical observations on memory is not only revealed by his ability to argue as we have seen in his *De umbris* and which heralds a redefinition of the order in which the elements of human-world-God occur. It is rather the awareness with which Bruno links his philosophical thought to that of the development and history of the writing technique that shows us how deep and radical his reconsideration of the mnemonic tradition must have been.

Precisely because of the radical nature of his reflection I deemed it appropriate to focus the discussion on Bruno on what I termed the hermeneutic hypothesis in my introduction, namely that the leading paradigm to understand memory is the one for writing. For the same reason I proposed to examine some features of Giordano Bruno's first work on mnemonics that would reduce to a minimum the historical and philosophical contextualization of his thought. I also wished to guide the reader's attention at this stage to view the paradigmatic function of the metaphor of inner writing in the *ars memoriae*, as well as to follow the construction of what Blumenberg termed the "metakinetics of historical horizons of meaning," that is the subtle shift of the signifieds so that concepts also have histories. Finally, this is why I insisted on defining the nature of the relation between Bruno's mnemonic systems and the mnemotechnic tradition.

3. Even if Hans Blumenberg's metaphorology is the research methodology adopted to identify my research objective, at the same time my interpretation of Bruno is however rather critical of Blumenberg's. Indeed, my critique is that Blumenberg interprets absolute metaphors in a one-dimensional way, whereas I believe that absolute metaphors should always be studied under the premise that they are multi-dimensional, precisely owing to Blumenberg's "metakinetics of historical horizons of meaning." To illustrate this, if we take the metaphor of the book, we have seen that it becomes an absolute metaphor if we relate it to the metaphor of writing, and in turn this relates to reading. Another example is the metaphor of light that needs to interact with the metaphor of the shadow (and vice versa) in order to acquire paradigmatic force. Hence, although Blumenberg seeks to convey in a historical and philosophical context the abundance and various layers of the meaning of concepts and ideas through the recovery of metaphors that have shaped them, he tends to reduce absolute metaphors to one single dimension of meaning.

This reduction fails to work if we wish to understand the thought of a philosopher like Giordano Bruno and will not work for reasons that are innate to Bruno's reflections themselves, Bruno being familiar with language issues and closely bound up with them.[278] According to Bruno it is reasonable to believe that there are many languages and that philosophy itself may be expressed through different languages resulting in the conviction that different philosophical traditions may equally refer to the same truth. Moreover, each individual is expected to take part in philosophical research and to contribute to it with their own words, even using linguistic contamination between the different kinds of philosophy.

This polymorphic feature of language more generally also concerns the relationship between signs (between letters and symbols, between *poiesis* and *pictura*) and is evident in the structure of the *ars memoriae* from the introduction to the three technical innovations (*subiectum*, *adiectum* and *organum*). In this theoretical context the image of printed writing, where the letters are also geometrical figures, serves both as an aid to comprehension and as a guide to conceptual formulation.

278 Michele Ciliberto *La ruota del tempo: Interpretazione di Giordano Bruno* (Rome: Editori Riuniti, 1986), 208; Michele Ciliberto, *Umbra profunda: Studi su Giordano Bruno* (Rome: Edizioni di Storia e di Letteratura, 1999), 109.

When the metaphor of inner writing is associated with the metaphor of the shadow, Bruno transfers the polymorphism of language analogically to the polymorphism of nature, thus justifying the memory process. Nature's productivity is transposed analogically also to human productivity and this is why I use *creativity* as a synonym for *praxis.*

4. The findings of this research open three further directions for research in the history of ideas and in Bruno studies: 1. The exploration of that highly intricate domain that is Bruno's philosophy through exploiting the use of the inner writing metaphor and its interplay with the other fundamental metaphor of the shadow to interpret the notion of order, nature, language, and creativity in his philosophical works; 2. Bruno's awareness of the history of writing techniques leads to an aspect of Bruno's life that has been little studied and seems worth investigating, namely the world of printing houses and printers where Bruno arranged to have his works printed and where he also worked. Indeed, as I have tried to highlight, the awareness of the link between artificial memory and inner writing was fostered not just in the Dominican environment, but also in Bruno's experience in the printing houses. Even the idea itself that letters are images and their composition occurs when moving them from one place to another resembles the work of a compositor in a printing house who assembles the typesetting; 3. A wider historical reconstruction of the connection between the development of the technique of writing, of philosophical and scientific theories on memory, and mnemonics.

Bibliography

Primary sources

[Cicero]. *Rhetorica ad Herennium.* Translated by Harry Caplan. Loeb Classical Library 403. Cambridge, MA: Harvard University Press, 1954.

Aesop. "The Poor Man and Death." In *Aesop's Fables.* Translated by Laura Gibbs. Oxford: Oxford University Press, 2002.

Albertus Magnus. *Opera omnia. Tomus 28: De bono.* Edited by Heinrich Kühle, Carl Feckes, Bernhard Geyer, and Wilhelm Kübel. Monasterii Westfalorum in aedibus Aschendorff, 1951.

Aristotle. *On the Soul. Parva Naturalia. On Breath.* Translated by W. S. Hett. Loeb Classical Library 288. Cambridge, MA: Harvard University Press, 1957.

Aristotle, Longinus, Demetrius. *Poetics. Longinus: On the Sublime. Demetrius: On Style.* Translated by Stephen Halliwell, W. Hamilton Fyfe, Doreen C. Innes, W. Rhys Robert. Revised by Donald A. Russell. Loeb Classical Library 199. Cambridge, MA: Harvard University Press, 1995.

Aristotle. *Posterior Analitics. Topica.* Translated by Hugh Tredennick and E. S. Forster. Loeb Classical Library 391. Cambridge, MA: Harvard University Press, 1960.

Aristotle. *Art of Rhetoric.* Translated by John Henry Freese. Revised by Gisela Striker. Loeb Classical Library 193. Cambridge, MA: Harvard University Press, 2020.

Augustine. *Confessions.* Translated by Carolyn J.-B. Hammond. Loeb Classical Library 26–27. Cambridge, MA: Harvard University Press, 2014–2016.

Blumenberg, Hans. "'Säkularisation'. Kritik einer Kategorie historischer Illegitimität." In *Die Philosophie und die Frage nach dem Fortschritt*, edited by Helmut Kuhn and Franz Wiedmann, 240–265. Munich: Pustes, 1964.

Blumenberg, Hans. "Approccio antropologico all'attualità della retorica." *Il Verri*, no. 35/36 (1971): 49–72.

Blumenberg, Hans. "Augustinus Anteil an der Geschichte des Begriffs der theoretischen Neugierde." *Revue des Études Augustiniennes* 7, (1961): 35–70.

Blumenberg, Hans. "Beobachtungen an Metapher." *Archiv für Begriffsgeschichte* 15, no. 2 (1971): 161–214.

Blumenberg, Hans. "Curiositas und Veritas. Zur Ideengeschichte von Augustin, Confessiones X 35." In *Studia Patristica VI: Texte und Untersuchungen zur altchristlichen Literatur*, edited by F.L. Cross, 294–302. Berlin: Akademie, 1962.

Blumenberg, Hans. "Das Universum eines Ketzers." Introduction in Giordano Bruno, *Das Aschermittwochsmahl*, 9–51. Translated by Ferdinand Fellmann. Frankfurt am Main: Insel, 1969.

Blumenberg, Hans. "Der kopernikanische Umsturz und die Weltstellung des Menschen. Eine Studie zum Zusammenhang von Naturwissenschaft und Geistesgeschichte." *Studium Generale* 8, (1955): 637–648.

Blumenberg, Hans. "Der Sturz des Protophilosophen. Zur Komik der reinen Theorie." In *Das Komische ("Poetik und Hermeneutik", Band 7.)*, edited by Wolfgang Preisendanz and Rainer Warning, 11–64. Munich: Wilhelm Fink, 1976.

Blumenberg, Hans. "Die ontologische Distanz. Eine Untersuchung über die Krisis der Phänomenologie Husserls" (Habilitationsschrift, Universität Kiel, 1950).

Blumenberg, Hans. "Die Vorbereitung der Neuzeit." *Philosophische Rundschau* 9, (1962): 81–133.

Blumenberg, Hans. "Einleitung." In Nicolaus von Cues, *Die Kunst der Vermutung*, edited by Hans Blumenberg, 7–69. Bremen: Dieterich, 1957.

Blumenberg, Hans. "Ernst Cassirers Gedenkend. Rede bei Entgegennahme des Kuno-Fischer Preises der Universität Heidelberg im Juli 1974." *Revue Internationale de Philosophie* 28, (1974): 456–463.

Blumenberg, Hans. "Kopernikus im Selbstverständnis der Neuzeit." In Akademie der Wissenschaften und der Literatur in Mainz, *Abhandlungen der geistes- und sozialwissenschaftlichen Klasse, Jahrgang 1964*, no. 5 (1965): 339–368.

Blumenberg, Hans. "Kopernikus und das Pathos der Vernunft. Das Denken der Neuzeit im Zeichen der kopernikanischen Wende." *Evangelische Kommentare* 6, (1973): 460–465.

Blumenberg, Hans. "Kosmos und System. Aus der Genesis der Koperikanischen Welt." *Studium Generale* 10, (1957): 61–80.

Blumenberg, Hans. "Kritk und Rezeption antiker Philosophie in der Patristik. Strukturanalysen zur einer Morphologie der Tradition." *Studium Generale* 12, no. 8 (1959): 485–497.

Blumenberg, Hans. "Licht als Metapher der Wahrheit. Im Vorfeld der philosophischen Begriffsbildung." *Studium Generale* 10, (1957): 432–447.

Blumenberg, Hans. "Nachbemerkung zum Bericht über das Archiv für Begriffsgeschichte." In *Jahrbuch der Akademie der Wissenschaften und der Literatur in Mainz*, 79–80. Mainz: Akademie der Wissenschaften und der Literatur, 1967.

Blumenberg, Hans. "Nachdenklichkeit." *Neue Zürcher Zeitung*, Zürich, November 21, 1980.

Blumenberg, Hans. "Nachruf auf Erich Rothacker." In *Jahrbuch der Akademie der Wissenschaften und der Literatur in Mainz*, 70–76. Mainz: Akademie der Wissenschaften und der Literatur, 1966.

Blumenberg, Hans. "Neoplatonismen und Pseudoplatonismen in der Kosmologie und Mechanik der frühen Neuzeit." In *Le Néoplatonisme*, edited by M.P.M. Schuhl and M.P. Hadot, 447–471. Paris: Éditions du CNRS, 1971.

Blumenberg, Hans. "Neugierde und Wissenstrieb. Supplemento zu 'Curiositas'." *Archiv für Begriffsgeschichte* 14, (1970): 7–40.

Blumenberg, Hans. "Ordnungsschwund und Selbstbehauptung. Über Weltverstehen und Weltverhalten im Werden der technischen Epoche." In *Das Problem der Ordnung*, edited by Helmut Kuhn and Franz Wiedmann, 37–57. Meisenheim am Glan: A. Hain, 1962.

Blumenberg, Hans. "Paradigmen zu einer Metaphorologie." *Archiv für Begriffsgeschichte* 6, (1960): 7–142. Translated by Robert Savage as *Paradigms for a Metaphorology*. Ithaca, NY: Cornell University Press, 2010.

Blumenberg, Hans. "Säkularisationsthese und Topoforschung: zur Substantialisierung der Geschichte." In *Topoforschung: eine Dokumentation*, edited by Peter Jehn, 150–154. Frankfurt am Main: Athenäum, 1972.

Blumenberg, Hans. "Selbsterhaltung und Beharrung. Zur Konstitution der neuzeitlichen Rationalität." In *Abhandlungen der Geistes- und Sozialwissenschaftlichen Klasse*, Jahrgang 1969, no. 11, 333–383. Mainz: Akademie der Wissenschaften und der Literatur, 1970.

Blumenberg, Hans. "Versuch zu einer immanenten Geschichte der kopernikanischen Theorie." *Studia Copernicana*, no. 16 (1978): 473–486.

Blumenberg, Hans. "Weltbilder und Weltmodelle." *Nachrichten der Gießener Hochschulgesellschaft* 30, (1961): 67–75.

Blumenberg, Hans. *Arbeit am Mythos*. Frankfurt am Main: Suhrkamp, 1979.

Blumenberg, Hans. *Beiträge zum Problem der Ursprünglichkeit der mittelalterlich-scholastischen Ontologie*. Edited by Benjamin Dahlke and Matthias Laarmann. Frankfurt am Main: Suhrkamp, 2020.

Blumenberg, Hans. *Beschreibung des Menschen*. Edited by Manfred Sommer. Frankfurt am Main: Suhrkamp, 2006.

Blumenberg, Hans. *Das Lachen der Thrakerin: Eine Urgeschichte der Theorie*. Frankfurt am Main: Suhrkamp, 1987.

Blumenberg, Hans. *Die Genesis der kopernikanischen Welt*. Frankfurt am Main: Suhrkamp, 1975.

Blumenberg, Hans. *Die kopernikanische Wende*. Frankfurt am Main: Suhrkamp, 1965.

Blumenberg, Hans. *Die Legitimität der Neuzeit*. 2nd revised edition. Frankfurt am Main: Suhrkamp, 1988. Translated by Robert M. Wallace as *The Legitimacy of the Modern Age*. First MIT Paperback edition. Cambridge, MA: MIT Press, 1985.

Blumenberg, Hans. *Die Lesbarkeit der Welt*. Second edition, revised. Frankfurt am Main: Suhrkamp, 1983.

Blumenberg, Hans. *Die Sorge geht über den Fluß*. Frankfurt am Main: Suhrkamp, 1987.

Blumenberg, Hans. *Höhlenausgänge*. Frankfurt am Main: Suhrkamp, 1989.

Blumenberg, Hans. *Lebenszeit und Weltzeit*. Frankfurt am Main: Suhrkamp, 1986.

Blumenberg, Hans. *Matthäuspassion*. Frankfurt am Main: Suhrkamp, 1988.

Blumenberg, Hans. *Schiffbruch mit Zuschauer: Paradigma einer Daseinsmetapher*. Frankfurt am Main: Suhrkamp, 1979.

Blumenberg, Hans. *Wirklichkeiten in denen wir leben*. Stuttgart: Reclam, 1981.

Bruno, Giordano. *De umbris idearum*. Edited by Rita Sturlese. Florence: Leo S. Olschki, 1991.

Bruno, Giordano. *Dialoghi filosofici italiani*. Edited and with an introduction by Michele Ciliberto. 5th ed. Milan: Mondadori, 2005.

Bruno, Giordano. *Dialoghi italiani*. Edited by Giovanni Aquilecchia and annotated by Giovanni Gentile. 2nd ed. Florence: Sansoni, 1985.

Bruno, Giordano. *Le ombre delle idee, Il canto di Circe, Il sigillo dei sigilli*. Translated and edited by Nicoletta Tirinnanzi. With an introduction by Michele Ciliberto. Milan: Biblioteca Universale Rizzoli, 1997.

Bruno, Giordano. *Opere latine.* Edited by Carlo Monti. Turin: UTET, 1980.
Bruno, Giordano. *Opere lulliane.* Edited by Marco Matteoli, Rita Sturlese, and Nicoletta Tirinnanzi. Milan: Adelphi, 2012.
Bruno, Giordano. *Opere magiche.* Edited by Simonetta Bassi, Rita Sturlese, and Nicoletta Tirinnanzi. Milan: Adelphi, 2000.
Bruno, Giordano. *Opere mnemotecniche.* 2 vols. Edited by di Marco Matteoli, Rita Sturlese, and Nicoletta Tirinnanzi. Milan: Adelphi, 2004–2009.
Bruno, Giordano. *The Ash Wednesday supper.* Translated, annotated and with an introduction by Hilary Gatty. Toronto, ON: University of Toronto Press, 2018.
Jordani Bruni Nolani. *Opera latine conscripta. Publicis sumptibus edita.* 3 vols. Recensebat F. Fiorentino [Felice Tocco, H. Vitelli, V. Imbriani, C. M. Tallarigo]. Neapoli–Florentiae: 1879–91.
- Vol. 1 – Pars 1 continens: 1. *Oratio valedictoria*, 2. *Oratio consolatoria*, 3. *Acrotismus Camoeracensis*, 4. *De immenso et innumerabilibus (Lib. 1, 2, 3)*, publicis sumptibus edita recensebat F. Fiorentino, Neapoli, Morano 1879.
- Vol. 1 – Pars 2 continens: 1. *De immenso et innumerabilibus (Lib. 4, 5, 6, 7, 8)*, 2. *De monade, numero et figura*, Neapoli, Morano 1884.
- Vol. 1 – Pars 3 continens: 1. *Articuli adversus mathematicos*, 2. *De triplici minimo et mensura*, publicis sumptibus edita curantibus F. Tocco et H. Vitelli, Florentiae, Typis Successorum Le Monnier 1889.
- Vol. 1 – Pars 4 continens: 1. *Summa terminorum Metaphysicorum*, 2. *Figuratio physici auditus Aristotelis*, 3. *Mordentium et de Mordentii circino*, publicis sumptibus edita curantibus F. Tocco et H. Vitelli, Florentiae, Typis Successorum Le Monnier 1889.
- Vol. 1: *Dialoghi metafisici.* Bari: Laterza, 1925.
- Vol. 2 – Pars 1 continens: 1. *De umbris idearum*, 2. *Ars memoriae*, 3. *Cantus Circaeus*, publicis sumptibus edita recensebat V. Imbriani et C.M. Tallarigo, Neapoli, Morano 1886.
- Vol. 2 – Pars 2 continens: 1. *De architectura Lulliana*, 2. *Ars reminiscendi*, 3. *Triginta sigilli etc.*, 4. *Sigillus sigillorum*, 5. *Centum et viginti articuli de natura et mundo*, 6. *De lampade combinatoria et De specierum scrutinio*, 7. *Animadversiones in lampadem Lullianam ex codice Augustano nunc primum editae*, curantibus F. Tocco et H. Vitelli, Florentiae, Typis Successorum Le Monnier 1890.
- Vol. 2 – Pars 3 continens: 1. *De lampade venatoria*, 2. *De imaginum compositione*, 3. *Artificium perorandi*, publicis sumptibus edita curantibus F. Tocco et H. Vitelli, Florentiae, Typis Successorum Le Monnier 1889.
- Vol. 2: *Dialoghi morali.* Bari: Laterza, 1927.
- Vol. 3 continens: 1. *Lampas triginta statuarum*, 2. *Libri physicorum Aristotelis explanati*, 3. *De magia et Theses de magia*, 4. *De magia mathematica*, 5. *De principium rerum, elementis et causis*, 6. *Medicina Lulliana*, 7. *De vinculis in genere*, Florentiae, Typis Successorum Le Monnier 1891.
Œuvres complètes de Giordano Bruno. Introduction philologique rigée par Giovanni Aquilecchia, texte établi par Giovanni Aquilecchia, collection dirigée par Yves Hersant et Nuccio Ordine. Paris: Les Belles Lettres, 1993–2000.
- Tome I: *Chandelier.* Introduction philologique générale par Giovanni Aquilecchia, texte établi par Giovanni Aquilecchia, introduction et notes par Giorgio Bárberi Squarotti,

avec un esssai de Nuccio Ordine, traduction de Yves Hersant. 2nd ed. Paris: Les Belles Lettres, 2003.
- Tome II: *Le souper des cendres.* Texte établi par Giovanni Aquilecchia, notes de Giovanni Aquilecchia, préface de Adi Ophir, traduction de Yves Hersant. Paris: Les Belles Lettres, 1994.
- Tome III: *De la cause, du principe et de l'un.* Texte établi par Giovanni Aquilecchia, notes de Giovanni Aquilecchia, introduction de Michele Ciliberto, traduction de Luc Hersant. Paris: Les Belles Lettres, 1996.
- Tome IV: *De l'infini, de l'univers et des mondes.* Texte établi par Giovanni Aquilecchia, notes de Jean Seidengart, introduction de Miguel Angel Granada, traduction de Jean-Pierre Cavaillé. Paris: Les Belles Lettres, 1995.
- Tome V.1: *Expulsion de la bête trionphante, Dialogue 1.* Texte établi par Giovanni Aquilecchia, notes de Maria Pia Ellero, introduction de Nuccio Ordine, traduction de Jean Balsamo. Paris: Les Belles Lettres, 1999.
- Tome V.2: *Expulsion de la bête trionphante, Dialogue 2–3.* Texte établi par Giovanni Aquilecchia, notes de Maria Pia Ellero, introduction de Nuccio Ordine, traduction de Jean Balsamo. Paris: Les Belles Lettres, 1999.
- Tome VI: *Cabale du cheval pégaséen.* Texte établi par Giovanni Aquilecchia, préface et notes de Nicola Badaloni, traduction de Tristan Dagron. Paris: Les Belles Lettres, 1993.
- Tome VII: *Des Fureurs héroiques.* Introduction et notes de Miguel Angel Granada, traduction de Paul-Henri Michel revue par Yves Hersant. Paris: Les Belle Lettres, 1999.

Cicero. *On Invention. The Best Kind of Orator. Topics.* Translated by H. M. Hubbel. Loeb Classical Library 386. Cambridge, MA: Harvard University Press, 1949.

Cicero. *On the Orator: Books 1–2.* Translated by E. W. Sutton and H. Rackham. Loeb Classical Library 348. Cambridge, MA: Harvard University Press, 1942.

Plato. *Euthyphro. Apology. Crito. Phaedo. Phaedrus.* Translated by Harold North Fowler. Loeb Classical Library 36. Cambridge, MA: Harvard University Press, 1914.

Plato. *Laches. Protagoras. Meno. Euthydemus.* Translated by W. R. M. Lamb. Loeb Classical Library 165. Cambridge, MA: Harvard University Press, 1924.

Plato. *Phaedrus.* Edited with and introduction, translation, and commentary by C. J. Rowe. Oxford: Aris and Phillips, 2013.

Plato. *Statesman. Philebus. Ion.* Translated by Harold North Fowler, W. R. M. Lamb. Loeb Classical Library 164. Cambridge, MA: Harvard University Press, 1925.

Plato. *Timaeus.* Translated by R. G. Bury. Loeb Classical Library. Cambridge, MA: Harvard University Press, 1966.

Thomas Aquinas, *Summa theologiae.* Edited by Thomas Gilby. Cambridge: Blackfriars, 1964–1981.

Secondary literature

"Briefwechsel Rigotti–Blumenberg (1983)." In *Nachlaß Blumenberg.* Marbach am Neckar: Deutsches Literaturarchiv.

Adams, David, and Peter Behrenberg. "Bibliographie Hans Blumenberg zum 70. Geburtstag." *Zeitschrift für philosophische Forschung* 44, no. 4 (1990): 647–661.

Adams, David. "Metaphern für den Menschen. Die Entwicklung der anthropologischen Metaphorologie Hans Blumenbergs." *Germanica*, no. 8 (1990): 171–191.

Aquilecchia, Giovanni. "Lo stampatore londinese di Giordano Bruno e altre note per l'edizione della 'Cena'." *Studi di filologia italiana* 18, (1960): 101–162.

Aquilecchia, Giovanni. *Schede bruniane (1950–1991).* Milan: Vecchiarelli, 1993.

Aretin, Johann Christoph. *Systematische Anleitung zur Theorie und Praxis der Mnemonik: nebst den Grundlinien zur Geschichte u. Kritik dieser Wissenschaft: mit 3 Kupfertaf.* Sulzbach, 1810.

Barthes, Roland. "L'ancienne rhétorique." *Communications* 16, (1970): 172–223.

Bassi, Simonetta, ed. *Bruno nel XXI secolo: Interpretazioni e ricerche.* Atti delle giornate di studio, Pisa 15–16 ottobre 2009. Istituto Nazionale di Studi sul Rinascimento, Atti di convegni, vol. 26. Florence: Leo S. Olschki, 2012.

Bassi, Simonetta. "Ancora su Bruno e Copernico." *Rinascimento* 47, (2007): 107–121.

Bassi, Simonetta. "Editoria e filosofia nella seconda metà del '500: Giordano Bruno e i tipografi londinesi." *Rinascimento* 37, (1997): 437–458.

Bassi, Simonetta. *L'arte di Giordano Bruno: Memoria, furore, magia.* Florence: Leo S. Olschki, 2004.

Bernecker, Sven and Kourken Michaelian, eds. *The Routledge Handbook of Philosophy of Memory.* London and New York: Taylor and Francis, 2017.

Betzler, Monika. "Ökonomisierung der Geschichte? Überlegungen zur Metaphorologie Hans Blumenbergs." *Prima Philosophia* 4, no. 2 (1991): 219–249.

Black, Max. *Models and Metaphor.* Ithaca, NY: Cornell University Press, 1962.

Blair, Anna M. *Too much to know: Managing Scholarly Information before the Modern Age*, New Haven and London: Yale University Press, 2010.

Bodei, Remo. "Distanza di sicurezza." Introduction in *Naufragio con spettatore: Paradigma di una metafora dell'esistenza*, by Hans Blumenberg, 7–23. Bologna: Il Mulino, 1985.

Bodei, Remo. "Il libro come metafora del mondo." Introduction in *La leggibilità del mondo: Il libro come metafora della natura*, by Hans Blumenberg, ix–xxv. Bologna: Il Mulino, 1999.

Bodei, Remo. "Il viaggio della vita: Blumenberg e le metafore." In *La filosofia del Novecento*, 151–153. Milan: Donzelli, 1997.

Bolzoni, Lina, Vittorio Erlindo, and Marcello Morelli. *Memoria e memorie.* Convegno internazionale di studi, Accademia Nazionale dei Lincei, Roma 18–19 maggio 1995, Florence: L. S. Olschki, 1998.

Bolzoni, Lina. "A Reply to Mary Carruthers Inventional Mnemonics and the Ornaments of Style." *Connotations* 3, no. 1 (1993/1994): 37–42.

Bolzoni, Lina. "Come costruire il tesoro della memoria. La tradizione mnemotecnica." In *Ricerche sulle selve rinascimentali*, edited by Paolo Cherchi, 157–173. Ravenna: Longo 1999.

Bolzoni, Lina. "Fresken, illustrierte Bücher und mnemonische Systeme. Die Gedächtniskunst und die Kunst der Transkodifikation." In *Seelen, Maschinen: Gattungstraditionen, Funktionen und Leistungsgrenzen der Mnemotechniken vom späten Mittelalter bis zum Beginn der Moderne*, edited by Jörg Jochen Berns and Wolfgang Neuber, 463–480. Vienna: Böhlau, 2000.

Bolzoni, Lina. "L'arte della memoria nell'età della stampa: parole e immagini, memoria e invenzione." In *Scienza e cultura italiana*, edited by Raffaella Castagnola, Paolo Parachini, 77–102. Lugano, CH: G. Casagrande, 2005.

Bolzoni, Lina. "Les images du livre et les images de la mémoire." In *Le livre illustré italien au XVIe siècle. Texte/Image*, edited by M. Plaisance, 151–176. Paris: Klienсksieck, 1999.

Bolzoni, Lina. "Macchine per la memoria e per l'invenzione fra Quattro e Cinquecento." In *Machina: XI Colloquio internazionale del lessico intellettuale europeo*, edited by M. Veneziani, 273–296. Florence: Leo S. Olschki, 2005.

Bolzoni, Lina. "The Play of Memory between Word and Images." In *Memory and Oblivion*, edited by Reinik Wessel and Jeroen Stumpel, 11–18. Proceedings of the 21st International Congress of the History of Art held in Amsterdam, 1-7 September 1996. Boston: Kluwer Academic Publisher, 1999.

Bolzoni, Lina. *La rete delle immagini: Predicazione in volgare dalle origini a Bernardino da Siena.* Turin: Einaudi, 2002.

Buch, Robert, and Daniel Weidner, eds. *Blumenberg lesen: Ein Glossar.* Frankfurt am Main: Suhrkamp, 2014.

Canone, Eugenio, ed. *Brunus redivivus: Momenti della fortuna di Giordano Bruno nel XIX secolo.* Rome: Istituti editoriali e poligrafici internazionali, 1998.

Canone, Eugenio, ed. *Giordano Bruno: Gli anni napoletani e la 'peregrinatio' europea; Immagini, testi, documenti.* Cassino: Università degli Studi, 1992.

Carchia, Gianni. "Variazioni intorno al concetto di 'autoaffermazione'." *Iride*, no. 12, 1994: 451–456.

Carr, Nicholas. *The Shallows: What the Internet Is Doing to Our Brains.* New York: W.W. Norton, 2011.

Carruthers, Mary and Jon Ziolkowski, eds. *The Medieval Craft of Memory: An Anthology of Texts and Pictures.* Philadelphia, PA: University of Pennsylvania Press, 2002.

Carruthers, Mary. *The Book of Memory.* Cambridge: Cambridge University Press, 2008.

Carruthers, Mary. *The Craft of Thought: Meditation, Rhetoric, and the Making of Images, 400–1200.* Cambridge: Cambridge University Press 2003.

Cassirer, Ernst. *An Essay on Man: An Introduction to a Philosophy of Human Culture.* New Haven, CT: Yale University Press, 1944.

Cassirer, Ernst. *Gesammelte Werke. Hamburger Ausgabe.* Edited by Birgit Recki. Hamburg: Felix Meiner, 1998–2009.

Cassirer, Ernst. *Individuum und Kosmos in der Philosophie der Renaissance.* Leipzig: G.B. Teubner, 1927.

Cassirer, Ernst. *Substanzbegriff und Funktionsbegriff.* Berlin: Bruno Cassirer, 1910.

Castelli, Enrico, ed. *Umanesimo e simbolismo.* Padua: CEDAM, 1958.

Catanorchi, Olivia, and Diego Pirillo, eds. *Favole, metafore, storie: Seminario su Giordano Bruno.* Pisa: Edizioni della Normale, 2007.

Ciliberto, Michele, and Nicholas Mann, eds. *Giordano Bruno, 1583–1585: The English Experience/L'esperienza inglese.* Atti del convegno, Londra 3–4 giugno 1994. Istituto Nazionale di Studi sul Rinascimento, Atti di Convegno, vol. 20. Florence: Leo S. Olschki, 1997.

Ciliberto, Michele. *Il Rinascimento: Storia di un dibattito.* Firenze: La Nuova Italia, 1975.

Ciliberto, Michele, ed. *Giordano Bruno: Parole concetti immagini.* 3 vols. Pisa: Edizioni della Normale, 2014.

Ciliberto, Michele. "... Per speculum et in aenigmate ..." Introduction in *Opere mnemotecniche: Tomo II* by Giordano Bruno, ix–xlvi. Milan: Adelphi, 2009.

Ciliberto, Michele. "Bruno nel XX secolo. Filosofia, magia, ermetismo." In *La mente di Giordano Bruno*, edited by Fabrizio Meroi, vii–xxxvi. Florence: Leo S. Olschki, 2004.

Ciliberto, Michele. "Fortune (e sfortune) di un maestro 'onnisciente' e 'quasi divino'." Introduction in *Opere Lulliane* by Giordano Bruno, xi–xli. Milan: Adelphi, 2012.

Ciliberto, Michele. *Giordano Bruno.* Rome/Bari: Laterza, 1990.

Ciliberto, Michele. *Introduzione a Giordano Bruno.* Rome/Bari: Laterza, 2010.

Ciliberto, Michele. *L'occhio di Atteone: Nuovi studi su Giordano Bruno.* Rome: Edizioni di Storia e di Letteratura, 2002.

Ciliberto, Michele. *La ruota del tempo: Interpretazione di Giordano Bruno.* Rome: Editori Riuniti, 1986.

Ciliberto, Michele. *Lessico di Giordano Bruno.* 2 vols. Rome: Edizioni dell'Ateneo e Bizzarri, 1979.

Ciliberto, Michele. *Pensare per contrari: Disincanto e utopia nel Rinascimento.* Rome: Edizioni di Storia e di Letteratura, 2005.

Ciliberto, Michele. *Umbra profunda: Studi su Giordano Bruno.* Rome: Edizioni di Storia e di Letteratura, 1999.

Cox, Virginia and John O. Ward, eds. *The Rhetoric of Cicero in its Medieval and Early Renaissance Commentary Tradition.* Leiden: Brill, 2006.

Curtius, Ernst Robert. "Schrift- und Buchmetaphorik in der Weltliteratur." *Deutsche Vierteljahresschrift* 20, no. 4, (1942): 359–411.

Daston, Lorraine. "The sciences of the archive." *Osiris* 7, no. 1 (2012): 156–187.

Daston, Lorraine, ed. *Science in the Archives: Pasts Presents Futures.* Chicago: University of Chicago Press, 2015.

Davidson, Donald. *Inquiries into Truth and Interpretation.* Oxford: Oxford University Press, 1985.

Dell'Omodarme, Francesca. "Frances A. Yates interprete di Giordano Bruno: appunti per una ricerca." *Rinascimento* 41, (2001): 353–374.

Derrida, Jacques. "La mythologie blanche. La métaphore dans le texte philosophique." In *Marges de la philosophie*, 247ff. Paris: Les Éditions de Minuit, 1972.

Derrida, Jacques. "Le retrait de la métaphore." In *Psyché: Inventions de l'autre*, 63–93. Paris: Galilée, 1987–1988.

Descartes, René. *A Discourse on the Method of Correctly Conducting One's Reason and Seeking Truth in the Sciences.* Translated by Ian Maclean. Oxford: Oxford University Press, 2006.

Dougherty, Carol. "Ships, Walls, Men Classical Athens and the Poetics of Infrastructure." In *Space, Place, and Landscape in Ancient Greek Literature and Culture*, edited by Kate Gilhuly and Nancy Worman, 130–170. Cambridge: Cambridge University Press, 2014.

Eco, Umberto. "Bruno: combinatoria e mondi infiniti." In *La ricerca della lingua perfetta nella cultura europea*, 145–151. Rome/Bari: Laterza, 1993.

Eco, Umberto. "Metafora e semiosi." In *Semiotica e filosofia del linguaggio*, 141–198. Turin: Einaudi, 1997.

Eco, Umberto. "Mnemotecniche come semiotiche." In *La cultura della memoria*, edited by Lina Bolzoni and Pietro Corsi, 35–56. Bologna: Il Mulino, 1992.

Ellero, Maria Pia. "Tra parola e immagine. Retorica e arte della memoria nell'*Artificium perorandi* e negli scritti magici." In *La mente di Giordano Bruno*, edited by Fabrizio Meroi, 343–368. Florence: Leo Olschki, 2004.

Eusterschulte, Anne. "Bruno." In *NaturStücke: Zur Kulturgeschichte der Natur*, edited by Werner Ingensiep and R. Hoppe-Salier, 69–100. Stuttgart: Edition Tertium, 1996.

Eusterschulte, Anne. *Analogia entis seu mentis: Analogie als erkenntnistheorethisches Prinzip in der Philosophie Giordano Brunos.* Würzburg: Königshausen und Neumann, 1997.

Eusterschulte, Anne. *Giordano Bruno zur Einführung.* Hamburg: Junius, 1997.

Ferrari, G. R. F. *Listening to the Cicadas: A Study of Plato's* Phaedrus. Cambridge: Cambridge University Press, 1990.

Fintoni, Monica. "'Mnemosine': dal *Sigillus sigillorum* ai *Dialoghi italiani.*" In *Giordano Bruno, 1583–1585: The English Experience*, edited by Michele Ciliberto and Nicholas Mann, 23–35. Florence: Leo S. Olschki, 1997.

Firpo, Luigi. *Il processo di Giordano Bruno.* Rome: Salerno Editrice, 1993.

Floridi, Luciano. *Information: A Very Short Introduction.* Oxford: Oxford University Press, 2010.

Floridi, Luciano. *The Ethics of Information.* Oxford: Oxford University Press, 2013.

Floridi, Luciano. *The Fourth Revolution: How the Infosphere Is Reshaping Human Reality.* Oxford: Oxford University Press, 2016.

Floridi, Luciano. *The Philosophy of Information.* Oxford: Oxford University Press, 2013.

Freud, Sigmund. *Gesammelte Werke: chronologisch geordnet.* Edited by Anna Freud, et al. Frankfurt am Main: S. Fischer, 1968–1978.

Gadamer, Hans Georg. Review of *Die Legitmität der Neuzeit*, by Hans Blumenberg. *Philosophische Rundschau* 15, (1968): 201–209.

Galilei, Galileo. *The Assayer.* Translated by Stillman Drake. New York: Anchor Book, 1957.

Garin, Eugenio. "La nuova scienza e il simbolo del 'libro'." *Rivista Critica di Storia della Filosofia* 29, no. 3 (July-September, 1974): 328–339.

Garin, Eugenio. *La cultura filosofica del Rinascimento: Ricerche e documenti.* 2nd edition. Florence: Sansoni, 1979.

Garin, Eugenio. *Medioevo e Rinascimento.* Bari: Laterza, 1954.

Giglioni, Guido. "Who is afraid of Frances Yates? 'Giordano Bruno and the Hermetic tradition' (1964) fifty years later." *Bruniana and Campanelliana* 20, no. 2 (2014): 421–432.

Goethe, Johann Wolfgang. *West-Östlicher Divan: 2. Noten und Abhandlungen.* Berlin: Akademie, 1952.

Goldmann, Luzia, ed. *Phänomen und Begriff der Metapher: Vorschlag zur Systematisierung der Theoriegeschichte.* Berlin: De Gruyter, 2018.

Habermas, Jürgen. *Postmetaphysical Thinking: Philosophical Essays.* Translated by William Mark Hohengarten. Cambridge, MA: MIT Press, 1992.

Haefliger, Jürg. *Imaginationssysteme: Erkenntnistheoretische, anthropologische und mentalitätshistorische Aspekte der Metaphorologie Hans Blumenbergs.* Bern: Lang, 1996.

Hajdu, Helga. *Das Mnemotechnische Schrifttum des Mittelalters.* Vienna: F. Leo and Comp., 1936.

Haverkamp, Anselm, "Paradigma Metapher, Metapher Paradigma. Zur Metakinetik hermeneutischer Horizonte (Blumenberg/Derrida, Kuhn/Foucault, Black/White)." In

Epochenschwelle und Epochenbewusstsein ('Poetik und Hermeneutik', 12), edited by Reinhart Herzog and Reinhart Koselleck, 547–560. Paderborn: Wilhelm Fink, 1987.

Hegel, G.W.F. "Glauben und Wissen oder die Reflexionsphilosophie der Subjectivität, in der Vollständigkeit ihrer Formen, als Kantische, Jakobische und Fichtesche Philosophie." In *Gesammelte Werke, Bd. 4*, by Georg W.F. Hegel, 315–324. Edited by Hartmut Buchner and Otto Pöggeler. Hamburg: Felix Meiner Verlag, 1968.

Hufnagel, Henning and Anne Eusterschulte, eds. *Turning Tradition Upside Down: Rethinking Giordano Bruno's Enlightment.* Budapest: Central European University Press, 2013.

Ingram, David. "Blumenberg and the Philosophical Grounds of Historiography." *History and Theory* 29, no. 1, (1990): 1–15.

Ingram, David. "The Copernican Revolution Revisited: Paradigm, Metaphor and Incommensurability in the History of Science. Blumenberg response to Kuhn and Davidson." *History of the Human Sciences* 6, no. 4 (1993): 11–35.

Jaeschke, Walter. "Säkularisierung." In *Handbuch religionswissenschaftlicher Grundbegriffe. Band 5.* Edited by Hubert Cancik, Burkhard Gladigow, and Karl-Heinz Kohl, 9–20. Stuttgart: W. Kohlkammer, 1998.

Jaeschke, Walter. *Hegel Handbuch: Leben, Werk, Wirkung.* Stuttgart: J.B. Metzler, 2003.

Jauss, Hans Robert. "Eine doppelte Konjunktur: Goethe und Napoleon–Valéry und Blumenberg." *Akzente* 37, no. 3 (1990): 216–220.

Johnson, Mark, ed. *Philosophical Perspective on Metaphor.* Chicago, IL: Minnesota University Press, 1981.

Jong, Irene J. F., ed. *Space in Ancient Greek Literature: Studies in Ancient Greek Narrative.* Leiden/Boston: Brill, 2012.

Kandel, Eric R. *In Search of memory: The Emergence of a New Science of Mind.* New York: W.W. Norton, 2006.

Kant, Immanuel. *Critique of the Power of Judgement.* Cambridge: Cambridge University Press, 2000.

Kant, Immanuel. *Prolegomena zu einer jeden künftigen Metaphysik, die als Wissenschaft wird auftreten können.* Edited by Konstantin Pollok. Hamburg: Felix Meiner, 2001.

Koerner, Joseph Leo. "Ideas about the Thing, Not the Thing Itself: Hans Blumenberg's Style." *History of the Human Sciences* 6, no. 4, (1993): 1–10. This number contains a monographic section dedicated to Hans Blumenberg, pp. 1–116, with contributions by David Ingram, Robert B. Pippin, Charles Turner, Bruce Krajewski, Donald R. Kelley, Wayne Hudson.

Konersmann, Ralf. "Geduld zur Sache. Ausblick auf eine Philosophie für Leser." *Neue Rundschau* 109, no. 1, (1998): 30–46.

Kuhn, Thomas S. *The Copernican Revolution: Planetary Astronomy in the Development of Western Thought.* Cambridge, MA: Harvard University Press, 1995.

Lakoff, George and Mark Johnson. *Metaphors We Live By.* Chicago: University of Chicago Press, 1980.

Leinkauf, Thomas, ed. *Der Naturbegriff in der Frühen Neuzeit: Semantische Perspektiven zwischen 1500 und 1700.* Tübingen: Max Niemeyer, 2005.

Leinkauf, Thomas, ed. *Giordano Bruno in Wittenberg (1586–1588): Aristoteles, Raimundus Lullus, Astronomie.* Pisa: Istituti Editoriali e Poligrafici Internazionali, 2004.

Leinkauf, Thomas. "Die episthemische Funktion der 'imaginatio' bei Giordano Bruno. Überlegungen zu *De imaginum compositione*." In *Imagination und Repräsentation: Zwei Bildsphären der Frühen Neuzeit*, edited by Horst Bredekamp, Pablo Schneider, and Christiane Kruse, 13–33. Paderborn: Wilhelm Fink, 2010.

Lewitscharoff, Sibylle. *Blumenberg*. Frankfurt am Main: Suhrkamp, 2011.

Löwith, Karl. *Meaning in History*. Chicago: University of Chicago Press, 1949.

Löwith, Karl. Review of *Die Legitmität der Neuzeit*, by Hans Blumenberg. *Philosophische Rundschau* 15, (1968): 196–201.

Lübbe, Anders H. *Säkularisierung: Geschichte eines ideenpolitischen Begriffs*. 3. Auflage mit einem neuen Nachwort. Freiburg: Alber, 2003.

Mann, Thomas. *Joseph and His Brothers*. Translated by John E. Woods. New York: Everyman's Library, 2005.

Marquard, Odo. "Lebenszeit und Lesezeit: Bemerkungen zum Oeuvre Hans Blumenberg." *Akzente* 37, no. 3, (1990): 268–271.

Matteoli, Marco and Rita Sturlese, "La nuova 'arte' del Bruno in tre enigmi." *Rinascimento* 41, (2001): 113–165.

Matteoli, Marco. *Nel tempio di Mnemosine: L'arte della memoria di Giordano Bruno*. Pisa: Edizioni della Normale, 2019.

Matteoli, Marco. "arte della memoria, mnemotecnica." *Bruniana and Campanelliana* 14, no. 1, (2008): 83–89.

Matteoli, Marco. "Geometrie della memoria. Schemi, ordini e figure della mnemotecnica di Giordano Bruno." In *Aspetti della geometria nell'opera di Giordano Bruno*, edited by Ornella Pompeo Faracovi, 129–170. Lugano: Agorà, 2012.

Matteoli, Marco. "Il canto di Circe e la 'magia' della nuova arte della memoria del Bruno." In *La magia nell'Europa moderna: Tra antica sapienza e filosofia naturale*, edited by Fabrizio Meroi, 467–488. Florence: Leo S. Olschki, 2007.

Matteoli, Marco. "Immaginazione, conoscenza e filosofia: l'arte della memoria di Giordano Bruno." In *Bruno nel XXI secolo: Interpretazioni e ricerche*, edited by Simonetta Bassi, 17–38. Atti delle giornate di studio, Pisa 15–16 ottobre 2009, Istituto Nazionale di Studi sul Rinascimento, Atti di convegni, vol. 26. Florence: Leo S. Olschki, 2012.

Matteoli, Marco. "L'arte della memoria nei primi scritti mnemotecnici di Bruno." *Rinascimento* 40, (2000): 75–122.

Matteoli, Marco. "Principio di mediazione e posizioni antigerarchiche in Raimondo Lullo e Giordano Bruno." In *La mente di Giordano Bruno*, edited by Fabrizio Meroi, 397–408. Florence: Leo Olschki, 2004.

Melandri, Enzo. "Per una filosofia della metafora." Introduction in *Paradigmi per una metaforologia* by Hans Blumenberg, vii–xiv. Bologna: Il Mulino, 1969.

Meroi, Fabrizio, ed. *La mente di Giordano Bruno*. Florence: Leo S. Olschki, 2004.

Metaphor and Symbolic Activity. A Quarterly Journal. 1986/1996. Currently known as *Metaphor and Symbol* (1997/current).

Michaelian, Kourken, Dorothea Debus, and Denis Perrin, eds. *New Directions in the Philosophy of Memory*. London and New York: Taylor and Francis, 2018.

Monod, Jean-Claude. *La querelle de la sécularisation de Hegel à Blumenberg*. Paris: Vrin, 2002.

Montiglio, Silvia. *Wandering in Ancient Greek Culture*. Chicago: University of Chicago Press, 2005.

Moxter, Michael. "Die schönen Ungenauigkeiten. Hans Blumenbergs phänomenologische Variationen." *Neue Rundschau* 109, no. 1 (1998): 83–93.

Müller, Severin. "Paradigmenwechsel und Epochenwandel. Zur Struktur wissenschaftshistorischer und geschichtlicher Mobilität bei Thomas S. Kuhn, Hans Blumenberg und Hans Freyer." *Saeculum* 32, (1981): 1–30.

Noël, Marie-Pierre. "Plato, Alcidamas, and Isocrates on Logography." In *New Chapters in the History of Rhetoric*, 91–107. Edited by Laurent Pernot. Leiden: Brill, 2009.

Nuzzo, Enrico. "Le figure metaforiche nel linguaggio filosofico di Giordano Bruno." In *La mente di Giordano Bruno*, edited by Fabrizio Meroi, 13–60. Florence: Leo S. Olschki, 2004.

Oliveiro, Alberto. "Dall'arte della memoria alla biologia della memoria." *Physis. Rivista internazionale di storia della scienza* 38, no. 1/2, (2001): 111–132.

Ortony, Andrew. *Metaphor and Thought.* Cambridge: Cambridge University Press, 1979.

Paprotté, Wolf and René Dirven, editors. *The Ubiquity of Metaphor: Metaphor in Language and Thought.* Amsterdam: John Benjamins: 1985.

Pick, Edward. *Memory and its Doctors.* London: Thurber, 1888.

Pöggeler, Otto. "Dialektik und Topik." In *Hermeneutik und Dialektik: Aufsätze: Hans-Georg Gadamer zum 70. Geburtstag. Vol 2: Sprache und Logik, Theorie der Auslegung und Probleme der Einzelwissenschaften*, edited by Rüdiger Bubner, Konrad Kramer, Reiner Wiehl, 273–310. Tübingen: Mohr, 1970.

Quintilian. *The Orator's Education.* Edited and translated by Donald A. Russell. 5 vols. Loeb Classical Library 124–127, 494. Cambridge, MA: Harvard University Press, 2001.

Regius, Raphael. *Raphaelis Regii ducenta problemata in totidem institutionis oratoriæ Quintiliani deprauationes. Eiusdem quæstio Utrum ars rhetorica ad Herenium falso Ciceroni inscribatur. Eiusdem de laudibus eloquentiæ panegyricus.* Venice, 1492.

Ricci, Saverio. *Giordano Bruno nell'Europa del Cinquecento.* Rome: Salerno Editrice, 2000.

Ricœur, Paul. *La métaphore vive.* Paris: Seuil, 1975.

Rolf, Eckard, ed. *Metapherntheorien: Typologie – Darstellung – Bibliographie.* Berlin: De Gruyter, 2005.

Romberch, Johannes. *Congestiorum artificiose memorie.* Venice, 1520.

Rorty, Richard. "Against Belatedness." *London Review of Books*, June/July 1983: 3–5.

Rosselli, Cosma. *Thesaurus artificiosae memoriae.* Venice, 1519 [or 1579].

Rossi, Paolo. *Clavis universalis: Arti della memoria e logica combinatoria da Lullo a Leibniz.* 3rd ed. Bologna: Il Mulino, 2000. Translated by Stephen Clucas as *Logic and the Art of Memory: The Quest for a Universal Language.* Chicago: Chicago University Press, 2000.

Rossi, Paolo. *Francesco Bacone: Dalla magia alla scienza.* Turin: Einaudi, 1974.

Rossi, Paolo. *Il passato, la memoria, l'oblio: Sei saggi di storia delle idee.* Bologna: Il Mulino, 2001.

Rothacker, Eric. *Das Buch der Natur: Materialien und Grundsätzliches zur Metapherngeschichte.* Edited by Wilhelm Perpeet. Bonn: Bouvier, 1979.

Rothacker, Eric. *Mensch und Geschichte: Studien zur Anthropologie und Wissenschaftsgeschichte.* Bonn: Athenäum, 1950.

Rothacker, Eric. *Zur Genealogie des menschlichen Bewusstseins.* Bonn: Bouvier, 1966.

Rothe, Richard. *Die Anfänge der christlichen Kirche und ihrer Verfassung: Ein geschichtlicher Versuch. Band 1.* Wittenberg: Zimmermann, 1837.

Schlaffer, Hannelore. "Ein Grund mehr zur Sorge. Hans Blumenberg jüngste Veröffentlichungen." *Merkur* 42, no. 4 (1998): 328–332.

Schmidt-Biggemann, Wilhelm. *Philosophia perennis: Historische Umrisse abendländischer Spiritualität in Antike, Mittelalter und Früher Neuzeit.* Frankfurt am Main: Suhrkamp, 1988.

Schmitt, Carl. *Political Theology: Four Chapters on the Concept of Sovereignity.* Edited and translated by George Schwab. With a foreword by Tracy B. Strong. Chicago: University of Chicago Press, 2005.

Shibles, Warren A. *Metaphor: An Annotated Bibliography and History.* Whitewater, WI: Language Press, 1971.

Sorabji, Richard. *Aristotle on Memory.* Chicago: University of Chicago Press, 2004.

Specht, Benjamin, ed. *Epoche und Metapher: Systematik und Geschichte Kultureller Bildlichkeit.* Berlin: De Gruyter, 2014.

Sturlese, Rita. "Arte della natura e arte della memoria in Giordano Bruno." *Rinascimento,* n.s., 40, (2000): 123–141.

Tessicini, Dario. *I dintorni dell'infinito: Giordano Bruno e l'astronomia del Cinquecento.* Pisa: Fabrizio Serra, 2007.

Tirinnanzi, Nicoletta. "'*Ars*' e '*Phantasia*' in Giordano Bruno." *Esercizi filosofici,* 1 (1992): 109–131.

Tirinnanzi, Nicoletta. "L'occhio e la pagina scritta. Aspetti della riflessione di Bruno sulla memoria tra il *De umbris idearum* e il *De magia naturali.*" In *Tracce della mente: Teorie della memoria da Platone ai moderni.* Edited by Maria Michela Sassi, 541–566. Pisa: Edizioni della Normale, 2007.

Tirinnanzi, Nicoletta. Introduction to *Opere mnemotecniche: Tomo I,* by Giordano Bruno, xiv–xix. Edited by Marco Matteoli, Rita Sturlese, and Nicoletta Tirinnanzi. Milan: Adelphi, 2004.

Tirinnanzi, Nicoletta. *Umbra naturae: L'immaginazione da Ficino a Bruno.* Rome: Edizioni di Storia e Letteratura, 2000.

Tocco, Felice. *Le opere latine di Giordano Bruno esposte e confrontate con le italiane.* Florence: Le Monnier, 1889.

van Noppen, Jean-Pierre and Edith Hols, eds. *Metaphor II: A Classified Bibliography of Publications from 1985 to 1990.* Amsterdam: John Benjamins, 1990.

van Noppen, Jean-Pierre. "More Books on Metaphor." *Revue Belge de philologie et d'histoire* 66, no. 3 (1988): 618–645.

van Noppen, Jean-Pierre. *Metaphor: A Bibliography of post-1970 Publications.* Amsterdam: John Benjamins, 1985.

Vasoli, Cesare. "Arte della memoria e predicazione." *Lettere Italiane* 38, no. 4 (October/December 1986): 478–499.

Vasoli, Cesare. "Bruno e 'l'arte della memoria'." *Il veltro. Rivista della civiltà italiana* 44, no. 3/4 (2000): pp. 299–311.

Vasoli, Cesare. "Bruno e i suoi primi scritti sull'arte della memoria." *Physis,* n.s., 38, no. 1/2 (2001): 19–39.

Vasoli, Cesare. "La metafora nel linguaggio magico rinascimentale." In *Simbolo, metafora, allegoria,* edited by Daniela Goldin. Atti del 4. convegno italo-tedesco, Bressanone, 1976, 145–155. Padua: Liviana, 1980.

Vasoli, Cesare. *La dialettica e la retorica dell'Umanesimo: "Invenzione" e "Metodo" nella cultura del XV e XVI secolo.* Milan: Feltrinelli, 1968.

Voegelin, Eric. "Philosophie der Politik in Oxford." *Philosophische Rundschau* 1, no. 1, (1953/54): 23–48.

Volkmann, Ludwig. "Ars memorativa." *Jahrbuch des Kunsthistorischen Sammlungen in Wien*, n.s., 3 (1929): 111–200.

von Harnack, Adolf. *Lehrbuch der Dogmengeschichte.* 3 vols. Freiburg i. Br.: Mohr, 1886–1890.

von Harnack, Adolf. *Das Wesen des Christentums.* Leipzig: J.C. Hinrichs, 1900.

von Harnack, Adolf. *Die Mission und Ausbreitung des Christentums in den ersten drei Jahrhunderten.* Leipzig: J.C. Hinrichs, 1902.

von Harnack, Adolf. *Marcion: Das Evangelium von fremden Gott: eine Monographie zur Geschichte der Grundlegung der katholischen Kirche.* Leipzig: J.C. Hinrichs, 1921.

von Meiern, Johann Gotftried. *Acta Pacis Westphalicae publica oder Westphälische Friedens-Handlungen und Geschichte.* Hannover: 1734–1736.

von Samsonow, Elisabeth. "Einleitung." In *Über die Monas, die Zahl und die Figur als Elemente einer sehr geheimen Physik, Mathematik und Metaphysik*, by Giordano Bruno, ix–l. Translated and commented by Elisabeth von Samsonow, Martin Mulsow, Ingomar Lorch, and Matthias Reuss. Hamburg: Meiner, 1991.

Wallace, Robert. "Introduction to Blumenberg." *New German Critique*, no. 32 (Spring/Summer 1984): 93–108.

Wetz, Franz Joseph, and Hermann Timm, eds. *Die Kunst des Überlebens: Nachdenken über Hans Blumenberg.* Frankfurt am Main: Suhrkamp, 1999.

Wetz, Franz Joseph. *Hans Blumenberg zur Einführung.* Hamburg: Junius, 1993.

Yates, Frances A. "Giordano Bruno's conflict with Oxford." *Journal of the Warburg Institute* 2, no. 3 (January 1939): 227–242.

Yates, Frances A. *Giordano Bruno and the Hermetic Tradition.* Chicago: University of Chicago Press, 1964.

Yates, Frances A. *John Florio: The Life of an Italian in Shakespeare's England.* London: Cambridge University Press, 1934.

Yates, Frances A. *The Art of Memory.* London: Pimlico, 2000.

Zabel, Hermann. *Verweltlichung/Säkularisierung: Zur Geschichte einer Interpretationskategorie.* (PhD Diss. Münster: Fakultät der Westfälischen Wilhelms-Universität, 1968).

Figures

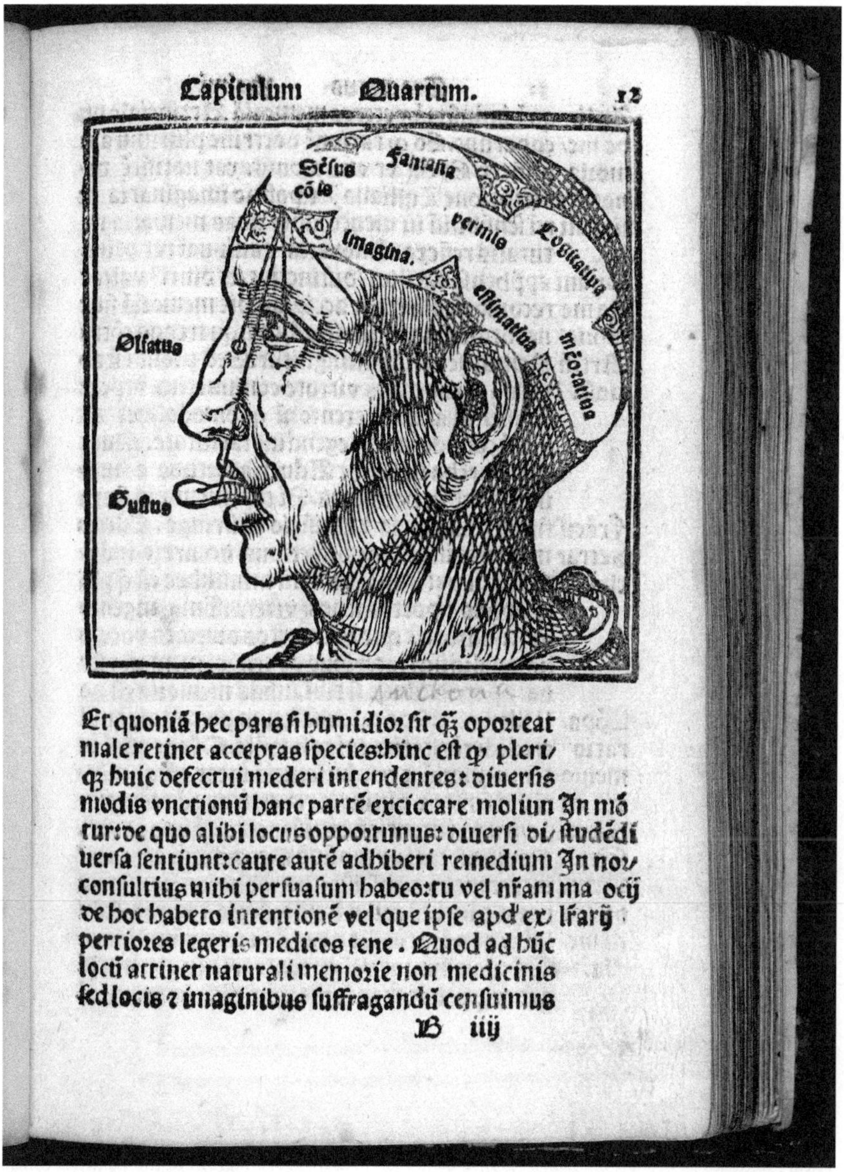
Capitulum Quartum. 12

Et quoniā hec pars si humidior sit q̄z oporteat male retinet acceptas species: hinc est q̄ plerique huic defectui mederi intendentes: diuersis modis vnctionū hanc partē exciccare moliuntur: de quo alibi locus opportunus: diuersi diuersa sentiunt: caute autē adhiberi remedium consultius mihi persuasum habeo: tu vel nostram de hoc habeto intentionē vel que ipse apud expertiores legeris medicos tene. Quod ad hūc locū attinet naturali memorie non medicinis sed locis & imaginibus suffragandū censuimus

In mō studēdi In nō ma ocij lr̄arū

B iiij

Figure 1. Johannes Romberch, *Congestorium artificiose memorie*, 1520. Head with areas annotated. Credit: Wellcome Collection, London.

Figure 2. Cosma Rosselli, *Thesaurus artificiosae memoriae*, 1579. Diagram of the faculties of the soul arranged in cells within the brain. Credit: Wellcome Collection, London. Public Domain Mark 1.0. No modifications have been made.

Tractatus Secundi

Quarta regula

Lucidi-tas no-cet

¶ Ea deniq3 locis inerit q̄litas ne vel nimis obſcura ſint
vel lucida nimis: aut figura vel forma ꝯſimili vel etiã ſphe
rica: Excellens quippe obiectum corrũpit ſenſum: ⁊ hic non
ꝓportionatum minus a potẽtia ſuſcipit. Nõ enim noctua
lumẽ ꝯtuetur ſolare: ⁊ exuperantia cãdoris ꝯturbat viſum
ne obiecta diſcernat: ita ⁊ in nimia claritate locoꝝ ꝯcepta:
reuerberationẽ patit fantaſia vt quodammodo imaginatio
ꝯturbet. Accedit inſup ꝙ mens in perpulchro (cuiuſmodi
eſt claritas) oblectata minus aduertat nõ tãto decore perſpi
cuũ: Vñ non viridia prata: ⁊ amenos cãpos ſeu iucunda

Figure 3. Johannes Romberch, *Congestorium artificiose memorie*, 1520. Illustration of the rule for choosing the *loci*, according to which the proportions of the human body should be respected to ensure that the mnemonic *locus* is suitable for its use. Credit: The Royal Danish Library, Copenhagen.

Figure 4. Johannes Romberch, *Congestorium artificiose memorie*, 1520. The shops in a city as a set of *loci* for the creation of an artificial memory system. Credit: The Royal Danish Library, Copenhagen.

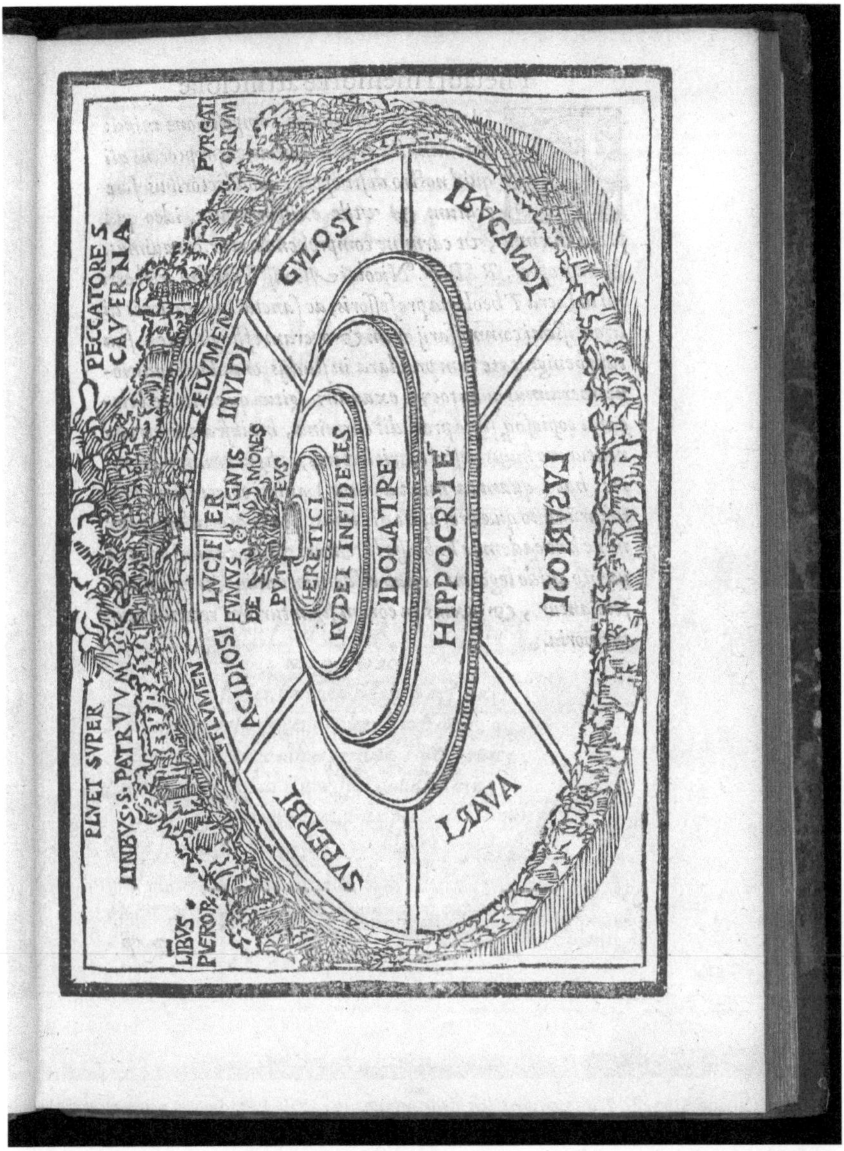

Figure 5. Cosma Rosselli, *Thesaurus artificiosae memoriae*, 1579. Hell as a set of *loci* for the creation of an artificial memory system. Credit: Wellcome Collection, London. Permanent link to the book: https://wellcomecollection.org/works/xqhchbzv.

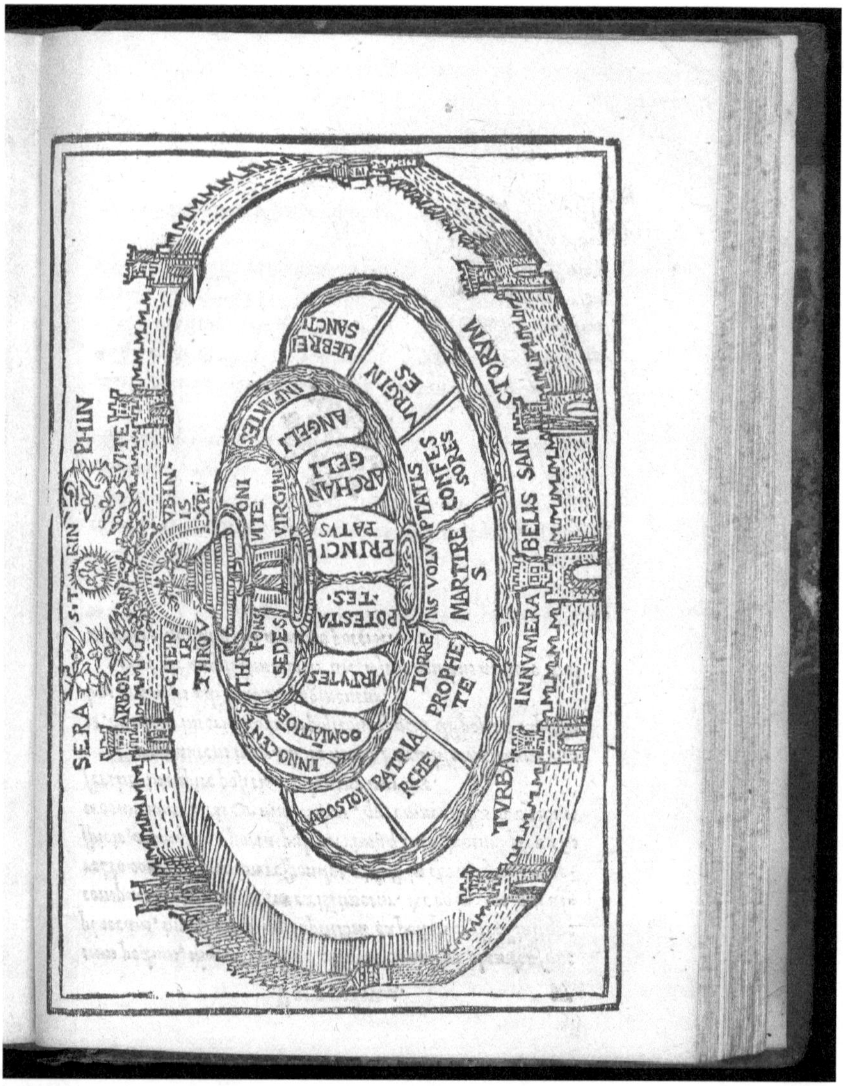

Figure 6. Cosma Rosselli, *Thesaurus artificiosae memoriae*, 1579. Paradise as a set of *loci* for the creation of an artificial memory system. Credit: Wellcome Collection, London. Permanent link to the book: https://wellcomecollection.org/works/xqhchbzv.

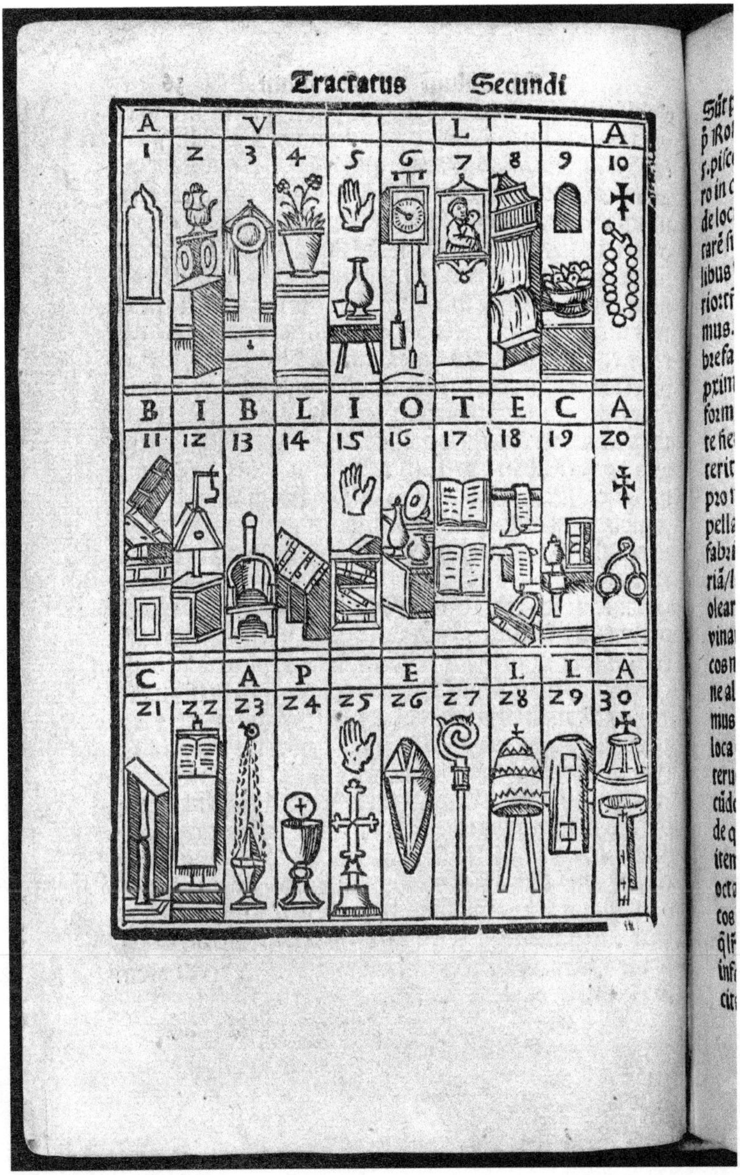

Figure 7. Johannes Romberch, *Congestorium artificiose memorie*, 1520. Visual alphabet. An example of images that may be used to count or assign an order to both the *loci* and *imagines*. Credit: Wellcome Collection, London. Attribution 4.0 International (CC BY 4.0). No modifications have been made.

Figure 8. Johannes Romberch, *Congestorium artificiose memorie*, 1520. Visual alphabet: V, X, Y. The letter "V" is an example of the rule for the choice of images that recommends using what is most impressed on the mind, so that one remembers more easily something that is funny, horrible, or grotesque, for example. In this case it is the amusing image of a man falling back with his legs in the air which helps to remember the letter "V". Credit: Wellcome Collection. Attribution 4.0 International (CC BY 4.0). No modifications have been made.